380 COUNTRY & FARMHOUSE HOME PLANS

TABLE OF CONTENTS

Library of Congress
Catalogue Card No.: 98-87397
IBSN: 1-58011-060-6

CREATIVE HOMEOWNER®
A Division of
Federal Marketing Corp.
24 Park Way,
Upper Saddle River, NJ 07458

Manufactured in the
United States of America

Current Printing (last digit)
10 9 8 7 6 5 4 3

Cover Photography by
Jon Riley
of Riley & Riley Photography

CRE▲TIVE
HOMEOWNER®

COPYRIGHT © 1999
CREATIVE HOMEOWNER®
A Division of Federal Marketing Corp.
Upper Saddle River, NJ

plan no. **price code F** ⚒ total living area: **2,614 sq. ft.**

98904

Quaint Dormers

Photography by John Ehrenclou

The foyer leads into the formal dining room, topped by a decorative ceiling, the library with a double door entry, and the master suite. The cooktop island kitchen has direct access to the formal dining room and flows into the breakfast bay and the family room. There is a deck expanding living space outside. Two secondary bedrooms, tucked into the left side of the home share the use of the full bath in the hall. There is room to expand into the second floor. The photographed home may have been modified to suit individual tastes.

plan info

First Floor	2,614 sq. ft.
Bonus Sec. Flr.	1,681 sq. ft.
Basement	2,563 sq. ft.
Garage	596 sq. ft.
Bedrooms	Three
Baths	2(full), 1(half)
Foundation	Basement

Unique window treatments, perfect fireplace placement, and access to a large deck are just some of the focal points in this elegant Family Room.

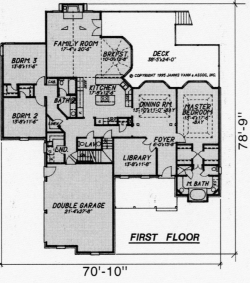

FAMILY ROOM
17'-4"x 20'-6"

BRKFST
10'-0"x12'-6"

DECK
38'-5"x24'-0"

© COPYRIGHT 1995 JANNIS VANN & ASSOC. INC.

BDRM 3
13'-8"x11'-6"

KITCHEN
17'-9"x17'-6"

BATH 2

DINING RM
13'-10"x13'-0" +BAY

MASTER BEDROOM
13'-4"x17'-4"
+BAY

BDRM 2
13'-8"x11'-6"

LINEN

LND.

FOYER
6'-0"x15'-8"

LIBRARY
13'-8"x11'-8"

M BATH

DOUBLE GARAGE
21'-4"x27'-8"

FIRST FLOOR

70'-10"

78'-9"

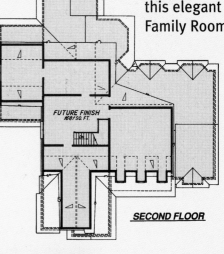

FUTURE FINISH
1681 SQ. FT.

SECOND FLOOR

The phenomenal detailing on this outstanding design makes it a standout in our collection. If you are looking for a unique home, this plan may be right for you!

price code **E**

total living area: **2,281 sq. ft.**

Gingerbread Charm

Photography by John Ehrenclou

Victorian elegance combines with a modern floor plan to make this a dream house without equal. A wrap-around porch and rear deck add lots of extra living space to the roomy first floor, which features a formal parlor and dining room just off the central entry. Informal areas at the rear of the house are wide-open for family interaction. Gather the crew around the fireplace in the family room, or make supper in the kitchen while you supervise the kids' homework in the sunwashed breakfast room. Three bedrooms, tucked upstairs for a quiet atmosphere, feature skylit baths. You'll love the five-sided sitting nook in your master suite, a perfect spot to relax after a luxurious bath in the sunken tub. The photographed home may have been modified to suit individual tastes.

plan info

First Floor	**1,260 sq. ft.**
Second Floor	**1,021 sq. ft.**
Basement	**1,186 sq. ft.**
Garage	**851 sq. ft.**
Bedrooms	**Three**
Baths	**2(full), 1(half)**
Foundation	**Basement, Slab, Crawl Space**

The family room with a cozy fireplace is separated from the Breakfast area by a half wall. This open arrangement adds to the spacious flow of this design.

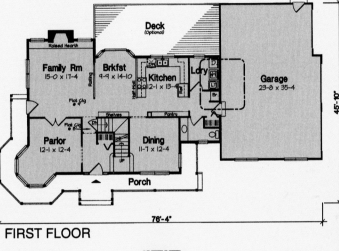

FIRST FLOOR

Alternate Crawl/Slab

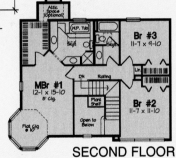

SECOND FLOOR

The Master Bedroom boasts a sitting nook for added charm. The Master Bath has an attached sunken tub that welcomes a relaxing soak after a long hard day.

plan no.

93182

price code **J**

total living area: **3,650 sq. ft.**

French Accents

Photography supplied by Ahmann Design

Traditional French touches adorn this country classic. From the stone and brick exterior, to the barrel vaulted ceiling in the Great room, it is filled with special features to accommodate your needs. One outstanding feature is the grand fireplace with built-in cabinetry in the Great room. The tremendous attention to detail in every aspect of this fireplace and mantel brings out the charm found in this home. For the busy professional, a main floor, den or office has been designed directly off the foyer; it has an exposed beam tray ceiling and fourteen feet of built-in cabinetry. Ready for entertaining, the large open kitchen, nook and Great room make it very functional. The kitchen has a large island with an oven and cooktop, and a curved counter. Just off the kitchen is a butler's pantry leading to the formal dining room. There is also a large walk-in pantry. Designed to be functional and elegant, the master bath includes a large whirlpool spa tub. No materials list is available for this plan. This plan is not to be built in 75 mile radius of Cedar Rapids, IA. The photographed home may have been modified to suit individual tastes.

plan info

Main Floor	**2,575 sq. ft.**
Second Floor	**1,075 sq. ft.**
Basement	**2,575 sq. ft.**
Bedrooms	**Four**
Baths	**3(full), 1(half)**
Foundation	**Basement**

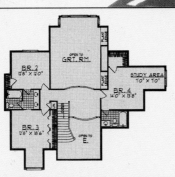

Let in the light! This massive wall of windows illuminates this richly accented Great Room. Coupled with the grand fireplace, warmth is not an issue even on the chilliest day!

A center work area simplifies even the most complex recipes. This kitchen is guaranteed to make you happy!

price code **C** ✕ total living area: **1,838** sq. ft.

Charming Two-Story

Photography by John Ehrenclou

Enter into the spacious foyer, walk past the powder room and sloped-ceilinged living/dining room arrangement and into the fireplaced family room. Look to your right and view the modern kitchen with plenty of counter space and a breakfast bar. Upstairs, you'll find two large bedrooms, and a master suite complete with a tub, a step-in shower and double vanity in the master bath. For more than ample storage space, use the spacious, two-car garage. The photographed home may have been modified to suit individual tastes.

plan info

First Floor	1,088 sq. ft.
Second Floor	750 sq. ft.
Basement	750 sq. ft.
Garage	517 sq. ft.
Bedrooms	Three
Baths	2(full), 1(half)
Foundation	Basement, Slab, Crawl Space

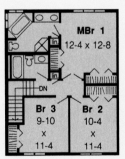

A charming living room with adjoining dining room will make entertaining a breeze.

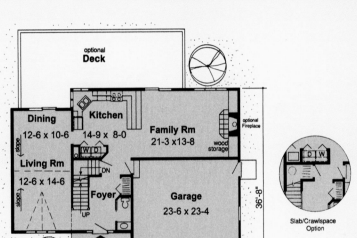

optional
Deck

Dining
12-6 x 10-6

Kitchen
14-9 x 8-0

Family Rm
21-3 x13-8

optional
Fireplace

wood
storage

Living Rm
12-6 x 14-6

W D

DN

Foyer

UP

Garage
23-6 x 23-4

36'-8"

D W

Slab/Crawlspace
Option

50'-0"

first floor

MBr 1
12-4 x 12-8

lin

lin

lin

DN

Br 3
9-10
x
11-4

Br 2
10-4
x
11-4

second floor

Open kitchen area adjoins the family room for a casual and comfortable atmosphere.

Country Comforts

Photography by Glen Graves

From the sprawling front porch to the two-way fireplace that warms the hearth room and living room, this house says "Welcome" to all who enter. Even your house plants will love the cozy, sunny atmosphere of this country classic. A central hallway links the formal, bayed dining room with the spacious kitchen at the rear of the house. Relax over an informal meal in the adjoining hearth room, or out on the deck when the weather's warm. It's accessible from both the hearth room and soaring, wide-open living room. Relish the privacy of your first floor master suite, which features a bath with every amenity, and a huge walk-in closet. Step upstairs for a great view of active areas, where you'll find three more bedrooms, each adjoining a full bath. The photographed home may have been modified to suit individual tastes.

plan info

First Floor	**1,737 sq. ft.**
Second Floor	**826 sq. ft.**
Basement	**1,728 sq. ft.**
Bedrooms	**Four**
Baths	**3(full), 1(half)**
Foundation	**Basement**

An
EXCLUSIVE DESIGN
By Karl Kreeger

Both the Living room and the Hearth room are warmed by the two-way stone fireplace.

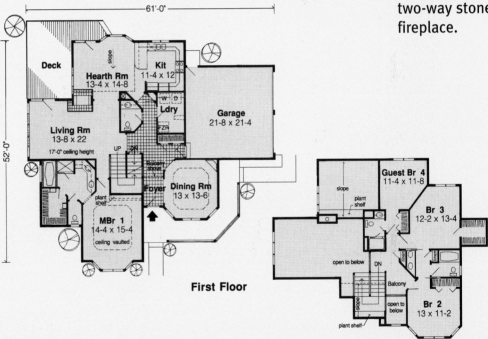

61'-0"

52'-0"

Deck

Hearth Rm
13-4 x 14-8

slope

Kit
11-4 x 12

W D

Ldry

FZR

Garage
21-8 x 21-4

Living Rm
13-8 x 22

17'-0" ceiling height

UP DN

Balcony above

Foyer

Dining Rm
13 x 13-6

plant shelf

MBr 1
14-4 x 15-4

ceiling vaulted

First Floor

slope

plant shelf

Guest Br 4
11-4 x 11-8

Br 3
12-2 x 13-4

open to below

DN

Balcony

open to below

Br 2
13 x 11-2

plant shelf

Second Floor

Love the outdoors? Invite the family over for a barbecue on your spacious rear deck.

plan no.

3 4 9 2 6

price code **F** ☒ ☒ **R** **total living area:** 2,525 sq. ft.

The Essence of Country

Photography supplied by John Ehrenclou

Y ou'll never get bored with the rooms in this charming, three-bedroom Victorian. The angular plan gives every room an interesting shape. From the wrap-around veranda, the entry foyer leads through the living room and parlor, breaking them up without confining them, and giving each room an airy atmosphere. In the dining room, with its hexagonal, recessed ceiling, you can enjoy your after-dinner coffee and watch the kids playing on the deck. Or eat in the sunny breakfast room off the island kitchen, where every wall has a window, and every window has a different view. You'll love the master suite's bump-out window, walk-in closets, and double sinks. The photographed home may have been modified to suit individual tastes.

An
EXCLUSIVE DESIGN
By Karl Kreeger

plan info

First Floor	1,409 sq. ft.
Second Floor	1,116 sq. ft.
Basement	1,409 sq. ft.
Garage	483 sq. ft.
Bedrooms	Three
Baths	2(full), 1(half)
Foundation	Basement, Slab Crawl Space

This quaint breakfast nook has easy access to the back deck. The center island provides ample counter space for all your enter-taining needs.

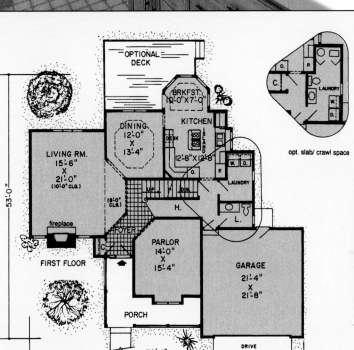

opt. slab/ crawl space

This lovely brick fireplace accents the spacious living room. This home is sure to please any homeowner.

99450

Magnificent Porch

Photography supplied by Design Basics, Inc.

© design basics, inc.

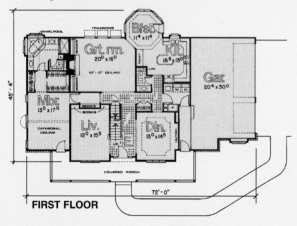

FIRST FLOOR

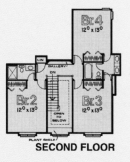

SECOND FLOOR

The volume entry of this home surveys the formal living and dining rooms. The formal living room features two bookcases. The impressive Great room includes three large windows and a raised hearth fireplace flanked by bookcases. The captivating gazebo dinette and island kitchen are equipped with a huge pantry and two lazy Susans. Upstairs, three secondary bedrooms enjoy ample bathroom accommodations and a gallery in the corridor. The first floor master suite includes a porch retreat access, a roomy dressing area, his-n-her vanity and a sunlit whirlpool. This plan is available with a basement or slab foundation. Please specify when ordering. The photographed home may have been modified to suit individual tastes.

plan info

First Floor	1,881 sq. ft.
Second Floor	814 sq. ft.
Basement	1,881 sq. ft.
Garage	534 sq. ft.
Bedrooms	Four
Baths	2(full), 1(half), 1(3/4)
Foundation	Basement or Crawl Space

total living area: 2,217 sq. ft.   **D** price code   plan no.

Neighborhood Beauty

Photography supplied by Studer Residential Design

This straight up two-story has an offset Great room that lends diversity to the front elevation. The boxed window in the dining room and front entry details accentuate the simple elegance of the exterior of this home. The sunken Great room is large enough for family gatherings that can be centered around the cozy fireplace. The second floor features the master bedroom suite with a garden bath and a library that can be designed to have access from the master bedroom for a private retreat, or it can be used as a fourth bedroom if the need arises. The traffic pattern of this home is designed for step-saving convenience while offering large rooms and amenities attractive to the discriminating family. No materials list is available for this plan. The photographed home may have been modified to suit individual tastes.

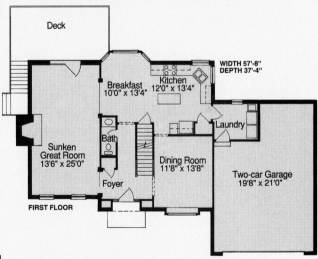

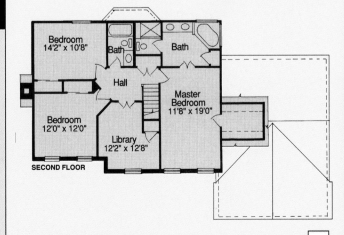

plan info

First Floor	**1,134 sq. ft.**
Second Floor	**1,083 sq. ft.**
Basement	**931 sq. ft.**
Garage	**554 sq. ft.**
Bedrooms	**Three**
Baths	**2(full), 1(half)**
Foundation	**Basement**

plan no.

3 4 0 2 7

price code **C** ☒ ☑ **R**   total living area: **1,960 sq. ft.**

Lots of Quaint Charm

Photography by John Ehrenclou

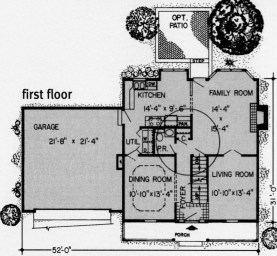

first floor

GARAGE
21'-8" x 21'-4"

OPT. PATIO

STEP

KITCHEN
14'-4" x 9'-6"

FAMILY ROOM
14'-4" x 15'-4"

UTIL

PAN.

P.R.

DINING ROOM
10'-10" x 13'-4"

LIVING ROOM
10'-10" x 13'-4"

FOYER

PORCH

52'-0"

31'-0"

This beautiful home accommodates the needs of a growing family and looks stunning in any neighborhood. The porch serves as a wonderful relaxing area to enjoy the outdoors. At the rear of the home is a patio, for a barbeque or more private time away from the kids. The inside is just as delightful. The dining room features a decorative ceiling and has easy entry to the kitchen. The kitchen/utility area has a side exit into the garage. The living room has double doors into the fireplaced, family room which features a back entrance to the patio. Upstairs is the sleeping area with three bedrooms plus a vaulted-ceiling master bedroom. The master bedroom has two enormous walk-in closets, as well as a dressing area and private bath. The photographed home may have been modified to suit individual tastes.

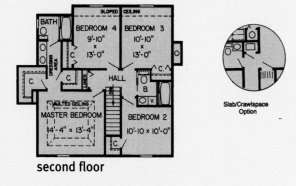

BATH

SLOPED CEILING

BEDROOM 4
9'-10" x 13'-0"

BEDROOM 3
10'-10" x 13'-0"

DRESSING AREA

HALL

C.

B.

V.

VAULTED CEILING
MASTER BEDROOM
14'-4" x 13'-4"

BEDROOM 2
10'-10 x 10'-0"

Slab/Crawlspace Option

second floor

An **EXCLUSIVE DESIGN** *By Karl Kreeger*

plan info

First Floor	**955 sq. ft.**
Second Floor	**1,005 sq. ft.**
Basement	**930 sq. ft.**
Garage	**484 sq. ft.**
Bedrooms	**Four**
Baths	**2(full), 1(half)**
Foundation	**Basement, Slab, Crawl Space**

total living area: 2,270 sq. ft.   ⚒   Ⓔ price code   plan no.

All American Beauty

9457

Photography supplied by Design Basics
Builder—Tweed & Construction

The spacious two-story entry surveys the formal dining room, enhanced by built-in hutch space. The Great room certainly lives up to its name. A built-in entertainment center, a see-through fireplace and an elegant bayed window highlight the room. The kitchen/breakfast/hearth room areas feature gazebo dining, wrapping counters and numerous amenities. The open layout gives an open, airy feeling to the living space. On the second floor the luxurious master suite is topped by a decorative ceiling and enjoys a lavish bath featuring a whirlpool tub, his-n-her vanity and a walk-in closet. The three additional bedrooms share the compartmented bath in the hall. The photographed home may have been modified to suit individual tastes.

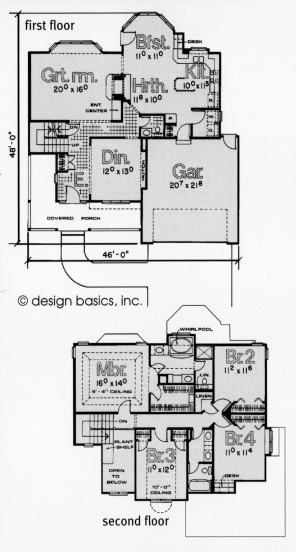

© design basics, inc.

plan info

First Floor	**1,150 sq. ft.**
Second Floor	**1,120 sq. ft.**
Basement	**1,150 sq. ft.**
Garage	**457 sq. ft.**
Bedrooms	**Four**
Baths	**2(full), 1(half)**
Foundation	**Basement**

second floor

17

plan no.   price code **D**   total living area: **2,101 sq. ft.**

92610

Moderate Size Luxury

Photography by Donna & Ron Kolb

first floor

Deck

Breakfast
9-2 x 16

Sunken
Great Room
16-10 x 21

Kitchen
8 x 13-4

Bath

Walk-in closet

Dining Room
16 x 11-8

Foyer

Master Bedroom
14 x 17-4

Bath

Hall

Laundry

Two-car Garage
21 x 20-8

Slope ceiling   Slope ceiling

second floor

Bedroom
15x 10-8

Great Room
Below

Bath

Bedroom
14x 10-6

Foyer Below

An octagonal master bedroom with a vaulted ceiling, a sunken Great room with a balcony above, and an exterior with an exciting roof line; provide this home with all the luxurious ammenities in a moderate size. The first floor master bedroom targets this home to the empty-nester market. The elegant exterior has a rich solid look that is very important to the discriminating buyer. The kitchen features a center island and a breakfast nook. The sunken Great room has a cozy fireplace. If you are looking for elegance and luxury in a moderate size, this home has it. No materials list is available for this plan. The photographed home may have been modified to suit individual tastes.

plan info

First Floor	1,626 sq. ft.
Second Floor	475 sq. ft.
Basement	1,512 sq. ft.
Garage	438 sq. ft.
Bedrooms	Three
Baths	2(full), 1(half)
Foundation	Basement

total living area: 2,562 sq. ft.

Modern Country

D price code

⚒

plan no. 99432

The cozy front porch and arched windows of this home provides a country feeling for this attractive elevation. Dazzling fifteen foot arched openings accent the Great room's entry. The formal dining room is easily accessible from the large island kitchen, offering ease in serving. Elegant French doors in the breakfast room open to the versatile office, which is topped by a ten foot ceiling. The luxurious master suite features a private entrance, a built-in dresser and a beautiful corner whirlpool tub.

plan info

First Floor	**1,875 sq. ft.**
Second Floor	**687 sq. ft.**
Basement	**1,875 sq. ft.**
Bedrooms	**Four**
Baths	**2(full), 1(half)**
Foundation	**Basement**

© design basics, inc.

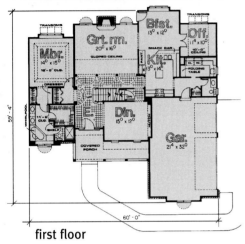

first floor

second floor

---

total living area: 2,692 sq. ft.

Interior Balcony

F price code

plan no. 92619

The veranda's six large round columns set the theme for this beautiful home. The foyer, nearly two stories high, is over-looked by the balcony above. The master bedroom is located on the first floor for seclusion and features a private bath, whirlpool, double vanity and a shower. The first floor laundry is close to the kitchen for maximum convenience. The expanded kitchen and sunken family room provide a center for family activities. No materials list is available for this plan.

plan info

First Floor	**1,746 sq. ft.**
Second Floor	**946 sq. ft.**
Basement	**1,589 sq. ft.**
Garage	**468 sq. ft.**
Bedrooms	**Four**
Baths	**2(full), 1(half)**
Foundation	**Basement**

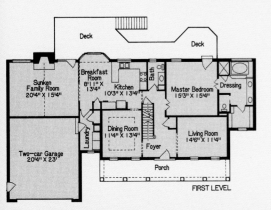

FIRST LEVEL

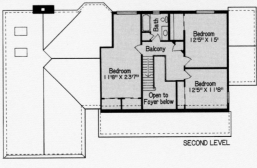

SECOND LEVEL

plan no.   price code **B** ⚒   total living area: 1,735 sq. ft.

**9
3
2
6
9**

Cozy Front Porch

Photography by John Ehrenclou

SUNDECK
16'-0"X12'-0"

BREAKFAST
9'0"X7'8"

KIT.
9'-0"X9'-6"

DINING
10'-0"X11'-4"

LIVING AREA
18'-0"X13'-6"

M.BDRM.
15'-6"X13'-6"

32'-0"

PORCH

first floor

40'-4"

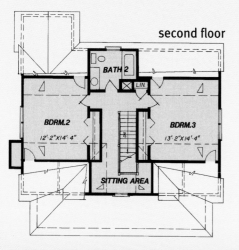

second floor

BATH 2

LIN.

BDRM.2
12'-2"X14'-4"

BDRM.3
13'-2"X14'-4"

SITTING AREA

From the cozy front porch, enter into an inviting living room with a large fireplace. The dining area is open to the living room, giving a spacious feeling to both rooms. An efficient kitchen includes ample counter and cabinet space as well as a double sink. A sunny breakfast area is available for informal eating. The sun deck expands your living area to the outdoors in the warmer weather. The master suite is located on the first floor insuring privacy from the other sleeping quarters. The private master bath is equipped with an oval tub and a double vanity. The first floor powder room includes a hideaway laundry center. The second floor bedrooms have ample closet space and share a full hall bath. The photographed home may have been modified to suit individual tastes.

An
EXCLUSIVE DESIGN
By Jannis Vann & Associates, Inc.

plan info

First Floor	1,045 sq. ft.
Second Floor	690 sq. ft.
Basement	465 sq. ft.
Garage	580 sq. ft.
Bedrooms	Three
Baths	2(full), 1(half)
Foundation	Basement

total living area: 1,312 sq. ft.

A Touch of Style

You don't have to sacrifice style when buying a smaller home. Notice the palladian window with a fan light above at the front of the home. The entrance porch includes a turned post entry. Once inside, the living room is topped by an impressive vaulted ceiling and accented by a fireplace. A decorative ceiling enhances both the master bedroom and the dining room. Efficiently designed, the kitchen includes a peninsula counter and serves the dining room with ease. A private bath and double closet highlight the master suite. Two additional bedrooms are served by a full hall bath.

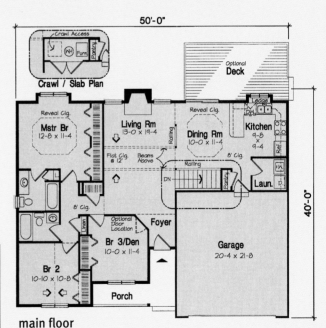

main floor

plan info

Main Floor	**1,312 sq. ft.**
Basement	**1,293 sq. ft.**
Garage	**459 sq. ft.**
Bedrooms	**Three**
Baths	**2(full)**
Foundation	**Basement, Slab, Crawl Space**

plan no. **price code** **D** ✕ 🗲 **total living area: 1,685 sq. ft.**

99810

Country Pleasures

© 1996 Donald A. Gardner Architects, Inc.

The foyer is open to the dramatic dormer and is defined by elegant columns, while the dining room is augmented by a tray ceiling. The front room does double duty as a bedroom or a study. A cathedral ceiling and a clerestory accentuating the rear porch expands the Great room. The Great room is further enhanced by the cased opening with accent columns into the open kitchen and breakfast room. The master suite, privately removed to one side of the house, features a tray ceiling in the bedroom. A garden tub with a picture window is the focal point of the master bath. Buyers will love the roomy walk-in closet. Two bedrooms on the other side of the home share a full bath and linen closet.

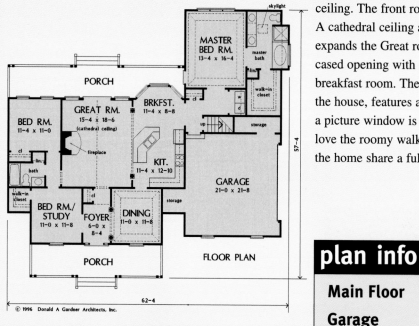

© 1996 Donald A Gardner Architects, Inc.

plan info

Main Floor	**1,685 sq. ft.**
Garage	**536 sq. ft.**
Bonus Room	**331 sq. ft.**
Bedrooms	**Three**
Baths	**2(full)**
Foundation	**Crawl Space**

Classic One Level Design

This convenient, one-level plan is perfect for the modern family with a taste for classic design. Traditional Victorian touches in this three-bedroom beauty include a romantic, railed porch and an intriguing breakfast tower just off the kitchen. You will love the step-saving arrangement of the kitchen between the breakfast and formal dining rooms. Enjoy the wide-open living room with sliders out to a rear deck, and the handsome master suite with its skylit, compartmentalized bath. Notice the convenient laundry location in the bedroom hall.

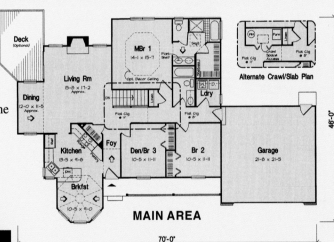

MAIN AREA

plan info

Main Area	**1,583 sq. ft.**
Basement	**1,573 sq. ft.**
Garage	**484 sq. ft.**
Bedrooms	**Three**
Baths	**2(full)**
Foundation	**Basement, Slab, Crawl Space**

An EXCLUSIVE DESIGN
By Karl Kreeger

20161

Detailed Charmer

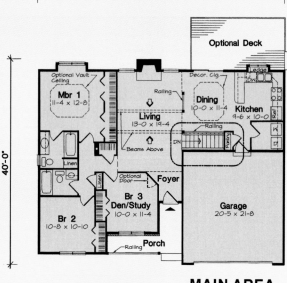

50'-0"

40'-0"

- Optional Vault Ceiling
- **Mbr 1** 11-4 x 12-8
- Optional Deck
- Decor. Clg.
- Ledge
- **Dining** 10-0 x 11-4
- **Kitchen** 9-6 x 10-0
- Railing
- **Living** 13-0 x 19-4
- Railing
- DN
- Beams Above
- Linen
- Optional Door
- **Foyer**
- **Br 3 Den/Study** 10-0 x 11-4
- **Garage** 20-5 x 21-8
- **Br 2** 10-8 x 10-10
- Railing **Porch**

MAIN AREA

Crawl Space Access

Pantry

Slab/Crawl Space Option

Walk past the charming front porch, in through the foyer and you'll be struck by the exciting, spacious living room. Complete with high sloping ceilings and a beautiful fireplace flanked by large windows. The large master bedroom shows off a full wall of closet space, its own private bath, and an extraordinary decorative ceiling. Just down the hall are two more bedrooms and another full bath. Take advantage of the accessibility off the foyer and turn one of these rooms into a private den or office space. The dining room provides a feast for your eyes with its decorative ceiling details, and a full slider out to the deck. Along with great counter space, the kitchen includes a double sink and an attractive bump-out window. The adjacent laundry room, optional expanded pantry, and a two-car garage make this Ranch a charmer.

plan info

Main Area	1,307 sq. ft.
Basement	1,298 sq. ft.
Garage	462 sq. ft.
Bedrooms	Three
Baths	2(full)
Foundation	Basement, Slab or Crawl Space

An EXCLUSIVE DESIGN *By Karl Kreeger*

24

total living area: 1,415 sq. ft. A price code plan no.

3
4
6
0
1

Quintessential Country

A large front porch is always an old-fashioned welcome to any home. This Cape provides such a welcome. Once inside the home, the vaulted ceiling and grand fireplace of the living room add to the character of this house. The efficient kitchen has a double sink and a peninsula counter that may double as an eating bar. A laundry center is conveniently located in the full bath. Two of the three bedrooms are located on the first floor. The second floor provides the privacy a master suite deserves. Sloping ceilings, a walk-in closet and a private master bath give the owner of this home a comfortable retreat on the second floor.

plan info

First Floor	**1,007 sq. ft.**
Second Floor	**408 sq. ft.**
Basement	**1,007 sq. ft.**
Bedrooms	**Three**
Baths	**2(full)**
Foundation	**Basement, Slab Crawl Space**

First Floor

Crawl Space Option

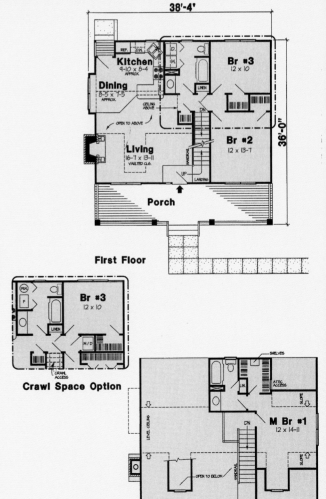

Second Floor

plan no. **price code B**   total living area: **1,576** sq. ft.

24708

Great Starter Home

This functional, one level home plan features a lovely country porch entry into a spacious living room that is accented by a fireplace. The efficient, U-shaped kitchen has direct access to both the dining and the living room. A screened porch is accessed directly from the kitchen. The master bedroom includes a private, double vanity bath with a whirlpool tub and a separate shower. The two additional bedrooms share a full double vanity bath which has the added convenience of a laundry center. No materials list is available for this plan.

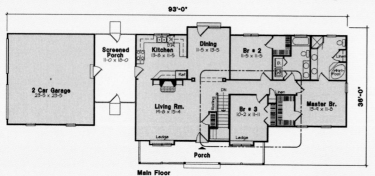

Main Floor

Alternate Crawl/Slab Plan

plan info

Main Floor	**1,576 sq. ft.**
Basement	**1,454 sq. ft.**
Garage	**576 sq. ft.**
Bedrooms	**Three**
Baths	**2(full)**
Foundation	**Basement, Slab or Crawl Space**

Brick, Wood and Gables

A classic design and spacious interior make this home attractive and exciting to the discriminating buyer. Brick and wood trim, multiple gables, and wing walls enhance the outside; while the interior offers features that are designed for entertaining guests. Sloped ceilings, a corner fireplace, windows across the rear of the Great room and a boxed window in the dining room area are all visible as you enter the open foyer. The large kitchen provides plenty of counter space, and a pantry. The breakfast area is surrounded by windows that flood the room with natural light. In the master bedroom suite you will find an ultra bath with a whirlpool tub, double sink, shower and walk-in closet. No materials list is available for this plan.

Width 65'-10"
Depth 56'-0"

main floor

plan info

Main Floor	**1,710 sq. ft.**
Basement	**1,560 sq. ft.**
Garage	**455 sq. ft.**
Bedrooms	**Three**
Baths	**2(full)**
Foundation	**Basement**

plan no. **99840**

price code **D**

total living area: **1,632 sq. ft.**

Beautiful Front & Back

© 1995 Donald A. Gardner Architects, Inc.

This country home is as beautiful from the back as it is from the front. Porches front and back, gables, and dormers provide special charm. The central Great room has a cathedral ceiling, fireplace, and a clerestory window which brings in lots of natural light. Columns divide the open Great room from the kitchen and breakfast bay. A tray ceiling and columns dress up the formal dining room. The master suite, with a tray ceiling and back porch access, is privately-located in the rear. The skylit master bath features a whirlpool tub, shower, dual vanity, and spacious walk-in closet. The front bedroom with walk-in closet doubles as a study. A garage with ample storage completes the plan.

FLOOR PLAN

MASTER BED RM. 13-4 x 16-4

BRKFST. 10-4 x 8-8

PORCH

BED RM. 11-4 x 11-0

GREAT RM. (cathedral ceiling) 15-4 x 18-6

fireplace

KIT. 11-4 x 12-10

UTIL.

storage

GARAGE 21-0 x 21-8

BED RM./ STUDY 11-0 x 11-8

FOYER 6-0 x 8-4

DINING 11-0 x 11-8

storage

PORCH

walk-in closet

master bath

skylight

62-4

55-2

(optional door location)

© 1995 Donald A Gardner Architects, Inc.

plan info

Main Floor	**1,632 sq. ft.**
Garage	**561 sq. ft.**
Bedrooms	**Three**
Baths	**2(full)**
Foundation	**Crawl Space**

total living area: 1,700 sq. ft.   Abundant Space

B price code
plan no. 24250

The design of this home allows for plenty of living space. This home makes use of custom, volume ceilings. The living room offers a sunk-in environment with a vaulted ceiling and fireplace. The oversized windows framing the fireplace enhance the room with natural light. The kitchen features a center island and eating nook. The master suite enjoys a vaulted ceiling. This suite is your own private get-away. The secondary bedrooms also have custom ceiling treatments and view the front porch.

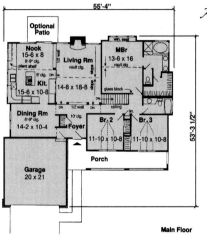

An EXCLUSIVE DESIGN
By Energetic Enterprises

Main Floor

plan info

Main Floor	1,700 sq. ft.
Basement	1,700 sq. ft.
Garage	462 sq. ft.
Bedrooms	Three
Baths	2(full)
Foundation	Basement or Crawl Space

---

total living area: 1,092 sq. ft.   Compact Ranch

A price code
plan no. 34328

A central entry opens to a spacious living room with ample windows and a handy closet nearby. The kitchen features a dining area with sliding glass doors to the backyard and optional deck. A hallway separates three bedrooms and a full bath from the active areas. The laundry facilities are tucked behind double doors for the slab/crawl space option.

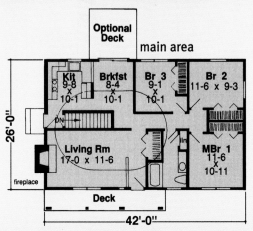

main area

ALTERNATE FLOOR PLAN
for Crawl Space

plan info

Main Area	1,092 sq. ft.
Basement	1,092 sq. ft.
Bedrooms	Three
Baths	1(full),
Foundation	Basement, Slab or Crawl Space

plan no.

10534

price code **I**

total living area: **3,440 sq. ft.**

Private Court & Hot Tub

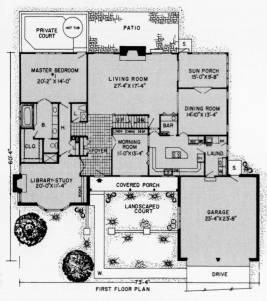

FIRST FLOOR PLAN

The luxurious master suite is secluded on the first floor. Elegant touches include a library, morning room with built-ins, a bar with wine storage, and a sun porch with French doors leading into the dining room. The living room and foyer rise to the second floor which is completed by three large bedrooms and two baths.

An EXCLUSIVE DESIGN
By Karl Kreeger

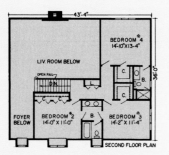

SECOND FLOOR PLAN

plan info

First Floor	**2,486 sq. ft.**
Second Floor	**954 sq. ft.**
Basement	**2,486 sq. ft.**
Garage	**576 sq. ft.**
Bedrooms	**Four**
Baths	**3(full), 1(half)**
Foundation	**Basement**

total living area: 1,787 sq. ft.

Classic Details

An
EXCLUSIVE DESIGN
By Karl Kreeger

Enjoy the beauty and tradition of a two-story home. From the spacious, tiled entry with coat closet to the seclusion of second floor bedrooms, you'll appreciate the classic features that distinguish a two-story home. You'll also delight in the modern touches that make this plan sparkle: the handsome window treatment in the living room; the oversized master bedroom with walk-in closet and deluxe, skylit bath; the efficient kitchen and charming breakfast nook; and the spacious outdoor deck.

plan info

First Floor	877 sq. ft.
Second Floor	910 sq. ft.
Basement	877 sq. ft.
Garage	458 sq. ft.
Bedrooms	Three
Baths	2(full), 1(half)
Foundation	Basement

---

total living area: 2,001 sq. ft.

Victorian Update

An
EXCLUSIVE DESIGN
By Karl Kreeger

Here's a compact Victorian charmer that unites tradition with today's needs. Imagine waking up in the roomy master suite with it's romantic bay and full bath with dual vanity. Two additional bedrooms, which feature huge closets, share the hall bath. The romance continues in the sunny breakfast room off the island kitchen, in the recessed ceilings of the formal dining room, and in the living room's cozy fireplace. Sun lovers will appreciate the sloping, skylit ceilings in the living room, and the rear deck.

plan info

First Floor	1,027 sq. ft.
Second Floor	974 sq. ft.
Basement	978 sq. ft.
Garage	476 sq. ft.
Bedrooms	Three
Baths	2(full), 1(half)
Foundation	Basement

Party Perfect

Designer - Jill Alcantara

Does your family enjoy entertaining? Here's your home! This handsome, rambling beauty can handle a crowd of any size. Greet your guests in a beautiful foyer that opens to the cozy, bayed living room and elegant dining room with floor-to-ceiling windows. Show them the impressive two-story gallery and book-lined study, flooded with sunlight from atrium doors and clerestory windows. Gather around the fire in the vaulted family room. The bar is located near the kitchen and just steps away from both nook and formal dining room. When the guests go home, you'll appreciate your luxurious first floor master suite and the cozy upstairs bedroom suites with adjoining sitting room.

FIRST FLOOR

SECOND FLOOR

plan info

First Floor	**2,310 sq. ft.**
Second Floor	**866 sq. ft.**
Garage	**679 sq. ft.**
Bedrooms	**Three**
Baths	**3(full), 1(half)**
Foundation	**Slab**

Sloped Ceiling Is Attractive Feature of Design

■ *Total living area 1,688 sq. ft.* ■ *Price Code B* ■

No. 10548

■ This plan features:

— Three bedrooms

— Two full and one half baths

■ A fireplace and sloped ceiling in
the Living Room

■ A Master Bedroom complete with
a full bath, shower and dressing
area

■ A decorative ceiling in the Dining
Room

Main area — 1,688 sq. ft.
Basement — 1,688 sq. ft.
Screened porch — 120 sq. ft.
Garage — 489 sq. ft.

An
EXCLUSIVE DESIGN
By Karl Kreeger

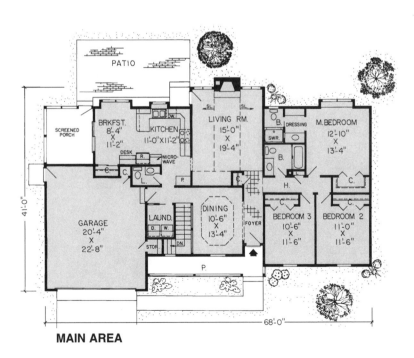

MAIN AREA

Yesteryear Flavor

Total living area 2,356 sq. ft. ■ **Price Code E**

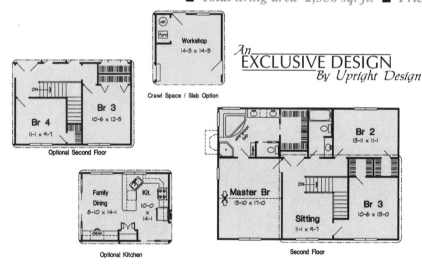

Workshop
14-5 × 14-5

Crawl Space / Slab Option

An
EXCLUSIVE DESIGN
By Upright Design

Br 3
10-6 × 12-5

Br 4
11-1 × 9-7

Optional Second Floor

Family
Dining
8-10 × 14-1

Kit.
10-0 × 14-1

desk

Optional Kitchen

Master Br
13-10 × 17-0

Br 2
13-11 × 11-1

Br 3
10-6 × 13-0

Sitting
11-1 × 9-7

Second Floor

No. 24404

■ **This plan features:**

— Three or four bedrooms

— Three full baths

■ Wrap-around Porch leads to Foyer with a landing staircase

■ Formal Living Room doubles as a Guest Room

■ Huge Family Room highlighted by a decorative ceiling, cozy fireplace and book shelves

■ Country-size Kitchen with island snackbar, built-in desk and nearby Dining Room, laundry/Workshop and Garage access

■ Master Bedroom with a large walk-in closet and a whirlpool tub

■ Two additional bedrooms with walk-in closets, share a full bath and Sitting area

First floor — 1,236 sq. ft.
Second floor — 1,120 sq. ft.

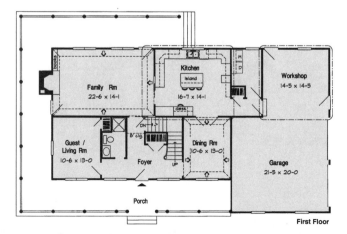

Family Rm
22-6 × 14-1

Kitchen
island
16-7 × 14-1

Workshop
14-5 × 14-5

Guest /
Living Rm
10-6 × 13-0

Foyer

Dining Rm
10-6 × 13-0

Garage
21-5 × 20-0

Porch

First Floor

Soft Arches Accent Country Design

■ Total living area 2,527 sq. ft. ■ Price Code F ■

No. 94233

■ This plan features:

— Four or five bedrooms

— Two full and one half baths

■ Entry Porch with double dormers and doors

■ Pillared arches frame Foyer, Dining Room and Great Room

■ Open Great Room with optional built-ins and sliding glass doors to Verandah

■ Kitchen with walk-in pantry and a counter/snackbar which opens to eating Nook and Great Room

■ Master Suite with his-n-her closets and vanities and a garden tub

■ An optional basement or slab foundation — please specify when ordering

■ No materials list is available for this plan

First floor — 1,676 sq. ft.
Second floor — 851 sq. ft.
Garage — 304 sq. ft.

SECOND FLOOR

FIRST FLOOR

Cabin in the Country

■ *Total living area 928 sq. ft.* ■ *Price Code A* ■

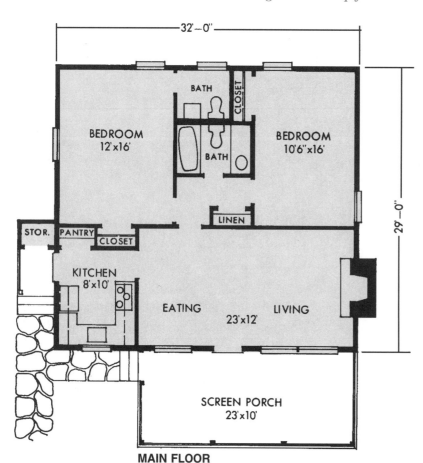

MAIN FLOOR

No. 90433

■ **This plan features:**

— Two bedrooms

— One full and one half baths

■ A screened Porch for enjoyment of your outdoor surroundings

■ A combination Living and Dining area with cozy fireplace for added warmth

■ An efficiently laid out Kitchen with a built-in Pantry

■ Two large bedrooms located at the rear of the home

■ An optional slab or crawl space foundation — please specify when ordering

Main floor — 928 sq. ft.
Screened porch — 230 sq. ft.
Storage — 14 sq. ft.

■ *Total living area 2,069 sq. ft.* ■ *Price Code D* ■

No. 96505 ⚒

■ This plan features:

— Three bedrooms

— Two full and one half baths

■ Secluded Master Bedroom tucked into the rear left corner of the home with a five-piece bath and two walk-in closets

■ Two additional bedrooms at the opposite side of the home sharing the full bath in the hall

■ Expansive Living Room highlighted by a corner fireplace and access to the rear Porch

■ Kitchen is sandwiched between the bright, bayed Nook and the formal Dining Room providing ease in serving

Main floor — 2,069 sq. ft.
Garage — 481 sq. ft.

WIDTH 70'-0"
DEPTH 58'-0"

MAIN FLOOR

Dramatic Ranch

■ *Total living area 1,792 sq. ft.* ■ *Price Code C* ■

An
EXCLUSIVE DESIGN
By Karl Kreeger

No. 20198

■ **This plan features:**

— Three bedrooms

— Two full baths

■ A large Living Room with a stone fireplace and a decorative beamed ceiling

■ A Kitchen/Dining Room arrangement which makes the rooms seem more spacious

■ A Laundry with a large Pantry located close to the bedrooms and the Kitchen

■ A Master Bedroom with a walk-in closet and a private master bath

■ Two additional bedrooms, one with a walk-in closet, that share the full hall bath

Main area — 1,792 sq. ft.
Basement — 818 sq. ft.
Garage — 857 sq. ft.

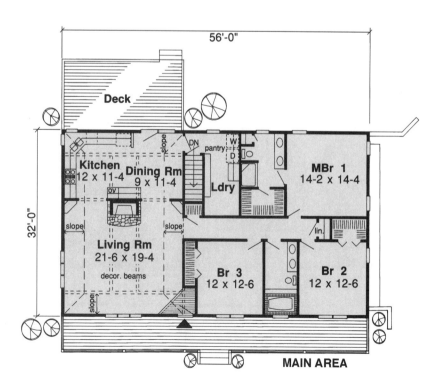

56'-0"

32'-0"

Deck

Kitchen
12 x 11-4

Dining Rm
9 x 11-4

Ldry

pantry

W
D

DN

MBr 1
14-2 x 14-4

Living Rm
21-6 x 19-4

decor. beams

slope

slope

slope

slope

lin.

Br 3
12 x 12-6

Br 2
12 x 12-6

ov

MAIN AREA

■ *Total living area 1,717 sq. ft.* ■ *Price Code B* ■

No. 91746 ⬣

■ This plan features:

— Three bedrooms

— Two full and one three quarter baths

■ A vaulted ceiling topping the Entry, Living and Dining Rooms

■ A lovely bay window in the Living Room, which includes direct access to a side deck

■ A Master Suite with a private compartmented bath with an oversized shower

■ Two additional bedrooms share a full hall bath topped by a skylight

■ A vaulted ceiling topping the Dining area

■ A walk-in pantry adds to the storage space of the cooktop island Kitchen

Main area — 1,717 sq. ft.
Garage — 782 sq. ft.

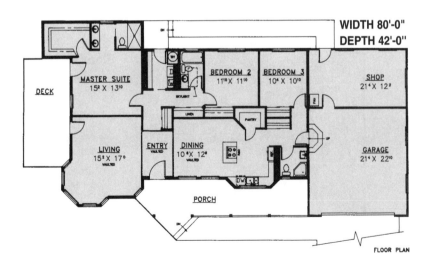

WIDTH 80'-0"
DEPTH 42'-0"

MASTER SUITE
15² X 13¹⁰

DECK

BEDROOM 2
11¹⁰ X 11¹⁰

BEDROOM 3
10⁴ X 10¹⁰

SHOP
21⁴ X 12²

LIVING
15² X 17⁰
VAULTED

ENTRY
VAULTED

DINING
10⁴ X 12⁸
VAULTED

PANTRY

GARAGE
21⁴ X 22¹⁰

PORCH

FLOOR PLAN

Ranch with Handicapped Access

■ *Total living area 1,734 sq. ft.* ■ *Price Code B* ■

No. 20403

■ This plan features:

— Three bedrooms

— One full and one three quarter baths

■ Ramps into the front Entry from the Porch; the Utility area and the Kitchen from the Garage; and the Family Room from the Deck

■ An open area topped by a sloped ceiling for the Family Room, the Dining Room, the Kitchen and the Breakfast alcove

■ Kitchen with a built-in pantry and an open counter

■ A Master Bedroom suite accented by a sloping ceiling above a wall of windows, offering access to the Deck

■ Two front bedrooms with sloped ceilings sharing a full hall

Main floor — 1,734 sq. ft.
Garage — 606 sq. ft.

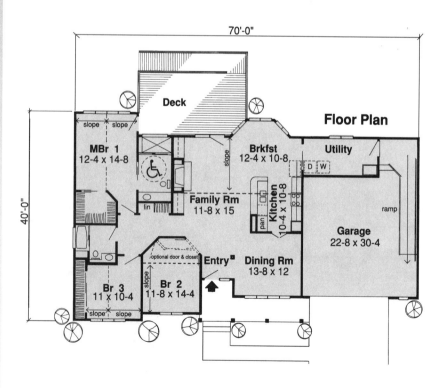

Floor Plan

70'-0"

40'-0"

Deck

MBr 1
12-4 x 14-8

slope   slope

Brkfst
12-4 x 10-8

Utility

D   W

Family Rm
11-8 x 15

Kitchen
10-4 x 10-8

lin

pan

ramp

Garage
22-8 x 30-4

optional door & closet

Entry

Dining Rm
13-8 x 12

Br 3
11 x 10-4

Br 2
11-8 x 14-4

slope   slope

Classic Country Farmhouse

© 1995 Donald A Gardner Architects, Inc.

■ *Total living area 1,832 sq. ft.* ■ *Price Code E* ■

No. 99808

■ This plan features:

— Three bedrooms

— Two full baths

■ Dormers, arched windows and multiple columns give this home country charm

■ Foyer, expanded by vaulted ceiling, accesses Dining Room, Bedroom/Study and Great Room

■ Expansive Great Room, with hearth fireplace topped by cathedral ceiling, opens to rear Porch and efficient Kitchen

■ Tray ceiling adds volume to the private Master Bedroom with a plush Bath and a walk-in closet

■ Extra room for growth offered by the Bonus Room with skylight

Main floor — 1,832 sq. ft.
Bonus room — 425 sq. ft.
Garage & storage — 562 sq. ft.

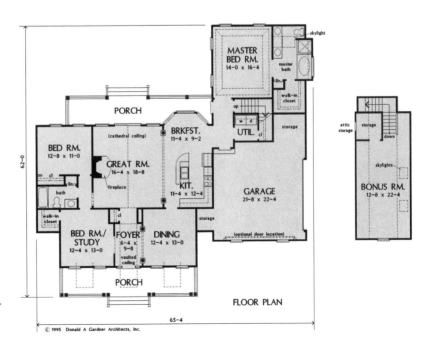

FLOOR PLAN

© 1995 Donald A Gardner Architects, Inc.

Sophisticated Southern Styling

■ *Total living area 2,858 sq. ft.* ■ *Price Code G* ■

First floor — 2,256 sq. ft.
Second floor — 602 sq. ft.
Bonus — 264 sq. ft.
Garage — 484 sq. ft.

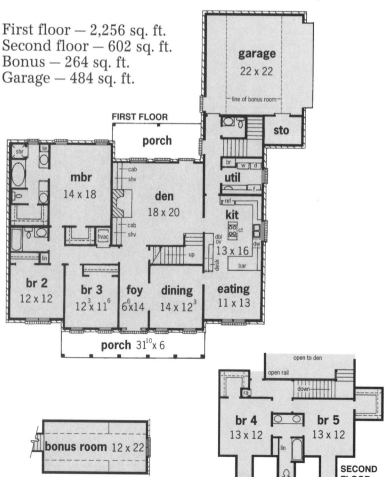

FIRST FLOOR

garage
22 x 22

line of bonus room

sto

porch

br   w   d

util

mbr
14 x 18

den
18 x 20

kit
13 x 16

cab
shv

cab
shv

ref

hvac

dbl
ov

desk

bar

up

br 2
12 x 12

br 3
12³ x 11⁶

foy
6³ x 14

dining
14 x 12³

eating
11 x 13

porch 31¹⁰ x 6

bonus room 12 x 22

open to den

open rail

down

ra

br 4
13 x 12

br 5
13 x 12

lin

SECOND
FLOOR

No. 92576

■ **This plan features:**

— Five bedrooms

— Three full and one half baths

■ Covered front and rear Porches expanding the living space to the outdoors

■ A Den with a large fireplace and built-in cabinets and shelves

■ A cooktop island, built-in desk, and eating bar complete the Kitchen

■ The Master Suite has two walk-in closets and a luxurious bath

■ Four additional bedrooms, two on the main level and two on the upper level, all have easy access to a full bath

■ An optional slab or crawl space foundation — please specify when ordering

■ *Total living area 1,625 sq. ft.* ■ ● *Price Code B* ■

No. 24701

■ This plan features:

- Three bedrooms

- Two full baths

■ Central Foyer leads to Den/Guest room with arched window and Living Room accented by two-sided fireplace

■ U-shaped Kitchen with peninsula counter/breakfast bar serves Dining Room

■ Master Suite features walk-in closet and private bath

■ Two additional bedrooms with ample closet space share full bath

Main floor — 1,625 sq. ft.
Basement — 1,625 sq. ft.
Garage — 455 sq. ft.

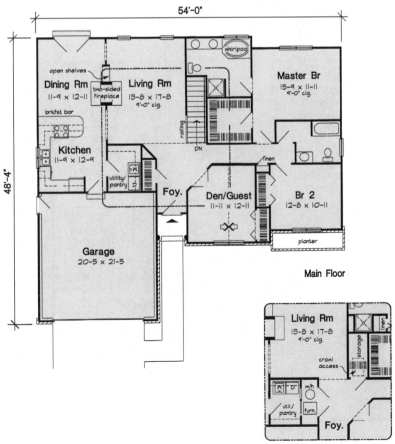

54'-0"

48'-4"

Dining Rm
11-9 x 12-11
open shelves
brkfst bar

two-sided fireplace

Living Rm
13-8 x 17-8
9'-0" clg.

whirlpool

Master Br
15-9 x 11-11
9'-0" clg.

Kitchen
11-9 x 12-9

railing

DN

utility/pantry

Foy.

linen

Den/Guest
11-11 x 12-11

Br 2
12-8 x 10-11

planter

Garage
20-5 x 21-5

Main Floor

Living Rm
13-8 x 17-8
9'-0" clg.

storage

crawl access

w/h

util/pantry

furn.

Foy.

Alternate Foundation Plan

Comfortable and Charming

■ *Total living area 1,964 sq. ft.* ■ *Price Code C* ■

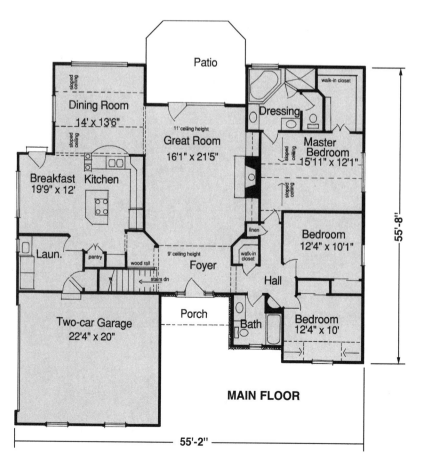

MAIN FLOOR

55'-2"

No. 92660

■ This plan features:

— Three bedrooms

— Two full baths

■ Great Room with massive fireplace and lots of windows with Patio access

■ Formal Dining Room with sloped ceiling and expansive view of backyard

■ Cooktop island and pantry in Kitchen efficiently serve Breakfast area and Dining Room

■ Corner Master Bedroom offers a sloped ceiling, walk-in closet and pampering bath with whirlpool tub and two vanities

■ No materials list is available for this plan

Main floor — 1,964 sq. ft.
Basement — 1,809 sq. ft.
Garage — 447 sq. ft.

■ *Total living area 2,563 sq. ft.* ■ *Price Code H* ■

No. 99843

■ This plan features:

— Four bedrooms

— Two full and one half baths

■ Bay windows and a long, skylit, screened Porch make this four bedroom country style home a haven for outdoor enthusiasts

■ Foyer is open to take advantage of the light from the central dormer with palladian window

■ Vaulted ceiling in the Great Room adds vertical drama to the room

■ Contemporary Kitchen is open to the Great Room creating a feeling of additional space

■ Master Bedroom is privately tucked away with a large luxurious bath complete with a bay window, corner shower and a garden tub

First floor — 1,907 sq. ft.
Second floor — 656 sq. ft.
Bonus room — 467 sq. ft.
Garage & storage — 580 sq. ft.

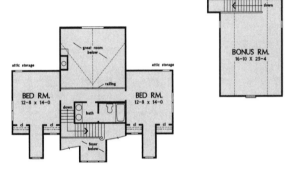

SECOND FLOOR PLAN

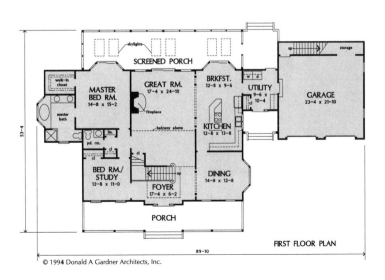

FIRST FLOOR PLAN

Country Style Charm

■ Total living area 1,857 sq. ft. ■ Price Code C ■

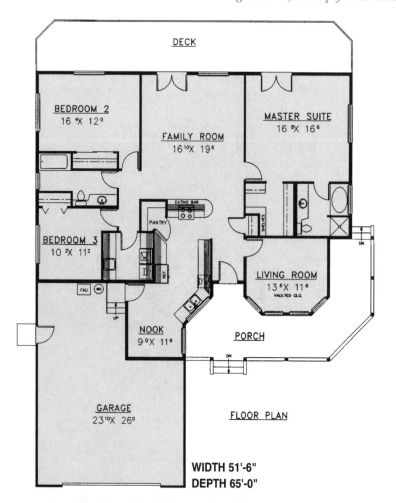

DECK

BEDROOM 2
16⁴X 12⁰

FAMILY ROOM
16¹⁰X 19⁶

MASTER SUITE
16⁶X 16⁶

EATING BAR

PANTRY

BEDROOM 3
10²X 11²

SHELVES

LIVING ROOM
13⁶X 11⁶
VAULTED CLG.

FAU

UP

NOOK
9⁰X 11⁶

PORCH

DN

GARAGE
23¹⁰X 26⁰

FLOOR PLAN

WIDTH 51'-6"
DEPTH 65'-0"

No. 91731

■ **This plan features:**

— Three bedrooms

— Two full baths

■ Brick accents, front facing gable, and railed wrap-around covered Porch

■ A built-in range and oven in a dog-leg shaped Kitchen

■ A Nook with garage access for convenient unloading of groceries and other supplies

■ A bay window wrapping around the front of the formal Living Room

■ A Master Suite with French doors opening to the Deck

Main area — 1,857 sq. ft.
Garage — 681 sq. ft.

An Open Concept Home

■ *Total living area 1,282 sq. ft.* ■ *Price Code A* ■

No. 93021

■ This plan features:

— Three bedrooms

— Two full baths

■ An angled Entry creating the illusion of space

■ Two square columns that flank the bar and separate the Kitchen from the Living Room

■ A Dining Room that may service both formal and informal occasions

■ A Master Bedroom with a large walk-in closet

■ A large master bath with double vanity, linen closet and whirlpool tub/shower combination

■ Two additional bedrooms that share a full bath

■ No materials list is available for this plan

Main floor — 1,282 sq. ft.
Garage — 501 sq. ft.

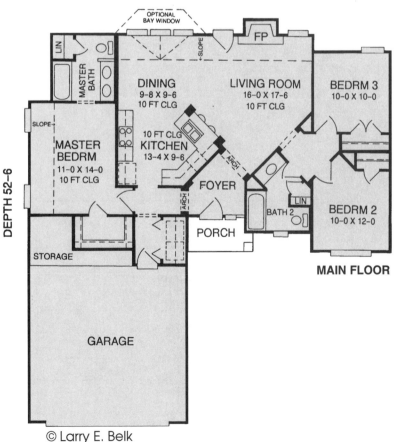

WIDTH 48–10

OPTIONAL BAY WINDOW

FP

LIN

MASTER BATH

DINING
9-8 X 9-6
10 FT CLG

LIVING ROOM
16-0 X 17-6
10 FT CLG

BEDRM 3
10-0 X 10-0

SLOPE

MASTER BEDRM
11-0 X 14-0
10 FT CLG

10 FT CLG
KITCHEN
13-4 X 9-6

ARCH

FOYER

DEPTH 52-6

ARCH

BATH 2

LIN

BEDRM 2
10-0 X 12-0

STORAGE

PORCH

GARAGE

MAIN FLOOR

© Larry E. Belk

47

Luxurious Yet Cozy

■ *Total living area 3,395 sq. ft.* ■ *Price Code I* ■

SECOND FLOOR

Bedroom 2
12⁴ x 13⁵

Great Room
Below

Shared
Bath

W.i.c.

Bedroom 3
12⁴ x 13⁵

Bath

Bedroom 4
13⁰ x 12⁸

Attic
Storage

Foyer
Below

Opt.
Bonus Room
12⁸ x 17⁴

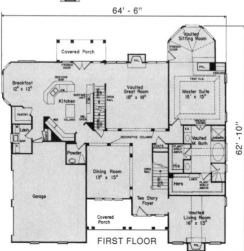

FIRST FLOOR

64' - 6"

62' - 10"

Covered Porch

Breakfast
12ʳ x 12²

Kitchen

Pantry

Laun.

Powder

Dining Room
13⁰ x 15⁴

Garage

Vaulted
Sitting Room

Vaulted
Great Room
18⁰ x 18⁰

Master Suite
16⁴ x 15⁰

Vaulted
M. Bath

His

Hers

Two Story
Foyer

Covered
Porch

Vaulted
Living Room
16⁴ x 13⁰

No. 98403

■ **This plan features:**

— Four bedrooms

— Three full and one half baths

■ Living Room is enhanced by a fieldstone fireplace and vaulted ceiling

■ Inviting fireplace between windows, and a vaulted ceiling enhance Great Room

■ Kitchen with a work island, serving bar, bright Breakfast Area and walk-in Pantry

■ Corner Master Suite includes a cozy fireplace, a vaulted Sitting Room and a lavish Dressing Area

■ Optional basement, crawl space or slab foundation — please specify when ordering

First floor — 2,467 sq. ft.
Second floor — 928 sq. ft.
Bonus — 296 sq. ft.
Basement — 2,467 sq. ft.
Garage — 566 sq. ft.

Brick Opulence and Grandeur

■ *Total living area 3,921 sq. ft.* ■ *Price Code K* ■

No. 92248

■ This plan features:

— Four bedrooms

— Three full and one half baths

■ Dramatic two-story glass Entry with a curved staircase

■ Both Living and Family rooms offer high ceilings, decorative windows and large fireplaces

■ Large, efficient Kitchen with a cooktop serving island, walk-in pantry, bright Breakfast Area and Patio access

■ Lavish Master Bedroom with a cathedral ceiling, two walk-in closets and large bath

■ Two additional bedrooms with ample closets share a double vanity bath

■ No materials list is available for this plan

First floor — 2,506 sq. ft.
Second floor — 1,415 sq. ft.
Basement — 2,400 sq. ft.
Garage — 660 sq. ft.

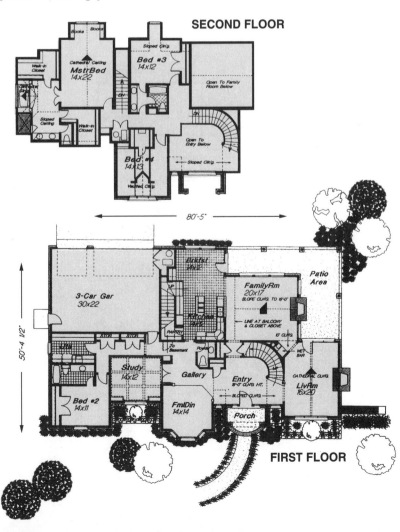

Entertaining is No Problem

■ *Total living area 2,346 sq. ft.* ■ *Price Code E* ■

SECOND FLOOR

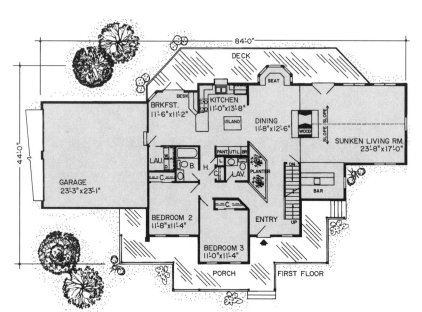

FIRST FLOOR

No. 10610

■ This plan features:

— Three bedrooms

— Two and one half baths

■ A Master Bedroom privately set with a sitting area, full bath and walk-in closet

■ An island Kitchen centered between the Dining Room and Breakfast area

■ A sunken Living Room with vaulted ceilings and a two-way fireplace

■ A covered porch and enormous deck

First floor — 1,818 sq. ft.
Second floor — 528 sq. ft.
Basement — 1,818 sq. ft.
Garage — 576 sq. ft.

■ *Total living area 3,504 sq. ft.* ■ *Price Code J* ■

No. 92505

■ This plan features:

— Four bedrooms

— Three full and one half baths

■ A unique facade created by arched windows, a copper roof over the two story bay, and a detailed mixture of stucco and stone

■ A Foyer with a two-story ceiling and a magnificent balcony

■ Elegant columns rising up two floors through the balcony define the entrance to a two-story Den

■ Den with a two-story fireplace, framed by sliding doors

■ A cozy, private Sitting area with a vaulted ceiling in the Master Suite

■ An optional slab or crawl space foundation — please specify when ordering

First floor — 2,442 sq. ft.
Second floor — 1,062 sq. ft.
Garage — 565 sq. ft.

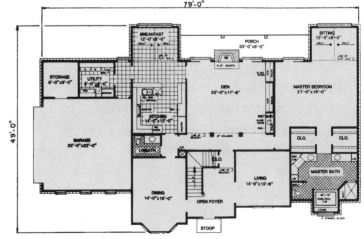

FIRST FLOOR PLAN

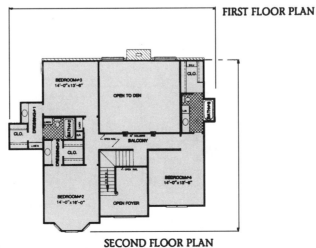

SECOND FLOOR PLAN

Columns Punctuate the Interior Space

S. NATHAN

■ *Total living area 2,188 sq. ft.* ■ *Price Code F* ■

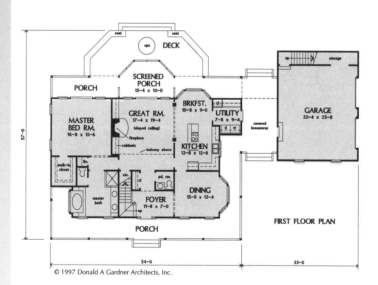

© 1997 Donald A Gardner Architects, Inc.

FIRST FLOOR PLAN

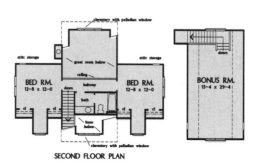

SECOND FLOOR PLAN

No. 99801

■ This plan features:

— Three bedrooms

— Two full and one half baths

■ A two-story Great Room and Foyer, both with dormer windows

■ Large Kitchen, featuring a center cooking island with counter and large Breakfast Area

■ Columns punctuate interior spaces

■ Master Bedroom, privately situated on the first floor, has a dual vanity, garden tub and separate shower

First floor — 1,618 sq. ft.
Second floor — 570 sq. ft.
Bonus room — 495 sq. ft.
Garage & storage — 649 sq. ft.

Total living area 2,455 sq. ft. ■ Price Code E

No. 98518

■ This plan features:

- Three bedrooms

- Two full and one half baths

■ Serve guests dinner in the bayed Dining Room and then gather in the Living Room which features a cathedral ceiling

■ The Family Room is accented by a fireplace

■ The Master Bedroom has a Sitting Area, walk-in closet, and a private bath

■ There is a Bonus Room upstairs for future expansion

■ An optional basement or slab foundation — please specify when ordering

■ No materials list is available for this plan

First floor — 1,447 sq. ft.
Second floor — 1,008 sq. ft.
Garage — 756 sq. ft.

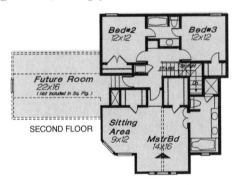

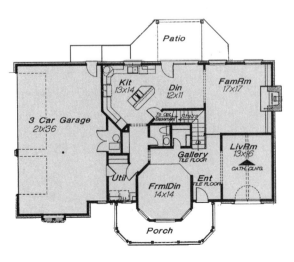

Roomy and Rustic Fieldstone

Total living area 3,079 sq. ft. ■ *Price Code H* ■

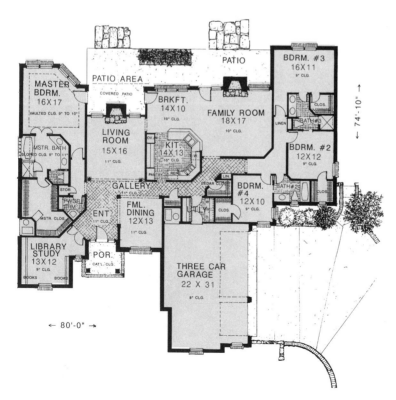

No. 92279

■ **This plan features:**

— Four bedrooms

— Three full and one half baths

■ Cathedral Porch leads into easy-care Entry and formal Living Room with fieldstone fireplace

■ Hub Kitchen with curved peninsula serving counter convenient to Breakfast area, Covered Patio, Family Room, Utility/Garage entry and Dining Room

■ Corner Master Bedroom enhanced by vaulted ceiling, plush bath and a huge walk-in closet

■ Three additional bedrooms with walk-in closets and private access to a full bath

■ No materials list is available for this plan

Main floor — 3,079 sq. ft.
Garage — 630 sq. ft.

■ *Total living area 3,012 sq. ft.* ■ *Price Code H* ■

No. 94715

■ This plan features:

— Four bedrooms

— Three full and one half baths

■ Old southern architecture incorporates today's open plan

■ Gracious two-story Foyer between formal Living and Dining rooms

■ Comfortable Great Room with a fireplace is nestled between French doors to the rear Decks

■ Hub Kitchen offers a cooktop island, an eating bar and a Breakfast area

■ Master Bedroom suite is enhanced by a fireplace and a plush bath

First floor — 2,094 sq. ft.
Second floor — 918 sq. ft.
Garage — 537 sq. ft.
Width — 71'-10"
Depth — 46'-0"

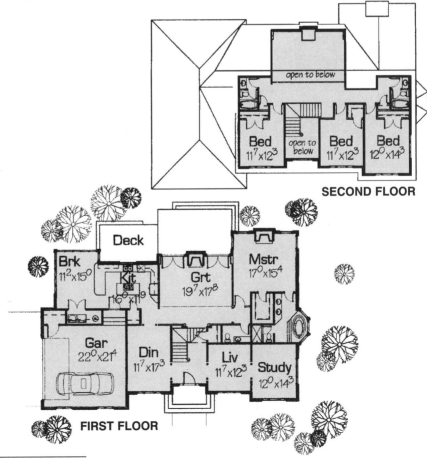

SECOND FLOOR

Bed 11⁷x12³ | Bed 11⁷x12³ | Bed 12⁰x14³

open to below

FIRST FLOOR

Deck

Brk 11²x15⁰
Kit 16⁰x11⁹
Grt 19⁷x17⁸
Mstr 17⁰x15⁴

Gar 22⁰x21⁴
Din 11⁷x17³
Liv 11⁷x12³
Study 12⁰x14³

An
EXCLUSIVE DESIGN
By United Design Associates

Welcoming Exterior

© 1995 Donald A. Gardner Architects, Inc.

■ *Total living area 2,832 sq. ft.* ■ *Price Code I* ■

SECOND FLOOR PLAN

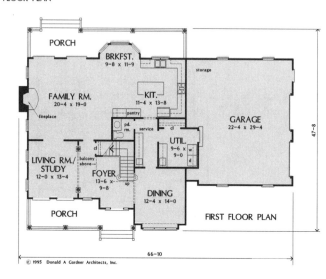

FIRST FLOOR PLAN

No. 96403

■ This plan features:

— Four bedrooms

— Two full and one half baths

■ Columns between the Foyer and Living Room/Study hint at all the extras in this four bedroom country estate with a warm, welcoming exterior

■ Transom windows over French doors open up the Living Room/Study to the front Porch, while a generous Family Room accesses the covered back Porch

■ Deluxe Master Suite is topped by a tray ceiling and includes a bath with a sunny garden tub bay and ample closet space

■ Bonus Room is accessed from the second floor

First floor — 1,483 sq. ft.
Second floor — 1,349 sq. ft.
Garage — 738 sq. ft.
Bonus — 486 sq. ft.

■ *Total living area 1,600 sq. ft.* ■ *Price Code B* ■

No. 10674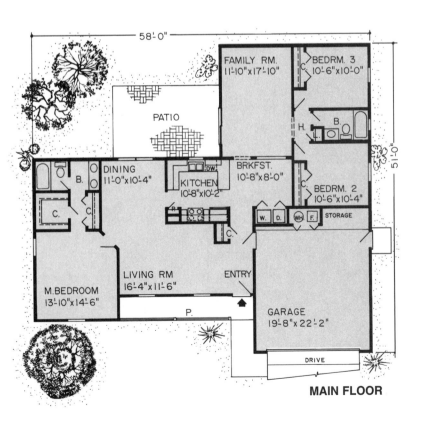

■ This plan features:

— Three bedrooms

— Two full baths

■ A galley Kitchen, centrally-located between the Dining, Breakfast and Living Room areas

■ A huge Family Room which exits onto the patio

■ A Master Suite with double closets and vanity

Main floor — 1,600 sq. ft.
Garage — 465 sq. ft.

MAIN FLOOR

Country Porch Topped by Dormer

■ *Total living area 1,470 sq. ft.* ■ *Price Code A* ■

No. 24706

■ This plan features:

— Three bedrooms

— Two full baths

■ **Front Porch** leads into tiled entry and spacious **Living Room** with focal point fireplace

■ **Side entrance** leads into **Utility Room** and central **Foyer** with a landing staircase

■ **Kitchen** with cooktop island, and a bright **Breakfast** area

■ Second floor **Master Bedroom** offers dormer window, vaulted ceiling, walk-in closet and double vanity bath

■ Two additional bedrooms with ample closets, share a full bath

First floor — 1,035 sq. ft.
Second floor — 435 sq. ft.
Basement — 1,018 sq. ft.

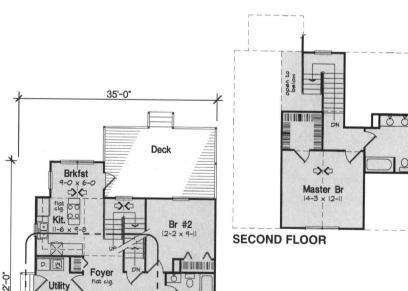

SECOND FLOOR

Master Br
14-3 × 12-11

35'-0"

Deck

Brkfst
9-0 × 6-0

Kit.
11-6 × 9-8

flat clg.

Br #2
12-2 × 9-11

UP

Foyer
flat clg.

Utility

DN

Living Rm
18-11 × 12-11

Br #3
12-2 × 9-3

42'-0"

Porch

FIRST FLOOR

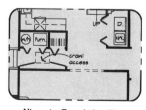

crawl access

Alternate Foundation Plan

■ *Total living area 2,277 sq. ft.* ■ *Price Code E* ■

No. 99431

■ This plan features:

— Four bedrooms

— Two full and one half baths

■ Wrap-around covered porch and windows create a striking appearance

■ Great Room features a cathedral ceiling, transom windows, and huge fireplace

■ Center-island kitchen has a lazy Susan and an ample pantry

■ Double doors access the Master Bedroom which is enhanced by a decorative boxed ceiling

■ Upstairs are three more bedrooms and a full bath

First floor — 1,570 sq. ft.
Second floor — 707 sq. ft.
Garage — 504 sq. ft.
Basement — 1,570 sq. ft.

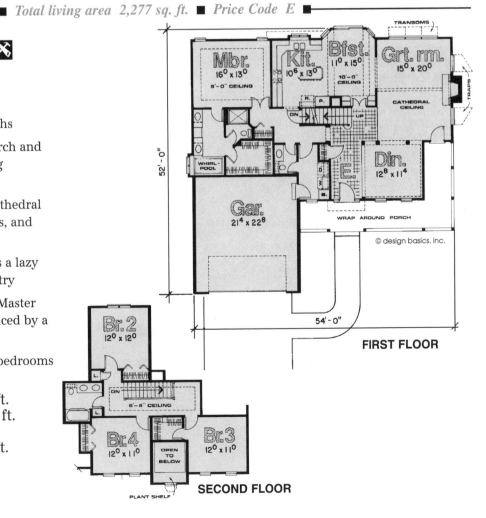

TRANSOMS

| Mbr. | Kit. | Bfst. | Grt. rm. |

Mbr. 16⁰ x 13⁰ 9'-0" CEILING

Kit. 10⁶ x 13⁰

Bfst. 11⁰ x 15⁰ 10'-0" CEILING

Grt. rm. 15⁰ x 20⁰ CATHEDRAL CEILING

WHIRL-POOL

Gar. 21⁴ x 22⁸

Din. 12⁸ x 11⁴

WRAP AROUND PORCH

© design basics, inc.

52'-0"

54'-0"

FIRST FLOOR

Br. 2 12⁰ x 12⁰

DN 8'-8" CEILING

Br. 4 12⁰ x 11⁰

OPEN TO BELOW

Br. 3 12⁰ x 11⁰

PLANT SHELF

SECOND FLOOR

59

Today's Amenities, Yesterday's Charm

■ *Total living area 2,778 sq. ft.* ■ *Price Code G* ■

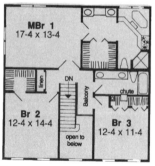

MBr 1
17-4 x 13-4

linen
DN
Balcony
chute

Br 2
12-4 x 14-4

open to
below

Br 3
12-4 x 11-4

Second Floor

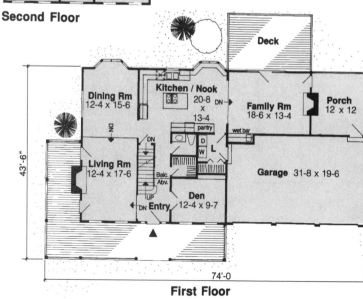

Deck

Dining Rm
12-4 x 15-6

Kitchen / Nook
20-8
x
13-4
pantry

DN

Family Rm
18-6 x 13-4

Porch
12 x 12

wet bar

43'-6"

DN

D
W
L

Living Rm
12-4 x 17-6

Balc.
Abv.

UP
DN **Entry**

Den
12-4 x 9-7

Garage 31-8 x 19-6

74'-0

First Floor

No. 10805

■ **This plan features:**

— Three bedrooms

— Two full and one half baths

■ Wide corner boards, clapboard
siding, and a full-length covered
porch lending a friendly air to
this classic home

■ A central entry opening to a cozy
Den on the right, a sunken Living
Room with adjoining Dining
Room on the left

■ An informal Dining Nook
accented by bay windows

■ A Master Suite spanning the rear
of the home including a huge,
walk-in closet, a private bath with
double vanities, and a whirlpool
tub

First floor — 1,622 sq. ft.
Second floor — 1,156 sq. ft.

Total living area 2,747 sq. ft. ■ Price Code F

No. 91109

■ This plan features:

— Five bedrooms

— Three full baths

■ A beautiful brick exterior is accentuated by double transoms over double windows

■ Big bedrooms and an oversized Great Room, desirable for a large family

■ Volume ceilings in the Master Suite, Great Room, Dining Room, Kitchen, Breakfast Nook and bedroom four

■ Three bathrooms, including a plush master bath, with a double vanity and knee space

■ Plenty of room to spread out in the Sun Room adjacent to the Great Room and the Game Room above the Garage

■ No materials list is available for this plan

First floor — 2,307 sq. ft.
Second floor — 440 sq. ft.
Garage & Storage — 517 sq. ft.

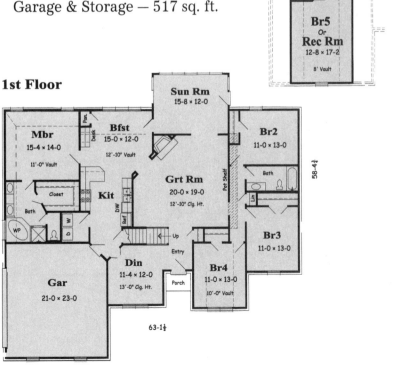

2nd Floor

Br5 Or Rec Rm
12-8 × 17-2
8' Vault

1st Floor

Sun Rm
15-8 × 12-0

Mbr
15-4 × 14-0
11'-0" Vault

Bfst
15-0 × 12-0
12'-10" Vault

Br2
11-0 × 13-0

Grt Rm
20-0 × 19-0
12'-10" Clg. Ht.

Kit

Br3
11-0 × 13-0

Din
11-4 × 12-0
13'-0" Clg. Ht.

Br4
11-0 × 13-0
10'-0" Vault

Gar
21-0 × 23-0

63-1¼

Lasting Elegance

Total living area 2,951 sq. ft. ■ **Price Code G**

SECOND FLOOR PLAN

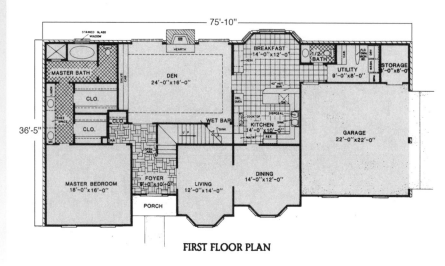

FIRST FLOOR PLAN

No. 92508

■ **This plan features:**

— Four bedrooms

— Three full and one half baths

■ Rich lines, bays and detailed window treatments add lasting elegance to this home

■ Huge den with hearth fireplace and built ins

■ Both the Living and Dining Rooms have bay windows

■ The convenient U-shaped Kitchen opens into a Nook

■ The large first floor Master Suite features a private bath

■ An optional slab or crawl space foundation — please specify when ordering

First floor — 2,008 sq. ft.
Second floor — 943 sq. ft.
Garage — 556 sq. ft.

Welcoming Wrap-Around Country Porch

■ *Total living area 2,083 sq. ft.* ■ *Price Code D* ■

No. 24245 X ⊠ ⓡ

■ **This plan features:**

— Three bedrooms

— Two full and one half baths

■ Formal areas flanking the entry hall

■ A Living Room that includes a wonderful fireplace

■ A U-shaped Kitchen including a breakfast bar, double sink, built-in pantry and planning desk

■ A Mudroom entry that will help keep the tracked-in dirt under control

■ An expansive Family Room with direct access to the rear Deck

■ A Master Suite highlighted by a walk-in closet and a private master bath

First floor — 1,113 sq. ft.
Second floor — 970 sq. ft.
Garage — 480 sq. ft.
Basement — 1,113 sq. ft.

Crawl Space/Slab Option

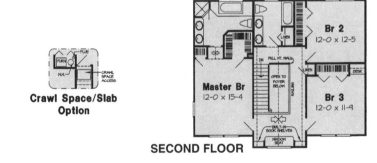

SECOND FLOOR

Master Br
12-0 x 15-4

Br 2
12-0 x 12-5

Br 3
12-0 x 11-9

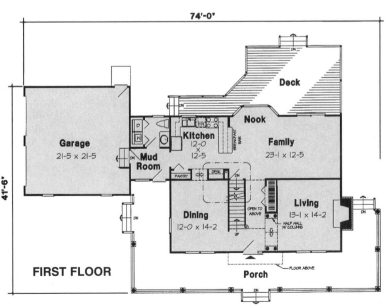

74'-0"

41'-6"

FIRST FLOOR

Garage
21-5 x 21-5

Mud Room

Kitchen
12-0 x 12-5

Deck

Nook

Family
23-1 x 12-5

Dining
12-0 x 14-2

Living
13-1 x 14-2

Porch

Traditional Brick with Detailing

■ *Total living area 1,869 sq. ft.* ■ *Price Code C* ■

No. 92536

■ **This plan features:**

— Three bedrooms

— Two full baths

■ Covered entry leads into the Foyer, the formal Dining Room and the Den

■ Expansive Den with a decorative ceiling over a hearth fireplace and sliding glass doors to the rear yard

■ Country Kitchen with a built-in Pantry, double ovens and a cooktop island easily serves the Breakfast Area and Dining Room

■ Private Master Suite with a decorative ceiling, a walk-in closet, a double vanity and a whirlpool tub

■ Two additional Bedrooms share a full Bath

■ An optional slab or crawl space foundation — please specify when ordering

Main floor — 1,869 sq. ft.
Garage — 561 sq. ft.

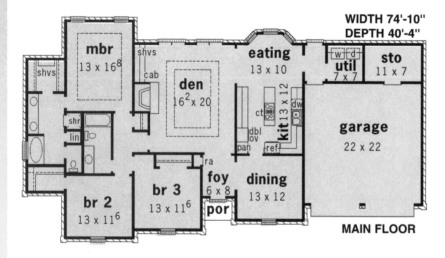

WIDTH 74'-10"
DEPTH 40'-4"

mbr
13 x 16⁸

shvs
cab

shvs

den
16² x 20

eating
13 x 10

w d
util
7 x 7

sto
11 x 7

shr
lin

ct
kit 13 x 12
dw

dbl
ov
pan
ref

garage
22 x 22

ra

br 2
13 x 11⁶

br 3
13 x 11⁶

foy
6 x 8
por

dining
13 x 12

MAIN FLOOR

■ *Total living area 1,670 sq. ft.* ■ *Price Code B* ■

No. 90409

■ This plan features:

— Three bedrooms

— Two full baths

■ A massive fireplace separating Living and Dining rooms

■ An isolated Master Suite with a walk-in closet and handy compartmentalized bath

■ A galley-type Kitchen between the Breakfast Room and Dining Room

■ An optional basement, slab or crawl space foundation — please specify when ordering

Main area — 1,670 sq. ft.
Basement — 1,670 sq. ft.
Garage — 427 sq. ft.

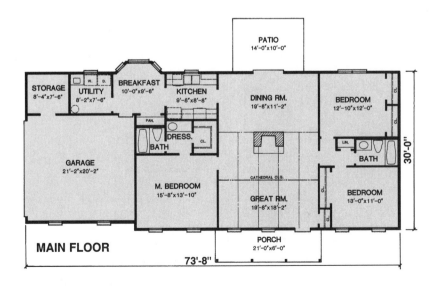

Home Sweet Home

■ *Total living area 2,588 sq. ft.* ■ *Price Code F* ■

FIRST FLOOR

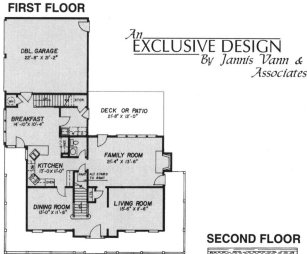

An
EXCLUSIVE DESIGN
*By Jannis Vann &
Associates, Inc.*

First floor — 1,320 sq. ft.
Second floor — 1,268 sq. ft.
Bonus room — 389 sq. ft.
Basement — 1,320 sq. ft.
Garage — 482 sq. ft.

SECOND FLOOR

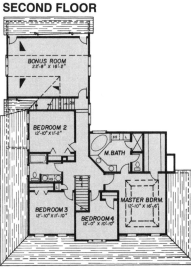

No. 93205

■ **This plan features:**

— Four bedrooms

— Two full and one half baths

■ Foyer with formal Living Room to the right

■ Dining Room convenient to the Kitchen

■ A U-shaped Kitchen equipped with a peninsula counter

■ A spacious Breakfast Room with direct access to the Garage

■ Family Room with a large fireplace and direct access to the rear Deck and Porch

■ Second floor Master Suite crowned by a decorative ceiling treatment

■ A Bonus Room for future expansion

■ An optional basement, crawl space or slab foundation — please specify when ordering

■ *Total living area 2,545 sq. ft.* ■ *Price Code F* ■

No. 93035

■ **This plan features:**

— Four bedrooms

— Two full and one half baths

■ An entrance flanked by columns and imposing gables, accented with dentil molding

■ An angled Foyer, drawing the eye to an arched passage in the Living Room

■ A large Kitchen/Family Room combination with an octagonal shaped breakfast area

■ A Master Bedroom that is entered through angled double doors and has a cathedral ceiling

■ A Master Bath with his-and-her vanities and walk-in closets

■ No materials list is available for this plan

Main floor — 2,545 sq. ft.
Garage — 436 sq. ft.

WIDTH 69'-0"

© Larry E. Belk

DEPTH 63'-6"

MAIN FLOOR

Exquisite Detail

■ *Total living area 3,262 sq. ft.* ■ *Price Code I* ■

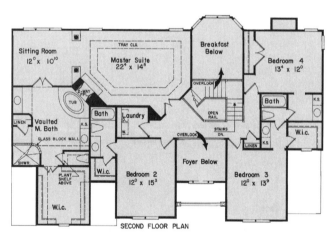

SECOND FLOOR PLAN

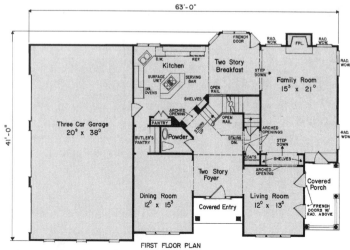

FIRST FLOOR PLAN

No. 98400

■ This plan features:

— Four bedrooms

— Three full and one half baths

■ Formal Living Room with access to Covered Porch

■ Radius windows and arches, huge fireplace enhance spacious Family Room

■ Kitchen has a Pantry, cooktop/serving bar and a two-story Breakfast Area

■ Expansive Master Bedroom offers a tray ceiling, a cozy Sitting Room, a luxurious bath and huge walk-in closet

■ An optional basement or crawl space foundation — please specify when ordering

First floor — 1,418 sq. ft.
Second floor — 1,844 sq. ft.
Basement — 1,418 sq. ft.
Garage — 820 sq. ft.

Out of the English Countryside

■ *Total living area 2,524 sq. ft.* ■ *Price Code F* ■

No. 98519

■ This plan features:

– Four bedrooms

– Three full and one half baths

■ From the Entry, is the Living Room/Study with a cozy fireplace, or left into the Dining Room, both rooms have lovely bay windows

■ The Family Room has a fireplace and a door that leads out onto a covered patio

■ The Breakfast Area is adjacent to the Family Room and the Kitchen which features a center island

■ The first floor Master Bedroom has two walk-in closets and an attached bath with a spa tub

■ Upstairs bedrooms each have walk-in closets and use of two full baths

■ Also located upstairs is a Bonus Room that would be a perfect Playroom

■ No materials list is available for this plan

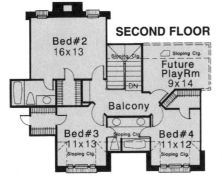

First floor — 1,735 sq. ft.
Second floor — 789 sq. ft.
Bonus — 132 sq. ft.
Garage — 482 sq. ft.

Covered Porch on Farm Style Traditional

■ Total living area 1,763 sq. ft. ■ Price Code C ■

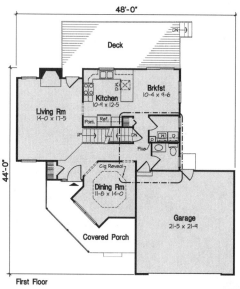

First Floor

Second Floor

No. 34901

■ This plan features:

– Three bedrooms

– Two full and one half baths

■ A Dining Room with bay window and elevated ceiling

■ A Living Room complete with gas-light fireplace

■ A two-car Garage

■ Ample storage space throughout the home

First floor — 909 sq. ft.
Second floor — 854 sq. ft.
Basement — 899 sq. ft.
Garage — 491 sq. ft.

An EXCLUSIVE DESIGN *By Karl Kreeger*

Master Retreat Welcomes You Home

■ *Total living area 1,486 sq. ft.* ■ *Price Code A* ■

No. 34154

■ This plan features:

— Three bedrooms

— Two full baths

■ Foyer opens into an huge Living Room with a fireplace below a sloped ceiling and Deck access

■ Efficient Kitchen with a Pantry, serving counter, Dining area, laundry closet and Garage entry

■ Corner Master Bedroom offers a walk-in closet and pampering bath with a raised tub

■ Two more bedrooms, one with a Den option, share a full bath

Main area — 1,486 sq. ft.
Garage — 462 sq. ft.

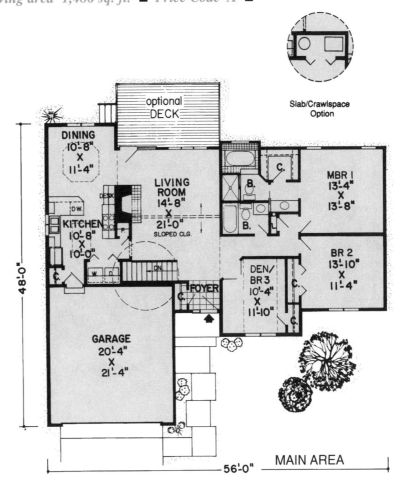

Slab/Crawlspace Option

MAIN AREA

Southern Hospitality

■ *Total living area 1,830 sq. ft.* ■ *Price Code C* ■

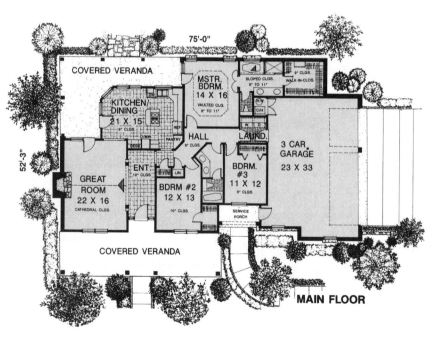

75'-0"

COVERED VERANDA

KITCHEN/
DINING
21 X 15
9" CLGS.

MSTR.
BDRM.
14 X 16
VAULTED CLG.
9" TO 11"

SLOPED CLGS.
9" TO 11"

WALK-IN-CLOS.

PANTRY

DESK

HALL
9" CLGS.

LAUND.

3 CAR
GARAGE
23 X 33

ENT
10" CLGS.

GREAT
ROOM
22 X 16
CATHEDRAL CLGS.

BDRM #2
12 X 13
10" CLGS.

BDRM.
#3
11 X 12
9" CLGS.

52'-3"

SERVICE
PORCH

COVERED VERANDA

MAIN FLOOR

No. 92220

■ **This plan features:**

— Three bedrooms

— Two full baths

■ Covered Veranda catches breezes

■ Tiled Entry leads into Great Room
with fieldstone fireplace, a
cathedral ceiling and atrium door
to another Covered Veranda

■ A bright Kitchen/Dining Room
includes a stovetop island/
snackbar, built-in Pantry and desk

■ Vaulted ceiling crowns Master
Bedroom that offers a plush bath
and huge walk-in closet

■ Two additional bedrooms with
ample closets share a double
vanity bath

■ No materials list is available for
this plan

Main floor — 1,830 sq. ft.
Garage — 759 sq. ft.

Columns Accentuate Southern Flair

■ *Total living area 2,400 sq. ft.* ■ *Price Code E* ■

No. 94641

■ **This plan features:**

— Four bedrooms

— Two full baths

■ Four columns accentuating the warm Southern welcome alluded to by the front Porch

■ Kitchen includes a peninsula counter, plenty of counter and storage space and an easy flow into the Breakfast Room

■ Master Bedroom topped by a decorative ceiling treatment and a compartmental master bath with a whirlpool tub

■ Two additional bedrooms with walk-in closets share a double vanity bath in the hall

■ No materials list is available for this plan

Main floor — 2,400 sq. ft.
Garage — 534 sq. ft.

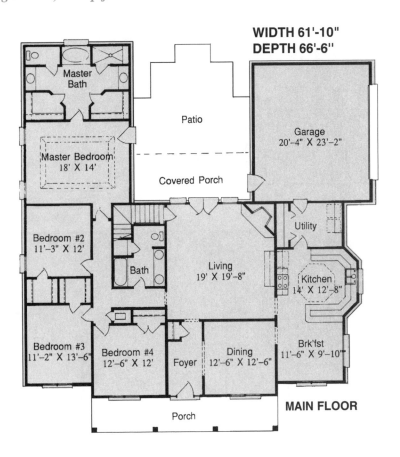

WIDTH 61'-10"
DEPTH 66'-6"

Master Bath

Patio

Garage
20'-4" X 23'-2"

Master Bedroom
18' X 14'

Covered Porch

Utility

Bedroom #2
11'-3" X 12'

Bath

Living
19' X 19'-8"

Kitchen
14' X 12'-8"

Bedroom #3
11'-2" X 13'-6"

Bedroom #4
12'-6" X 12'

Foyer

Dining
12'-6" X 12'-6"

Brk'fst
11'-6" X 9'-10"

Porch

MAIN FLOOR

Beckoning Country Porch

■ *Total living area 1,560 sq. ft.* ■ *Price Code B* ■

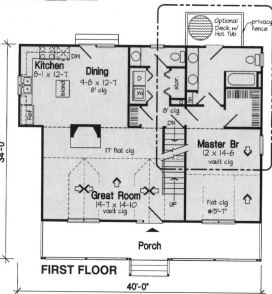

SECOND FLOOR

Br 2
10-10 x 12-6

Br 3
11-6 x 12-6

railing — DN

open to great room below

open to master bedroom below

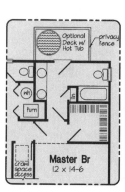

Alternate Foundation Plan

Optional Deck w/ Hot Tub — privacy fence

wh — furn

crawl space access

Master Br
12 x 14-6

FIRST FLOOR

Kitchen
8-1 x 12-7

Dining
9-8 x 12-7
8' clg

DW — island — Ref — D — W

stor.

8' clg

17' flat clg

DN

Master Br
12 x 14-6
vault clg

UP

flat clg @15'-7"

Great Room
19-7 x 14-10
vault clg

Optional Deck w/ Hot Tub — privacy fence

Porch

34'-0"

40'-0"

No. 34603

■ **This plan features:**

— Three bedrooms

— Two full and one half baths

■ Country style exterior with dormer windows

■ Vaulted ceiling and central fireplace in the Great Room

■ L-shaped Kitchen/Dining Room with work island and atrium door to backyard

■ First floor Master Suite with vaulted ceiling, walk-in closet, private bath and optional private Deck with hot tub

■ Two additional bedrooms on the second floor with easy access to full bath

First floor — 1,061 sq. ft.
Second floor — 499 sq. ft.
Basement — 1,061 sq. ft.

Elegant Window Treatment

■ *Total living area 1,492 sq. ft.* ■ *Price Code A* ■

No. 34150

An EXCLUSIVE DESIGN *By Karl Kreeger*

■ This plan features:

— Two bedrooms (optional third)

— Two full baths

■ An arched window that floods the front room with light

■ A homey, well-lit Office or Den

■ Compact, efficient use of space

■ The Kitchen has easy access to the Dining Room

■ A fireplaced Living Room with a sloping ceiling and a window wall

■ The Master Bedroom sports a private master bath and a roomy walk-in closet

Main floor — 1,492 sq. ft.
Basement — 1,486 sq. ft.
Garage — 462 sq. ft.

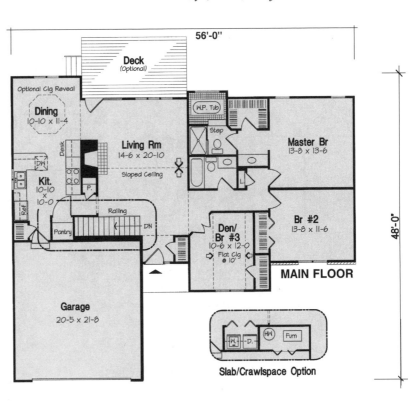

Your Classic Hideaway

■ *Total living area 1,773 sq. ft.* ■ *Price Code C* ■

No. 90423

■ **This plan features:**

— Three bedrooms

— Two full baths

■ A lovely fireplace in the Living Room which is both cozy and a source of heat

■ An efficient Country Kitchen, connects the large Dining and Living rooms

■ A lavish Master Suite enhanced by a step-up sunken tub, more than ample closet space, and separate shower

■ A screened Porch and Patio area for outdoor living

■ An optional basement, slab or crawl space foundation — please specify when ordering

Main floor — 1,773 sq. ft.
Screened porch — 240 sq. ft.

MAIN FLOOR

PATIO
16-0x10-0

GARAGE
21-0x21-0

SCR. PORCH
12-0x20-4

DINING
12-0x13-4

KITCHEN
10x13

UTILITY

BEDROOM
11-0x13-4

M. BATH

M. BEDROOM
12-0x18-0

LIVING ROOM
15-6x17-8

CLOSET

DRESSING

LINEN

BEDROOM
12-0x11-4

FOYER

BATH

PORCH
26-0x6-0

88'-8"

43'-8"

■ *Total living area 2,685 sq. ft.* ■ *Price Code F* ■

An
EXCLUSIVE DESIGN
By Westhome Planners, Ltd.

No. 90838

■ This plan features:

— Three bedrooms

— Three full baths

■ A corner gas fireplace in the spacious Living Room

■ A Master Suite including a private bath with a whirlpool tub, separate shower and a double vanity

■ An island Kitchen that is well-equipped to efficiently serve both formal Dining Room and informal Nook

■ Two additional bedrooms sharing a full bath on the second floor

First floor — 1,837 sq. ft.
Second floor — 848 sq. ft.
Basement — 1,803 sq. ft.
Bonus room — 288 sq. ft.

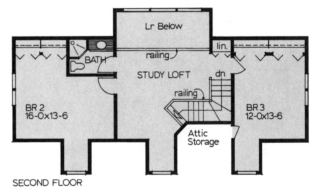

SECOND FLOOR

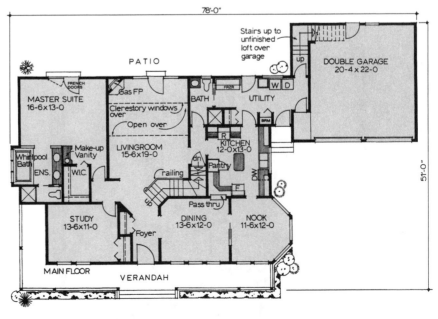

Impressive Fieldstone Facade

■ *Total living area 3,110 sq. ft.* ■ *Price Code H* ■

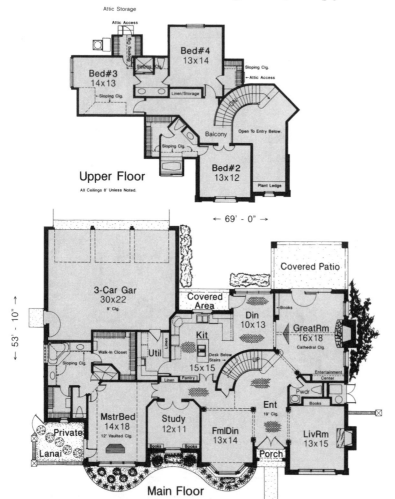

Attic Storage

Attic Access

Bed #4
13x14

Bed #3
14x13

Sloping Clg.

Linen/Storage

Balcony

Open To Entry Below

Upper Floor
All Ceilings 8' Unless Noted.

Bed #2
13x12

Plant Ledge

← 69' - 0" →

← 53' - 10" →

3-Car Gar
30x22
8' Clg.

Covered Area

Covered Patio

Din
10x13

Kit
15x15

GreatRm
16x18
Cathedral Clg.

Walk-in Closet

Util

Entertainment Center

Pantry

MstrBed
14x18
12' Vaulted Clg.

Study
12x11

FmlDin
13x12

Ent
19' Clg.

Pwdr

Books

LivRm
13x15

Private

Lanai

Porch

Main Floor

No. 92277

■ **This plan features:**

— Four bedrooms

— Three full and one half baths

■ Double door leads into two-story entry with an exquisite curved staircase

■ Formal Living Room features a marble hearth fireplace, triple window and built-in book shelves

■ Formal Dining Room defined by columns and a lovely bay window

■ Expansive Great Room with entertainment center, fieldstone fireplace and cathedral ceiling

■ Vaulted ceiling crowns Master Bedroom suite offering a plush bath and two walk-in closets

■ No materials list is available for this plan

Main floor — 2,190 sq. ft.
Upper floor — 920 sq. ft.
Garage — 624 sq. ft.

Gazebo Porch Creates Old-Fashioned Feel

■ *Total living area 1,452 sq. ft.* ■ *Price Code A* ■

No. 24718

■ **This plan features:**

— Three bedrooms

— Two full baths

■ An old-fashioned welcome is created by the covered Porch

■ The Breakfast Area overlooks the Porch and is separated from the Kitchen by an extended counter

■ The Dining Room and the Great Room are highlighted by a two sided fireplace

■ The roomy Master Suite is enhanced by a whirlpool bath with double vanity and a walk-in closet

■ Each of the two secondary bedrooms feature a walk-in closet

■ No materials list is available for this plan

Main floor — 1,452 sq. ft.
Garage — 584 sq. ft.

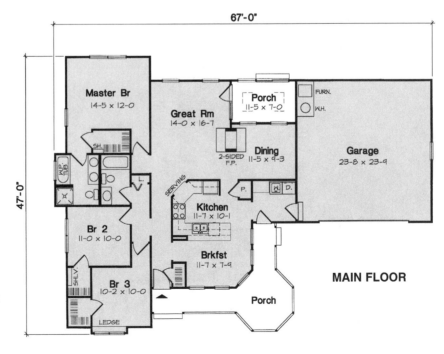

Country Brick

■ *Total living area 2,443 sq. ft.* ■ *Price Code E* ■

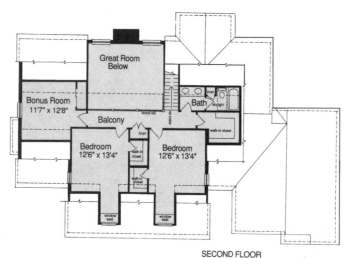

SECOND FLOOR

FIRST FLOOR

No. 92653

■ This plan features:

— Three or four bedrooms

— Two full and one half baths

■ Friendly front porch leads into a gracious open Foyer

■ Secluded Library offers a quiet space with built-in shelves

■ Great Room with a focal point fireplace topped by sloped ceiling

■ Kitchen with island snack bar, bright Breakfast area, pantry and nearby Laundry/Garage entry

■ Master Bedroom offers a deluxe bath and spacious walk-in closet

■ Two additional bedrooms with walk-in closets and window seats

■ No materials list is available for this plan

First floor — 1,710 sq. ft.
Second floor — 733 sq. ft.
Bonus — 181 sq. ft.
Basement — 1,697 sq. ft.
Garage — 499 sq. ft.

■ *Total living area 1,560 sq. ft.* ■ *Price Code B* ■

No. 34602 ◪◪

■ This plan features:

— Three bedrooms

— Two full and one half baths

■ A wrap-around Porch for views and visiting provides access into the Great Room and Dining area

■ A spacious Great Room with a two-story ceiling and dormer window above a massive fireplace

■ A combination Dining/Kitchen with an island work area and breakfast bar opening to a Great Room and adjacent to the Laundry/storage and half-bath area

■ A private two-story Master Bedroom with a dormer window, walk-in closet, double vanity bath and optional deck with hot tub

First floor — 1,061 sq. ft.
Second floor — 499 sq. ft.
Basement — 1,061 sq. ft.

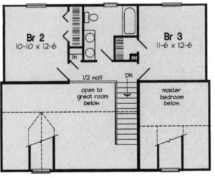

SECOND FLOOR

Alternate Foundation Plan

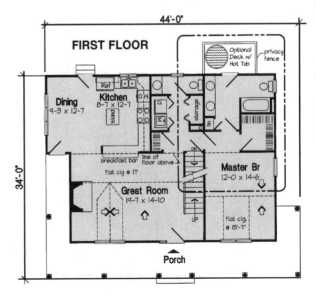

An Extraordinary Home

■ *Total living area 2,082 sq. ft.* ■ *Price Code D* ■

Bedroom
11'1" x 13'3"

Bedroom
11'5" x 12'0"

linen

Bath

bookshelves
computer desk

Balcony   Foyer Below

wood rail

Bonus
Room
11'0" x 22'0"

wood rail

SECOND FLOOR

Master Bedroom
13'6" x 15'1"

Triple French Doors
w/ arched window above

Great Room
17'4" x 21'2"

Dining
Room
10'10" x 14'0"

12' high ceiling

Bath

hanging
space

Bath

walk-in closet   Laun

pass thru

Kitchen
12'4" x 11'6"

Foyer

Two-car Garage
22'9" x 22'0"

Breakfast
11' x 9'4"

pantry

wood rail

FIRST FLOOR

50'4"

60'

No. 92642

■ **This plan features:**

— Three bedrooms

— Two full and one half baths

■ A grand entry into the formal Dining Room with a volume ceiling

■ A roomy, well-equipped Kitchen that includes a pass-through

■ Large windows in the Breakfast area flood the room with natural light

■ A private Master Bedroom with a luxurious, compartmented bath

■ Split stairs, graced with wood railings, lead to the second floor

■ No materials list is available for this plan

First floor — 1,524 sq. ft.
Second floor — 558 sq. ft.
Bonus room — 267 sq. ft.
Basement — 1,460 sq. ft.

Country Living in Any Neighborhood

■ *Total living area 2,181 sq. ft.* ■ *Price Code D* ■

No. 90436

■ **This plan features:**

— Three bedrooms

— Two full and two half baths

■ An expansive Family Room with fireplace

■ A Dining Room and Breakfast Nook lit by flowing natural light from bay windows

■ A first floor Master Suite with a double vanity bath that wraps around his-n-her closets

■ An optional basement, slab or crawl space foundation — please specify when ordering

First floor — 1,477 sq. ft.
Second floor — 704 sq. ft.
Basement — 1,374 sq. ft.
Garage — 528 sq. ft.

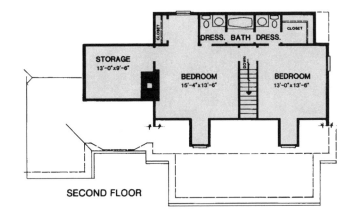

DRESS. BATH DRESS.

STORAGE
13'-0"x9'-6"

BEDROOM
15'-4"x13'-6"

BEDROOM
13'-0"x13'-6"

CLOSET

CLOSET

SECOND FLOOR

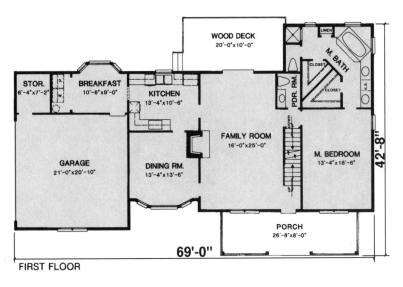

WOOD DECK
20'-0"x10'-0"

LINEN

M. BATH

STOR.
6'-4"x7'-2"

BREAKFAST
10'-6"x9'-0"

KITCHEN
13'-4"x10'-6"

CLOSET

CLOSET

PDR. RM.

GARAGE
21'-0"x20'-10"

DINING RM.
13'-4"x13'-6"

FAMILY ROOM
16'-0"x25'-0"

M. BEDROOM
13'-4"x18'-6"

42'-8"

PORCH
26'-8"x8'-0"

69'-0"

FIRST FLOOR

European Style

Total living area 2,727 sq. ft. ■ Price Code F

No. 92501

■ This plan features:

— Four bedrooms

— Three full and one half baths

■ Central Foyer between spacious Living and Dining rooms with arched windows

■ Hub Kitchen with extended counter and nearby Utility/Garage entry, easily serves Breakfast Area and Dining Room

■ Spacious Den with a hearth fireplace between built-ins and sliding glass doors to Porch

■ Master Bedroom wing with decorative ceiling, plush bath with two walk-in closets

■ Three additional bedrooms with ample closets and private access to a full bath

■ An optional slab or crawl space foundation — please specify when ordering

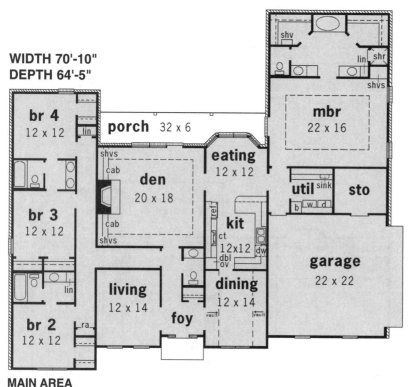

WIDTH 70'-10"
DEPTH 64'-5"

MAIN AREA

Main area — 2,727 sq. ft.
Garage — 569 sq. ft.

Wide Open and Convenient

■ *Total living area 1,737 sq. ft.* ■ *Price Code B* ■

No. 20100

■ This plan features:

— Three bedrooms

— Two full baths

■ Vaulted ceilings in the Dining Room and Master Bedroom

■ A sloped ceiling in the fireplaced Living Room

■ A skylight illuminating the Master Bath

■ A large Master Bedroom with a walk-in closet

Main floor — 1,737 sq. ft.
Basement — 1,727 sq. ft.
Garage — 484 sq. ft.

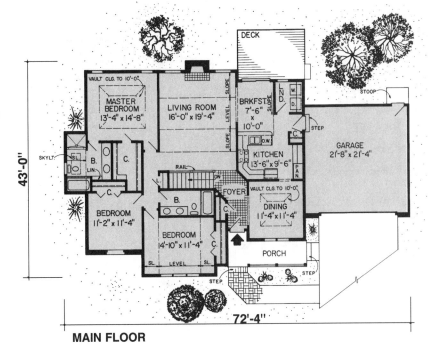

MAIN FLOOR

An
EXCLUSIVE DESIGN
By Karl Kreeger

Luxurious Masterpiece

■ *Total living area 3,818 sq. ft.* ■ *Price Code K* ■

No. 92265

■ **This plan features:**

— Four bedrooms

— Three full and one half baths

■ An elegant and distinguished exterior

■ An expansive formal Living Room with a 14' ceiling and a raised hearth fireplace

■ Informal Family Room offers another fireplace, wetbar and a cathedral ceiling

■ A hub Kitchen with a cooktop island, peninsula counter, and a bright breakfast area

■ Private Master Bedroom with a pullman ceiling, lavish his-n-her baths and a garden window tub

■ Three additional bedrooms with walk-in closets and private access to a full bath

■ No materials list is available for this plan

Main floor — 3,818 sq. ft.
Garage — 816 sq. ft.

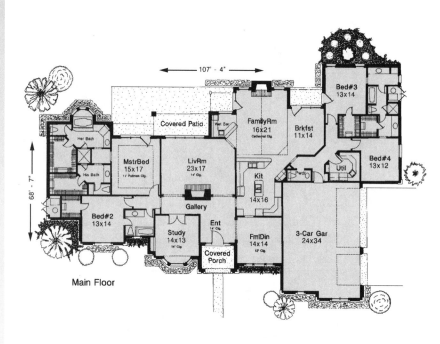

Main Floor

Grand Four Bedroom Farmhouse

© 1992 Donald A. Gardner Architects, Inc.

■ *Total living area 2,561 sq. ft.* ■ *Price Code H* ■

No. 99891

■ This plan features:

— Four bedrooms

— Two full and one half baths

■ Double gables, wrap-around Porch and custom window details add appeal to farmhouse

■ Formal Living and Dining rooms connected by Foyer in front, while casual living areas expand rear

■ Efficient Kitchen with island cooktop and easy access to all eating areas

■ Fireplace, wetbar and rear Porch and Deck provide great entertainment space

■ Spacious Master Bedroom features walk-in closet and pampering bath

First floor — 1,357 sq. ft.
Second floor — 1,204 sq. ft.
Garage & storage — 546 sq. ft.

SECOND FLOOR PLAN

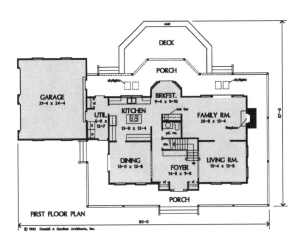

FIRST FLOOR PLAN

© 1992 Donald A Gardner Architects, Inc.

Relax on the Veranda

Total living area 3,051 sq. ft. ■ *Price Code H* ■

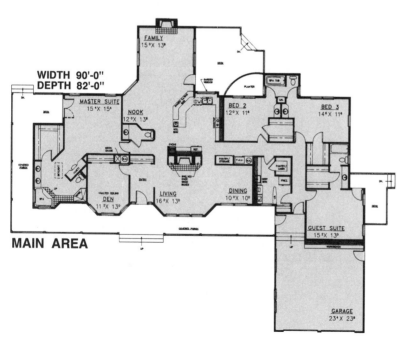

WIDTH 90'-0"
DEPTH 82'-0"

MASTER SUITE
15'X 15'

NOOK
12'X 13'

FAMILY
15'X 13'

BED 2
12'X 11'

BED 3
14'X 11'

DEN
11'X 13'

LIVING
16'X 13'

DINING
10'X 10'

GUEST SUITE
15'X 13'

GARAGE
23'X 23'

MAIN AREA

No. 91749 ✖

■ **This plan features:**

— Four bedrooms

— Three full and one half baths

■ A wrap-around veranda

■ A sky-lit Master Suite with elevated custom spa, twin basins, a walk-in closet, and an additional vanity outside the bathroom

■ A vaulted ceiling in the Den

■ A fireplace in both the Family Room and the formal Living Room

■ An efficient Kitchen with a peninsula counter and a double sink

■ Two additional bedrooms with walk-in closets, served by a compartmentalized bath

■ A Guest Suite with a private bath

Main Area — 3,051 sq. ft.
Garage — 646 sq. ft.

■ *Total living area 2,787 sq. ft.* ■ *Price Code G* ■

No. 92902

■ This plan features:

— Four bedrooms

— Three full baths

■ Family living area comprised of a family room, breakfast area, and island Kitchen

■ Formal Dining Room with easy access from the Kitchen

■ Pampering Master Suite with private master bath and an abundance of storage space

■ Screened Porch and covered Patio extending living space outdoors

■ No materials list is available for this plan

Main floor — 2,787 sq. ft.
Garage — 685 sq. ft.

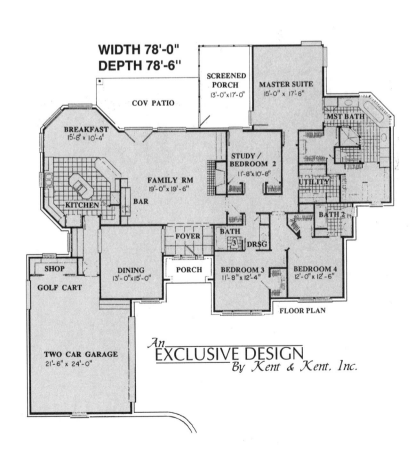

WIDTH 78'-0"
DEPTH 78'-6"

An EXCLUSIVE DESIGN
By Kent & Kent, Inc.

Luxuriant Living

© 1997 Donald A Gardner Architects, Inc.

■ *Total living area 2,869 sq. ft.* ■ *Price Code I* ■

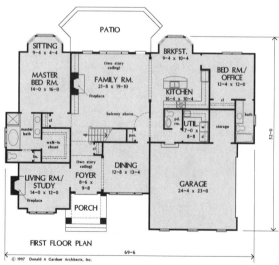

FIRST FLOOR PLAN

© 1997 Donald A Gardner Architects, Inc.

First floor — 2,249 sq. ft.
Second floor — 620 sq. ft.
Bonus — 308 sq. ft.
Garage — 642 sq. ft.

SECOND FLOOR PLAN

No. 99825

■ This plan features:

— Four bedrooms

— Three full and one half baths

■ French doors, windows and a high gabled Entry make a dramatic entrance

■ Living Room features a box bay window and a fireplace

■ Dining Room is illuminated by a bank of windows

■ Family Room has a two-story ceiling, a fireplace and access to the rear Patio

■ Kitchen and Nook adjoin handy Home Office

■ The Master Suite features a private bath and a Sitting Area

■ Upstairs find two bedrooms, each with a walk-in closet, a full bath and a Bonus Room

Unique and Desirable

© 1996 Donald A Gardner Architects, Inc.

■ *Total living area* *1,977 sq. ft.* ■ *Price Code* *E* ■

No. 99803 ✕ 🇺🇸 ℞

■ This plan features:

— Three bedrooms

— Two full baths

■ Private Master Bedroom has a walk-in closet and a skylit Bath

■ Two additional Bedrooms, one with a possible use as a Study, share a full Bath

■ From the Foyer columns lead into the Great Room with a cathedral ceiling and a fireplace

■ In the rear of the home is a skylit screen Porch and a Deck that features built-in seats and a spa

■ The Kitchen is conveniently located between the Dining Room and the skylit Breakfast Area

■ An optional basement or crawl space foundation — please specify when ordering

Main floor — 1,977 sq. ft.
Bonus room — 430 sq. ft.
Garage & storage — 610 sq. ft.

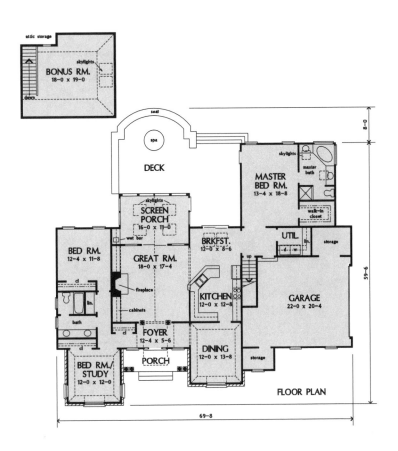

Covered Porch with Columns

Total living area 1,856 sq. ft. ■ Price Code C

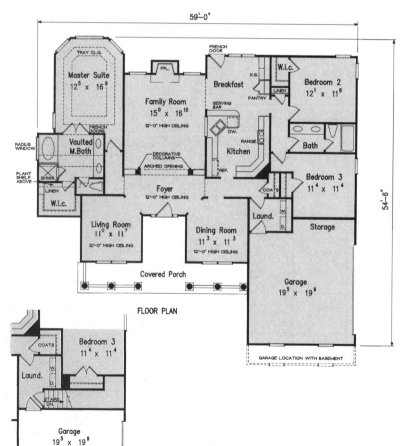

FLOOR PLAN

OPT. BASEMENT STAIR LOCATION

No. 98408

■ **This plan features:**

— Three bedrooms

— Two full baths

■ The foyer with 12' ceiling leads past decorative columns into the Family Room with a center fireplace

■ The Living and Dining rooms are linked by Foyer and have windows overlooking the front Porch

■ The Kitchen has a serving bar and is adjacent to the Breakfast Nook which has a French door that opens to the backyard

■ The private Master Suite has a tray ceiling and a vaulted bath with a double vanity

■ An optional basement, slab or a crawl space foundation — please specify when ordering

Main floor — 1,856 sq. ft.
Basement — 1,856 sq. ft.
Garage — 429 sq. ft.

Grand Design Highlighted by Turrets

■ *Total living area 4,759 sq. ft.* ■ *Price Code L* ■

No. 94230

■ **This plan features:**

— Four bedrooms

— Two full, one three-quarter and one half baths

■ Triple arches at entry lead into Grand Foyer and Gallery with arched entries to all areas

■ Triple French doors catch the breeze and access to rear grounds in Living and Leisure rooms

■ Spacious Kitchen with large walk-in Pantry, cooktop/work island and angled serving counter/snack bar, glass Nook, Utility Room and Garage entry

■ Master Suite wing offers Veranda access, two closets and vanities, and a garden window tub

■ Three second floor bedrooms with walk-in closets, balcony and full bath access

■ No materials list is available for this plan

First floor — 3,546 sq. ft.
Second floor — 1,213 sq. ft.
Garage — 822 sq. ft.

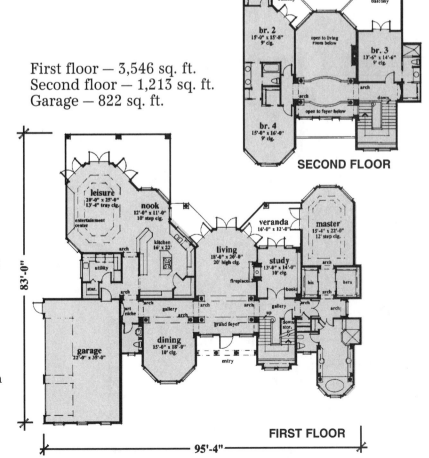

A Little Drama

■ *Total living area 1,768 sq. ft.* ■ *Price Code C* ■

No. 92609

■ This plan features:

— Three bedrooms

— Two full and one half baths

■ A 12' high Entry with transom and sidelights, multiple gables and a box window

■ A sunken Great Room with a fireplace and access to a rear Porch

■ A Breakfast Bay and Kitchen flowing into each other and accessing a rear Porch

■ A Master Bedroom with a tray ceiling, walk-in closet and a private master bath

■ No materials list is available for this plan

First floor — 960 sq. ft.
Second floor — 808 sq. ft.
Basement — 922 sq. ft.
Garage — 413 sq. ft.

■ *Total living area 2,095 sq. ft.* ■ *Price Code D* ■

No. 20136 ⚒

An EXCLUSIVE DESIGN
By Karl Kreeger

■ This plan features:

— Three bedrooms

— Two full and one half bath

■ Center Foyer with a lovely, landing staircase and balcony, flanked by Formal Parlor and Dining Room

■ Expansive Living Room with a cozy fireplace below decorative beams on sloped ceiling

■ Hub Kitchen with pantry and peninsula counter, easily serves Breakfast area, Dining Room

■ Private Master Bedroom offers a decorative ceiling, over-sized closet and double vanity bath

■ Two second floor bedrooms with ample closets, share a full bath

First floor — 1,556 sq. ft.
Second floor — 539 sq. ft.
Garage — 572 sq. ft.
Basement — 1,556 sq. ft.

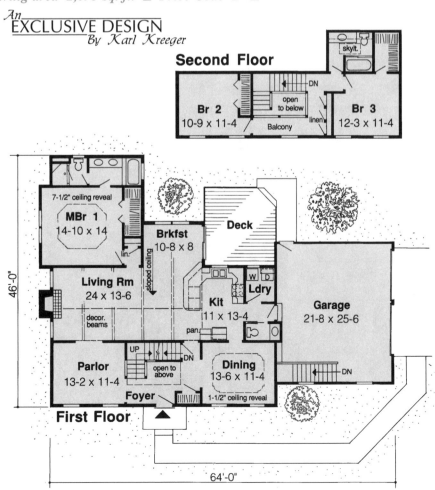

Second Floor

Br 2
10-9 x 11-4

Br 3
12-3 x 11-4

open to below

Balcony   linen   skylt.

DN

First Floor

MBr 1
14-10 x 14

7-1/2" ceiling reveal

Brkfst
10-8 x 8

Deck

Living Rm
24 x 13-6

sloped ceiling

decor. beams

Kit
11 x 13-4

Ldry
W D

Garage
21-8 x 25-6

pan.

Parlor
13-2 x 11-4

UP   open to above   DN

Dining
13-6 x 11-4

1-1/2" ceiling reveal

DN

Foyer

46'-0"

64'-0"

Living Room Features Vaulted Ceiling

■ *Total living area 1,246 sq. ft.* ■ *Price Code A* ■

No. 90353

■ **This plan features:**

— Three bedrooms

— Two full baths

■ A vaulted ceiling in the Living Room and the Dining Room, with a clerestory above

■ A Master Bedroom with a walk-in closet and private full bath

■ An efficient Kitchen, with a corner double sink and peninsula counter

■ A Dining Room with sliding doors to the deck

■ A Living Room with a fireplace that adds warmth to open areas

■ Two additional bedrooms that share a full hall bath

Main floor — 846 sq. ft.
Upper floor — 400 sq. ft.

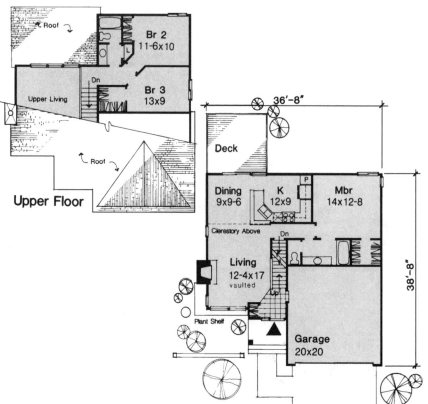

■ *Total living area 2,099 sq. ft.* ■ *Price Code C* ■

No. 91053 ⚒

■ This plan features:

— Three bedrooms

— Two full and one half baths

■ A classic Victorian exterior design accented by a wonderful turret room and second floor covered Porch above a sweeping veranda

■ A spacious formal Living Room

■ An efficient, U-shaped Kitchen with a peninsula snackbar, opens to an eating Nook and Family Room for informal gatherings

■ An elegant Master Suite with a unique, octagon Sitting area, a private Porch, an oversized, walk-in closet and private Bath with a double vanity and a window tub

■ Two bedrooms with ample closets sharing a full hall bath

First floor — 1,150 sq. ft.
Second floor — 949 sq. ft.
Garage — 484 sq. ft.

SECOND FLOOR

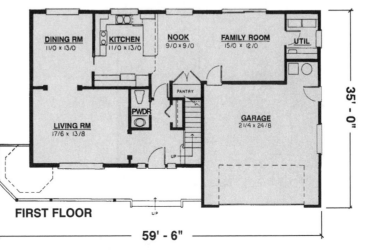

FIRST FLOOR

Arched Windows Abound

■ *Total living area 4,328 sq. ft.* ■ *Price Code F* ■

Patio

Media Room
17'10" x 21'6"

Bedroom
14'1" x 12'9"

Basement

Bath

Bedroom
10'9" x 14'10"

Bath

Billiard Room
15'8" x 16'8"

Exercise
Room
10'11" x 10'10"

Basement

LOWER LEVEL

Deck

Kitchen
15'1" x 18'7"

Breakfast
13'8" x 13'8"

Great Room
15'8" x 21'5"

Master
Bedroom
14'4" x 19'11"

walk in closet

Laun.

Hall

Bath

Gallery

Dressing

Three-car Garage
22'2" x 29'8"

Dining Room
16'2" x 14'2"

Foyer

Library
11'8" x 12'7"

Porch

FIRST FLOOR

70' - 8"

64' - 4"

No. 92657

■ **This plan features:**

— Three bedrooms

— Two full, one three quarter and one half baths

■ The large foyer and gallery area

■ The impressive master bedroom with a walk in closet, dressing area, and bath with dual vanities

■ Two bedrooms on the lower level share a full bath

■ Accented by columns, the dining room and great room, perfect for formal occasions

■ An exercise room, billiard room, media room, and full bath complete the lower level

■ No materials list is available for this plan

Main level — 2,582 sq. ft.
Lower level — 1,746 sq. ft.
Basement — 871 sq. ft.

■ *Total living area 3,034 sq. ft.* ■ *Price Code E* ■

No. 91111

■ This plan features:

— Four bedrooms

— Two full and one half baths

■ Dramatic roof lines and a seven foot tall arched transom above front door

■ Columns, arches, angled stairs, a high ceiling and a large plant ledge in the Foyer

■ High vaulted ceilings and an abundance of windows in the Sun Room, Breakfast Nook and Living Room

■ The Master Bedroom has a lavish whirlpool bath and a large walk-in closet

■ No materials list is available for this plan

First floor — 2,123 sq. ft.
Second floor — 911 sq. ft.
Garage & storage — 565 sq. ft.

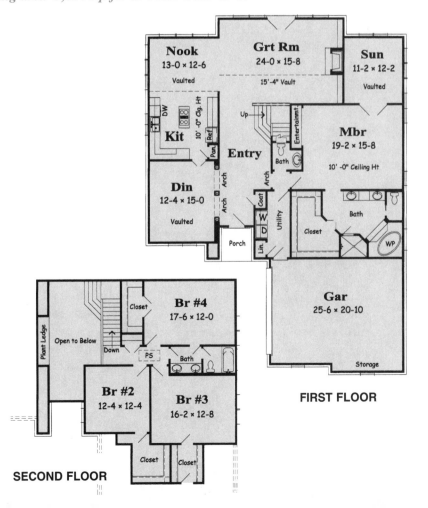

Stately Home

■ *Total living area 2,526 sq. ft.* ■ *Price Code E* ■

Main floor — 2,526 sq. ft.
Garage — 611 sq. ft.

ALTERNATE PLAN
FOR BASEMENT

FLOOR PLAN

No. 96435

■ This plan features:

— Four bedrooms

— Two full and one half baths

■ An elegant brick exterior and careful detailing

■ Arched window in the clerestory dormer above the foyer

■ Great Room topped by a cathedral ceiling boasting built-in cabinets and bookshelves

■ Through glass doors capped by an arched window the Sun Room is access from the Great Room

■ Both the Dining Room and the Bedroom/Study have tray ceilings

■ Master Suite includes a fireplace, access to the deck, his-n-her vanity, a shower and a whirlpool tub

■ An optional basement or crawl space foundation — please specify when ordering

■ *Total living area 2,082 sq. ft.* ■ *Price Code C* ■

No. 99500

■ **This plan features:**

—Three bedrooms

—Two full and one half baths

■ Charming porch and quaint dormers enhance curb appeal

■ Formal Foyer with half bath and staircase to the left and elegant Dining Room with a bay window to right

■ Open Great Room with a fireplace

■ First floor Master Suite has a five-piece bath and a walk-in closet

■ Entertainment room on second floor keeps the noise upstairs

■ Two additional bedrooms share a full bath

■ An optional slab or crawl space foundation — please specify when ordering

■ No materials list is available for this plan

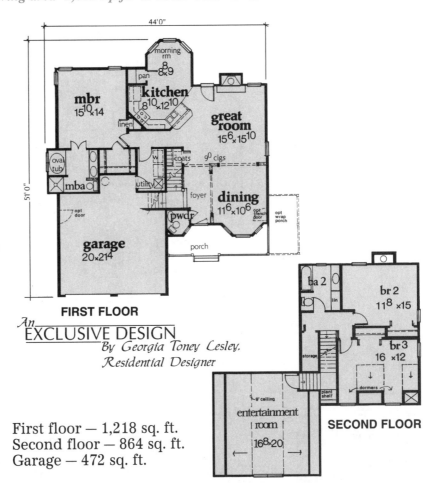

An EXCLUSIVE DESIGN
By Georgia Toney Lesley,
Residential Designer

First floor — 1,218 sq. ft.
Second floor — 864 sq. ft.
Garage — 472 sq. ft.

Classic Victorian

■ *Total living area 2,832 sq. ft.* ■ *Price Code E* ■

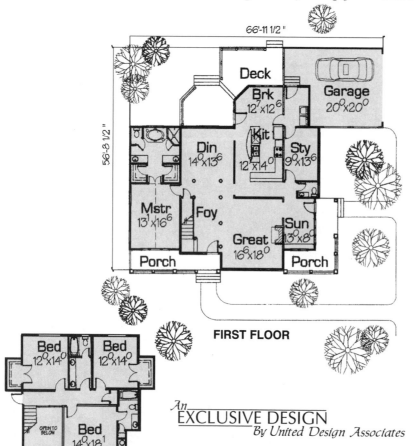

FIRST FLOOR

Deck
Brk 12⁷×12⁶
Garage 20⁰×20⁰
Kit 12⁰×14⁰
Din 14⁰×13⁶
Sty 9⁰×13⁶
Mstr 13¹×16⁶
Foy
Sun 13⁰×8⁰
Great 16⁶×18⁰
Porch
Porch

66'-11 1/2 "
56'-8 1/2 "

Bed 12⁰×14⁰
Bed 12⁰×14⁰
OPEN TO BELOW
Bed 14⁰×18¹

SECOND FLOOR

An EXCLUSIVE DESIGN
By United Design Associates

No. 94721

■ **This plan features:**

– Four bedrooms

– Three full and one half baths

■ Large open areas that are bright and free flowing

■ Great Room accented by a fireplace and large front window

■ Sun Room off of the Great Room viewing the porch

■ Dining Room in close proximity to the Kitchen

■ Efficient Kitchen flows into informal Breakfast Nook

■ Private first floor Master Suite highlighted by a plush master bath

■ Three bedrooms on the second floor, two with walk-in closets and one with a private bath

First floor — 1,868 sq. ft.
Second floor — 964 sq. ft.
Garage — 460 sq. ft.

Distinctive Brick with Room to Expand

■ *Total living area 2,645 sq. ft.* ■ *Price Code E* ■

No. 93206

■ This plan features:

— Four bedrooms

— Two full and one half baths

■ Arched entrance with decorative glass leads into two-story Foyer

■ Formal Dining Room with tray ceiling above decorative window

■ Efficient Kitchen with island cooktop, built-in desk and Pantry

■ Master Bedroom topped by tray ceiling with French door to Patio, huge private bath with garden tub and two walk-in closets

■ Optional space for Storage and Future Bedroom with full bath

■ An optional basement, crawl space or slab foundation — please specify when ordering

First Floor — 2,577 sq. ft.
Future Second Floor — 619 sq. ft.
Bridge — 68 sq. ft.
Basement — 2,561 sq. ft.
Garage — 560 sq. ft.

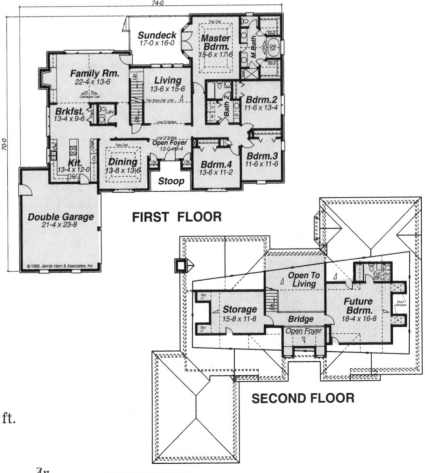

FIRST FLOOR

SECOND FLOOR

An
EXCLUSIVE DESIGN
By Jannis Vann &
Associates, Inc.

■ *Total living area 1,931 sq. ft.* ■ *Price Code C* ■

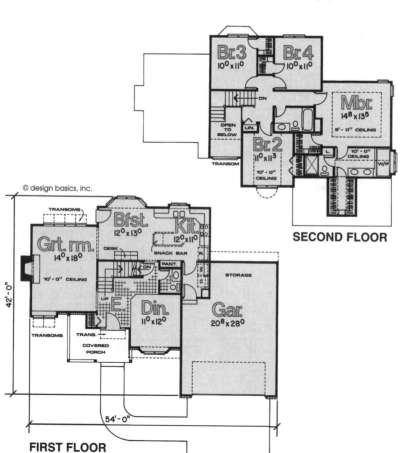

© design basics, inc.

Br. 3
10⁰ x 11⁰

Br. 4
10⁰ x 11⁰

OPEN TO BELOW

LIN.

ON

TRANSOM

Mbr.
14⁸ x 13⁵

9' - 0" CEILING

Br. 2
11⁰ x 11³

10' - 0" CEILING

10' - 0" CEILING

W/P

L.

SECOND FLOOR

TRANSOMS

Bfst.
12⁰ x 13⁰

Kit.
12⁰ x 11⁰

DESK

SNACK BAR

Grt. rm.
14⁰ x 18⁰

10' - 0" CEILING

ON

PANT.

STORAGE

UP

Din.
11⁰ x 12⁰

Gar.
20⁸ x 28⁰

TRANSOMS

TRANS.

COVERED PORCH

42'-0"

54'-0"

FIRST FLOOR

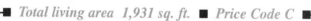

No. 94902

■ **This plan features:**

— Four bedrooms

— Two full and one half baths

■ Ten foot ceiling above transom windows and hearth fireplace accent the Great Room

■ Island counter/snack bar, pantry and desk featured in Kitchen/Breakfast area

■ Beautiful arched window under volume ceiling in Bedroom two

■ Master Bedroom suite features decorative ceiling to walk-in closets and double vanity bath with a whirlpool tub

■ Two additional bedrooms with ample closets share a full bath

First floor — 944 sq. ft.
Second floor — 987 sq. ft.
Basement — 944 sq. ft.
Garage — 557 sq. ft.

■ *Total living area 2,686 sq. ft.* ■ *Price Code E* ■

No. 98457

■ This plan features:

— Four bedrooms

— Three full and one half baths

■ A feeling of spaciousness is created by the two-story Foyer in this home

■ Arched openings and decorative windows enhance the Dining and Living rooms

■ The efficient Kitchen has a work island, Pantry and a Breakfast area

■ The plush Master Suite features a tray ceiling, an alcove of windows and a whirlpool bath

■ An optional basement or a crawl space foundation — please specify when ordering

First floor — 1,883 sq. ft.
Second floor — 803 sq. ft.
Basement — 1,883 sq. ft.
Garage — 495 sq. ft.

One-Story Farmhouse

Total living area 1,387 sq. ft. ■ Price Code A

No. 99661

■ This plan features:

— Three bedrooms

— Two full baths

■ Main activity space grouped to the right of the Foyer

■ Large Living Room with a corner fireplace and a front-facing bow window

■ Dining room enhanced by three French doors to the rear deck

■ Eat-in Kitchen directly accesses the Dining Room

■ Two bedrooms off a short hall sharing a full bath

■ Master Bedroom Suite with a vaulted ceiling, a decorative window, a walk-in closet and a private bath

Main floor — 1,387 sq. ft.
Basement — 1,387 sq. ft.
Garage — 493 sq. ft.

Floor plan labels

69'-4"

DECK

up

BED RM
10'x10-4"

DINING RM
10'-8" x 11'

KITCHEN
14'-4" x 10'-8"

dw

BED RM
10' x 11'

cl.
cl.
lin.

LDRY
9'-8x5-6'

D
W

STOR.

ref.
dn.

31'-0"

MASTER
BED RM
11' x 14'-6'

B.

W.I.C.

F

LIVING RM
13' x 22'

2-CAR GARAGE
20' x 20'

10 ft. high cell.

B.

cl.

f.p.

cl.

whirlpool tub

PORCH

up

FLOOR PLAN

■ *Total living area 2,759 sq. ft.* ■ *Price Code E* ■

No. 90443 ⊠

■ This plan features:

— Three bedrooms

— Three full and two half baths

■ A Master Suite with two closets and bath with separate shower, corner tub and dual vanity

■ A large Dining Room with a bay window, adjacent to the Kitchen

■ A formal Living Room for entertaining and a cozy Family Room with fireplace

■ Two upstairs bedrooms with walk-in closets and private baths

■ A Bonus Room to allow the house to grow with your needs

■ An optional basement or crawl space foundation — please specify when ordering

First floor — 1,927 sq. ft.
Second floor — 832 sq. ft.
Bonus room — 624 sq. ft.
Basement — 1,674 sq. ft.

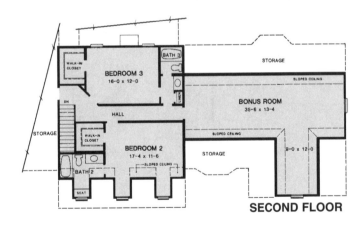

SECOND FLOOR

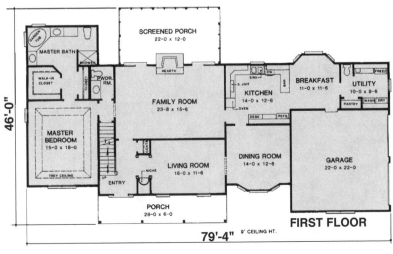

FIRST FLOOR

Eye-Catching Turret Adds to Master Suite

■ *Total living area 2,403 sq. ft.* ■ *Price Code D* ■

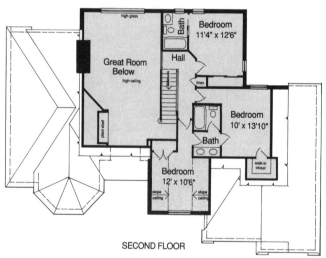

SECOND FLOOR

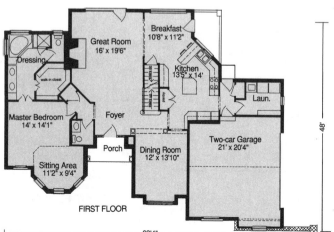

FIRST FLOOR

No. 92651

■ **This plan features:**

— Four bedrooms

— Three full and one half baths

■ Sheltered entry surrounded by glass leads into open Foyer and Great Room with high ceiling, hearth fireplace and atrium door to backyard

■ Columns frame entrance to Dining Room

■ Kitchen with built-in pantry, work island and bright Breakfast area

■ Master Bedroom wing with sitting area, walk-in closet and private bath with corner window tub and double vanity

■ Three bedrooms, one with a private bath

■ No materials list is available for this plan

First floor — 1,710 sq. ft.
Second floor — 693 sq. ft.
Basement — 1,620 sq. ft.
Garage — 467 sq. ft.

© 1991 Donald A. Gardner Architects, Inc.

■ *Total living area 1,898 sq. ft.* ■ *Price Code C* ■

No. 99852 ✖ ᴙ

■ This plan features:

— Three bedrooms

— Two full and one half baths

■ Ready, set, grow with this lovely Country home enhanced by wrap-around Porch and rear Deck

■ Palladian window in clerestory dormer bathes two-story Foyer in natural light

■ Private Master Bedroom offers everything; walk-in closet, whirlpool tub, shower and double vanity

■ Two upstairs bedrooms with dormers and storage access share a full bath

■ An optional basement or crawl space foundation — please specify when ordering

First floor — 1,356 sq. ft.
Second floor — 542 sq. ft.
Bonus room — 393 sq. ft.
Garage & storage — 543 sq. ft.

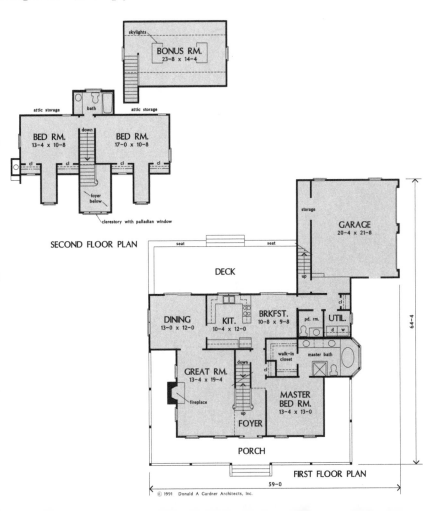

Windows Distinguish Design

■ *Total living area* 3,525 sq. ft. ■ *Price Code F* ■

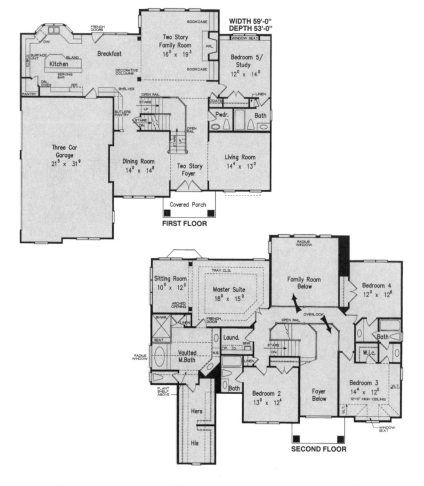

WIDTH 59'-0"
DEPTH 53'-0"

FIRST FLOOR

SECOND FLOOR

No. 98438

■ This plan features:

— Five bedrooms

— Four full and one half baths

■ Light shines into the Dining Room and the Living Room through their respective elegant windows

■ A hall through the Butler's Pantry leads the way into the Breakfast Nook

■ The two-story Family Room has a fireplace with built-in bookcases on either side

■ The upstairs Master Suite has a Sitting Room and a French door that leads into the vaulted master bath

■ An optional basement or crawl space foundation — please specify when ordering

First floor — 1,786 sq. ft.
Second floor — 1,739 sq. ft.
Basement — 1,786 sq. ft.
Garage — 704 sq. ft.

Brick Accents and Dormer Windows

■ Total living area 1,957 sq. ft. ■ Price Code C ■

No. 94906

■ This plan features:

— Four Bedrooms

— Two full and one half baths

■ A detailed Covered Porch leads into easy-care Entry

■ Formal Dining Room welcomes guests with decorative windows

■ A well integrated Family Room, Kitchen and Breakfast area accommodate many family activities

■ A private Master Bedroom suite accented by a transom window and plush bath with a whirlpool tub

■ Three secondary bedrooms share a full bath and an unfinished Storage room

First floor — 1,348 sq. ft.
Second floor — 609 sq. ft.
Storage room — 341 sq. ft.
Basement — 1,348 sq. ft.
Garage — 566 sq. ft.

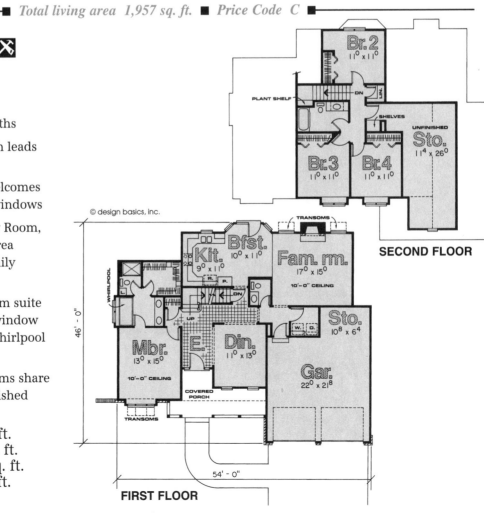

SECOND FLOOR

© design basics, inc.

FIRST FLOOR

Classic Exterior with Modern Interior

■ *Total living area 1,876 sq. ft.* ■ *Price Code C* ■

WIDTH 56'-2"
DEPTH 48'-0"

Screened-in Porch

Master Bedroom 14'1" x 15'1"

Great Room 16'8" x 15'4"
slope ceiling   slope ceiling

Dining Area 10'1" x 14'1"

Bath

Laun.

Dressing

Foyer

walk-in closet

Kitchen 13'2" x 11'8"

pantry

Porch

Two-car Garage 20' x 27'5"

FIRST FLOOR

Bedroom 10'5" x 12'

Bedroom 11'6" x 11'5"

Foyer Below

Hall

Bath

desk

Bonus Bedroom 10' x 18'2"

SECOND FLOOR

No. 92674

■ **This plan features:**

— Three or four bedrooms

— Two full and one half baths

■ Front Porch leads into an open Foyer and Great Room beyond accented by a sloped ceiling, corner fireplace and multiple windows

■ An efficient Kitchen with a cooktop island, walk-in pantry, a bright Dining Area and nearby Screened Porch, Laundry and Garage entry

■ Deluxe Master Bedroom wing with a decorative ceiling, large walk-in closet and plush bath

■ No materials list is available for this plan

First floor — 1,348 sq. ft.
Second floor — 528 sq. ft.
Bonus — 195 sq. ft.
Basement — 1,300 sq. ft.

Country Style Home With Corner Porch

© 1997 Donald A Gardner Architects, Inc.

■ *Total living area 1,815 sq. ft.* ■ *Price Code C* ■

No. 99804

■ **This plan features:**

— Three bedrooms

— Two full baths

■ Dining Room has four floor-to-ceiling windows that overlook front Porch

■ Great Room topped by a cathedral ceiling, enhanced by a fireplace, and sliding doors to the back Porch

■ Utility Room located near Kitchen and Breakfast Nook

■ Master Bedroom has a walk-in closet and private bath

■ Two additional bedrooms with ample closet space share a full bath

■ A skylight Bonus Room over the two-car Garage

Main floor — 1,815 sq. ft.
Garage — 522 sq. ft.
Bonus — 336 sq. ft.

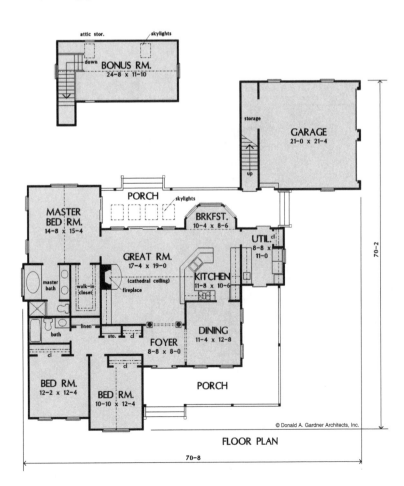

Covered Front Porch

■ *Total living area 2,725 sq. ft.* ■ *Price Code E* ■

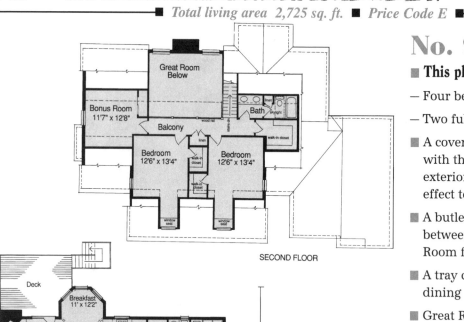

Great Room Below

Bonus Room 11'7" x 12'8"

Balcony

Bath

walk-in closet

Bedroom 12'6" x 13'4"

Bedroom 12'6" x 13'4"

walk-in closet

walk-in closet

linen

window seat

window seat

SECOND FLOOR

Deck

Breakfast 11' x 12'2"

Kitchen 16'6" x 13'6"

pantry

Bath

Hall

Laun.

Great Room 20'6" x 18'6"

Living Room 13'10" x 12'8"

Dining Room 13'4" x 16'2"

tray ceiling

Three-car Garage 20' x 34'1"

wood rail

butler's pantry

Porch

FIRST FLOOR

59'-6"

54'-0"

No. 92663

■ **This plan features:**

— Four bedrooms

— Two full and one half baths

■ A covered front porch coupled with the fieldstone and brick exterior provide a welcoming effect to this home

■ A butler's pantry is located between the Kitchen and Dining Room for ease in serving

■ A tray ceiling tops the formal dining area

■ Great Room with a fireplace

■ A sloped ceiling is featured in the Master Bedroom along with the luxurious dressing/bath area

■ No materials list is available for this plan

First floor — 1,573 sq. ft.
Second floor — 1,152 sq. ft.
Basement — 1,534 sq. ft.
Garage — 680 sq. ft.

■ *Total living area 2,496 sq. ft.* ■ *Price Code D* ■

No. 98733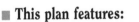

■ This plan features:

— Three bedrooms

— Two full baths

■ A sheltered entrance leading to a large Living Room topped by a vaulted ceiling and enhanced by a large bay window and a fireplace

■ A formal Dining Room with arched openings and a vaulted ceiling

■ A large fireplace in the Family Room is equipped with a built-in entertainment center

■ A cooktop island/eating bar and a walk-in pantry add to the Kitchen that is open to the Nook

■ A privately situated Master Suite including an ultra bath and direct access to the side Porch that is equipped with a hot tub

Main floor — 2,496 sq. ft.
Basement — 2,401 sq. ft.
Garage — 827 sq. ft.

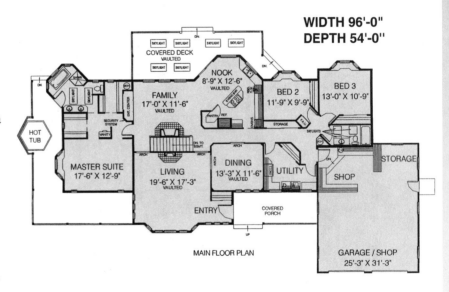

WIDTH 96'-0"
DEPTH 54'-0"

MAIN FLOOR PLAN

Compact One Level Home

■ *Total living area 1,442 sq. ft.* ■ *Price Code A* ■

No. 92685

■ **This plan features:**

— Three bedrooms

— Two full baths

■ Great Room combines with the Breakfast area to form a spacious gathering place

■ Sloped ceiling tops Great Room and reaches a twelve-foot height

■ Windows across the rear of home provide a favorable indoor/outdoor relationship

■ Step-saving Kitchen with a pantry

■ Master Suite includes a walk-in closet and a full bath

■ Two additional bedrooms share the full bath in the hall

■ No materials list is available for this plan

Main floor — 1,442 sq. ft.
Basement — 1,442 sq. ft.
Garage — 421 sq. ft.

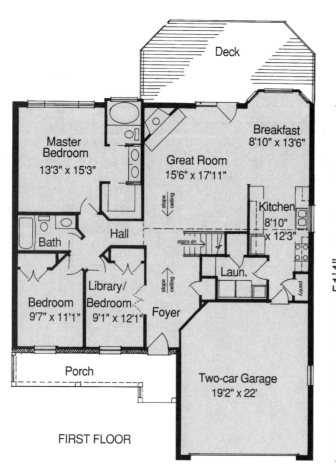

Deck

Master Bedroom
13'3" x 15'3"

Great Room
15'6" x 17'11"

Breakfast
8'10" x 13'6"

Bath

Hall

Kitchen
8'10" x 12'3"

slope ceiling

stairs dn.

Laun.

Bedroom
9'7" x 11'1"

Library/ Bedroom
9'1" x 12'1"

Foyer

slope ceiling

Porch

Two-car Garage
19'2" x 22'

51'4"

FIRST FLOOR

45'

Spacious and Convenient Ranch

■ *Total living area 1,720 sq. ft.* ■ *Price Code B* ■

No. 99057 ✖

■ This plan features:

— Three bedrooms

— One full and one three-quarter baths

■ Portico offers a sheltered entrance into Foyer and formal Living Room

■ Convenient Family Room with inviting fireplace, Patio access and nearby Laundry/Garage entry

■ Formal Dining Room highlighted by backyard view

■ U-shaped, efficient Kitchen with pantry and peninsula serving counter

■ Corner Master Bedroom offers three closets and a private bath

■ Two additional bedrooms share a full bath

Main floor — 1,720 sq. ft.
Basement — 1,630 sq. ft.

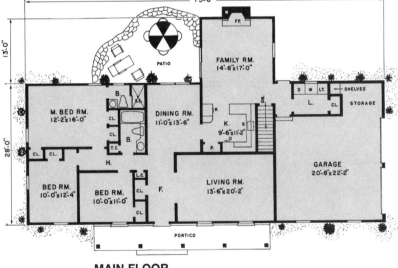

MAIN FLOOR

Stately Stone and Stucco

■ *Total living area 3,027 sq. ft.* ■ *Price Code F* ■

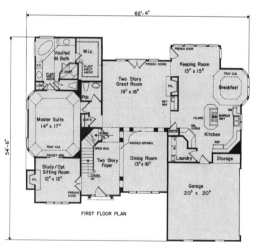

FIRST FLOOR PLAN

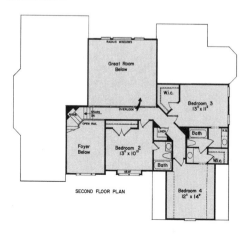

SECOND FLOOR PLAN

No. 98402

■ **This plan features:**

— Four bedrooms

— Three full and one half baths

■ Two-story Foyer with angled staircase welcomes all

■ Large Great Room has a fireplace, wetbar and French doors

■ Kitchen with a cooktop island, pantry and Breakfast alcove

■ Open Keeping Room accented by a wall of windows

■ Master Suite wing offers a tray ceiling, a plush bath and roomy walk-in closet

■ An optional basement, slab or crawl space foudation — please specify when ordering

First floor — 2,130 sq. ft.
Second floor — 897 sq. ft.
Garage — 494 sq. ft.
Basement — 2,130 sq. ft.

© 1990 Donald A. Gardner Architects, Inc.

■ *Total living area 2,692 sq. ft.* ■ *Price Code E* ■

No. 99853

■ This plan features:

— Four bedrooms

— Three full and one half baths

■ Impressive double gable roof with front and rear palladian windows and wrap-around Porch

■ Vaulted ceilings in two-story Foyer and Great Room accommodates Loft/Study area

■ Spacious, first floor Master Bedroom offers walk-in closet and luxurious bath

■ Living space extended outdoors by wrap-around Porch and large Deck

■ Upstairs, one of three bedrooms could be a second Master Suite

First floor — 1,734 sq. ft.
Second floor — 958 sq. ft.

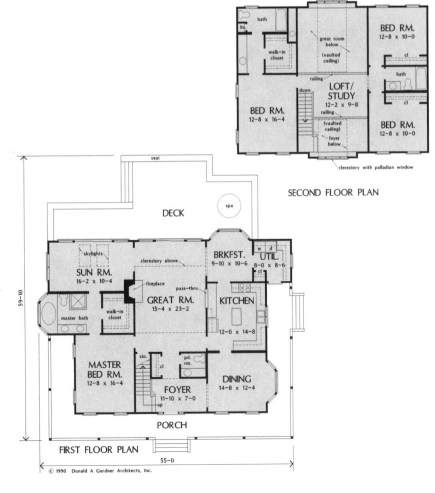

SECOND FLOOR PLAN

FIRST FLOOR PLAN

© 1990 Donald A Gardner Architects, Inc.

Style and Convenience

■ *Total living area 1,373 sq. ft.* ■ *Price Code A* ■

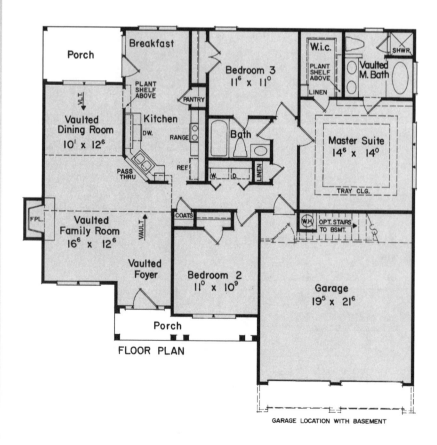

FLOOR PLAN

GARAGE LOCATION WITH BASEMENT

No. 98411

This plan features:

— Three bedrooms

— Two full baths

■ Large front windows, dormers and an old-fashioned Porch

■ A vaulted ceiling in the Foyer

■ A Formal Dining Room crowned in an elegant vaulted ceiling

■ An efficient Kitchen enhanced by a Pantry, and a pass-through to the Family Room

■ A decorative tray ceiling, a five-piece private bath and a walk-in closet in the Master Suite

■ An optional basement or crawl space foundation available — please specify when ordering

Main floor — 1,373 sq. ft.
Basement — 1,386 sq. ft.
Width — 50'-4"
Depth — 45'-0"

Total living area 3,870 sq. ft. ■ **Price Code F** ■

No. 92274

■ **This plan features:**

— Four bedrooms

— Three full and one half baths

■ Two-story glass Entry enhanced by a curved staircase

■ Open Living/Dining Room with decorative windows makes entertaining easy

■ Large, efficient Kitchen with cooktop/work island, huge walk-in Pantry, Breakfast Area, butler's Pantry and Utility/Garage entry

■ Comfortable Family Room with hearth fireplace, built-ins and access to covered Patio

■ Cathedral ceiling tops luxurious Master Bedroom offering a private Lanai, skylit bath, double walk-in closet and adjoining Study

■ No materials list is available for this plan

Main floor — 2,807 sq. ft.
Upper floor — 1,063 sq. ft.
Garage — 633 sq. ft.

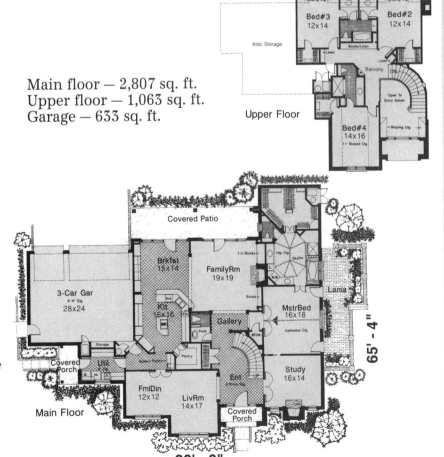

Attractive Combination of Brick and Siding

■ *Total living area 2,010 sq. ft.* ■ *Price Code C* ■

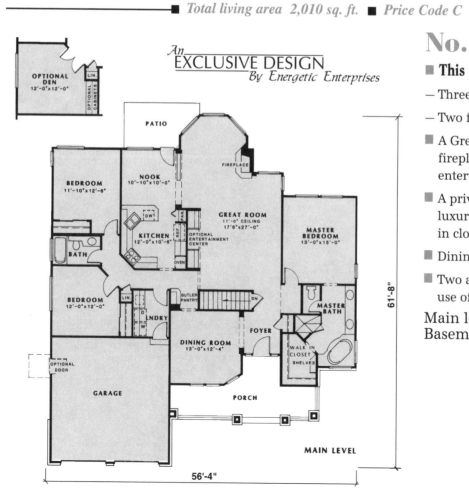

An
EXCLUSIVE DESIGN
By Energetic Enterprises

OPTIONAL DEN 12'-0"x12'-0"

OPTIONAL CABINETS

LIN.

PATIO

BEDROOM 11'-10"x12'-6"

NOOK 10'-10"x10'-0"

FIREPLACE

KITCHEN 12'-0"x10'-6"

OPTIONAL ENTERTAINMENT CENTER

REF. PAN.

OVEN

GREAT ROOM 11'-0" CEILING 17'6"x27'-0"

MASTER BEDROOM 13'-0"x15'-0"

BATH

BEDROOM 12'-0"x12'-0"

LIN.

LNDRY

BUTLER PANTRY

DN

MASTER BATH

FOYER

DINING ROOM 13'-0"x12'-4"

WALK IN CLOSET SHELVES

OPTIONAL DOOR

GARAGE

PORCH

MAIN LEVEL

56'-4"

61'-8"

No. 24259

■ **This plan features:**

— Three Bedrooms

— Two full Baths

■ A Great Room sunny bayed area, fireplace and built-in entertainment center

■ A private Master Bedroom with luxurious Master Bath and walk-in closet

■ Dining Room has a Butler Pantry

■ Two additional Bedrooms have use of hall full Bath

Main level — 2,010 sq. ft.
Basement — 2,010 sq. ft.

Total living area 1,388 sq. ft. ■ **Price Code A** ■

No. 93279

■ This plan features:

— Three bedrooms

— Two full baths

■ A central, double fireplace adding warmth and atmosphere to the Family Room, Kitchen and the Breakfast Area

■ An efficient Kitchen highlighted by a peninsula counter that doubles as a snack bar

■ A Master Suite that includes a walk-in closet, a double vanity, separate shower and tub in the bath

■ Two additional bedrooms sharing a full hall bath

■ A wooden Deck that can be accessed from the Breakfast Area

■ An optional crawl space or slab foundation — please specify when ordering

Main floor — 1,388 sq. ft.
Garage — 400 sq. ft.

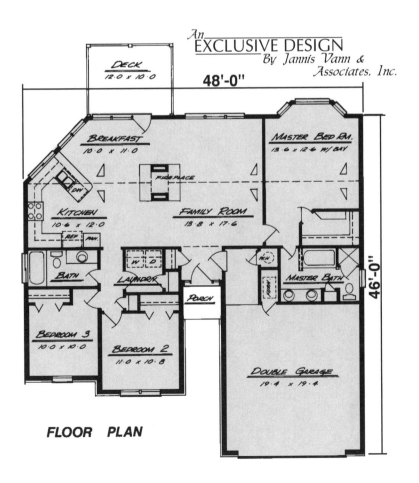

An
EXCLUSIVE DESIGN
By Jannis Vann & Associates, Inc.

FLOOR PLAN

Contemporary with Cozy Front Porch

■ *Total living area 2,041 sq. ft.* ■ *Price Code C* ■

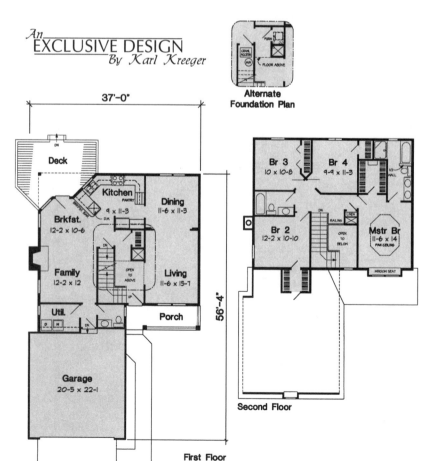

An
EXCLUSIVE DESIGN
By Karl Kreeger

37'-0"

56'-4"

Deck

Kitchen
PANTRY

Dining
11-6 x 11-3

Brkfst.
12-2 x 10-6

Family
12-2 x 12

Living
11-6 x 15-7

OPEN
TO
ABOVE

Ut4il.

Porch

Garage
20-5 x 22-1

First Floor

Alternate
Foundation Plan

Br 3
10 x 10-8

Br 4
9-9 x 11-3

Br 2
12-2 x 10-10

OPEN
TO
BELOW

Mstr Br
11-6 x 14

Second Floor

No. 20219

■ **This plan features:**

— Four bedrooms

— Two full and one half baths

■ A welcoming front porch

■ A Foyer that opens to a balcony

■ An efficient Kitchen is equipped with a peninsula counter that doubles as an eating bar

■ A Breakfast Area with easy access to a wood deck and a view of the fireplace in the Family Room

■ A Master Suite that includes a pan ceiling and a private Master Bath

■ Three additional bedrooms that share a full hall bath

■ No materials list is available for this plan

First floor — 1,028 sq. ft.
Second floor — 1,013 sq. ft.
Basement — 1,019 sq. ft.
Garage — 479 sq. ft.

Convenient Country

■ Total living area 1,767 sq. ft. ■ Price Code B ■

No. 99045

■ This plan features:

— Three bedrooms

— Two full and one half baths

■ Full front Porch provides comfortable visiting and a sheltered entrance

■ Expansive Living Room with an inviting fireplace opens to bright Dining Room and Kitchen

■ U-shaped Kitchen with peninsula serving counter and nearby Pantry

■ Secluded Master Bedroom with two closets and a double vanity bath

■ Two second floor bedrooms share a full bath

■ No materials list is available for this plan

First floor — 1,108 sq. ft.
Second floor — 659 sq. ft.
Basement — 875 sq. ft.

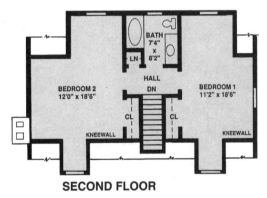

SECOND FLOOR

WIDTH 67'-0"
DEPTH 30'-0"

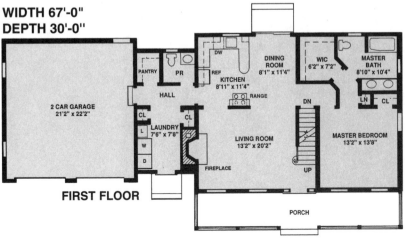

FIRST FLOOR

Affordable Style

■ *Total living area 1,490 sq. ft.* ■ *Price Code A* ■

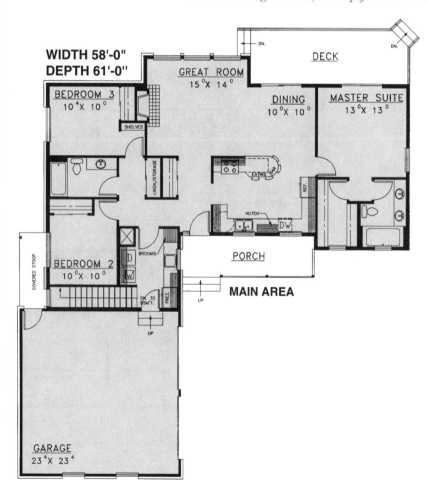

WIDTH 58'-0"
DEPTH 61'-0"

BEDROOM 3
10⁴X 10⁰

GREAT ROOM
15⁰X 14⁰

DECK

DINING
10⁰X 10⁰

MASTER SUITE
13⁰X 13⁰

SHELVES

LINEN/STORAGE

EATING BAR

REF.

HUTCH

DW

PORCH

BEDROOM 2
10⁰X 10⁰

BROOMS

COVERED STOOP

DN. TO BSM'T.

FREEZ.

UP

UP

MAIN AREA

GARAGE
23⁴X 23⁴

No. 91753

■ **This plan features:**

— Three bedrooms

— Two full baths

■ A well-appointed Kitchen boasts a double sink, ample counter and storage space, a peninsula eating bar and a built-in hutch

■ A terrific Master Suite including a private bath and a walk-in closet

■ A Dining Room that flows from the Great Room and into the Kitchen that includes sliding glass doors to the deck

■ A Great Room with a cozy fireplace that can also be enjoyed from the Dining area

■ No materials list is available for this plan

Main area— 1,490 sq. ft.
Covered porch — 120 sq. ft.
Basement — 1,490 sq. ft.
Garage — 579 sq. ft.

■ *Total living area* 2,212 sq. ft. ■ *Price Code* D ■

No. 99620

■ This plan features:

— Four bedrooms

— Two full and one half baths

■ Two bay windows in the formal Living Room with a heat-circulating fireplace to enhance the mood and warmth

■ A spacious formal Dining Room with a bay window and easy access to the Kitchen

■ An octagon-shaped Dinette defined by columns, dropped beams and a bay window

■ An efficient island Kitchen with ample storage and counter space

■ A Master Suite equipped with a large whirlpool tub plus a double vanity

■ Three additional bedrooms that share a full hall bath

First floor — 1,192 sq. ft.
Second floor — 1,020 sq. ft.

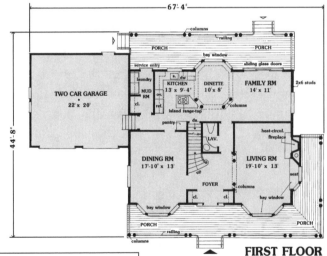

FIRST FLOOR

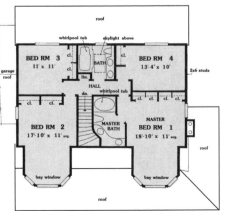

SECOND FLOOR

Basement — 1,026 sq. ft.
Garage & storage — 469 sq. ft.

Brick and Wood Highlighted by Sunbursts

■ *Total living area 1,813 sq. ft.* ■ *Price Code C* ■

No. 94104

■ **This plan features:**

— Three bedrooms

— Two full and one half baths

■ Sheltered Porch entrance leads
into two-story Foyer with lovely
landing staircase

■ Beautiful bay window brightens
Living Room opening into formal
Dining Room

■ L-shaped Kitchen with a built-in
pantry and Dining area with
sliding glass door to rear yard

■ Comfortable Family Room with
focal point fireplace topped by
cathedral ceiling

■ Corner master Bedroom offers
two closets and a private bath

■ No materials list is available for
this plan

First floor — 1,094 sq. ft.
Second floor — 719 sq. ft.
Basement — 1,078 sq. ft.
Garage — 434 sq. ft.

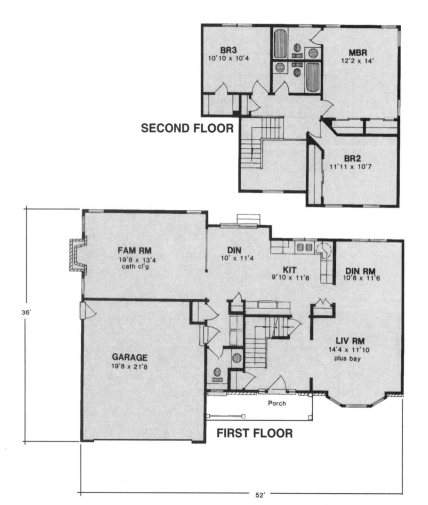

■ *Total living area 3,034 sq. ft.* ■ *Price Code E* ■

No. 93041

■ **This plan features:**

— Five bedrooms

— Two full and one half baths

■ A stucco designed accented by an arched, two-story Entry

■ The Kitchen, Breakfast Room and Family Room are adjacent and open to one another

■ An island cooktop and double sinks, along with an abundance of storage space in the Kitchen even more convenient

■ The Master Suite with an angled whirlpool tub, separate shower and his-n-her vanities

■ No materials list is available for this plan

First floor — 1,973 sq. ft.
Second floor — 1,060 sq. ft.
Garage — 531 sq. ft.
Width — 64'-4"
Depth — 53'-4"

FIRST FLOOR

SECOND FLOOR

Victorian Accents

■ *Total living area 1,768 sq. ft.* ■ *Price Code B* ■

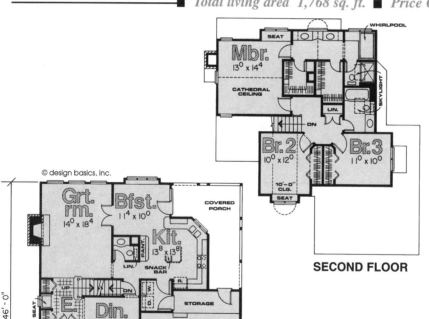

© design basics, inc.

SECOND FLOOR

FIRST FLOOR

No. 94907

■ This plan features:

— Three bedrooms

— Two full and one half baths

■ Covered porch and double doors lead into Entry accented by a window seat and curved banister stair case

■ Decorative windows overlooking backyard and a large fireplace highlight spacious Great Room

■ A hub Kitchen with an island/ snack bar and large pantry

■ Cathedral ceilings crown Master Bedroom suite with two walk-in closets and a whirlpool tub

■ Two additional bedrooms, one with a vaulted ceiling above a window seat, share a full bath

First floor — 905 sq. ft.
Second floor — 863 sq. ft.
Basement — 905 sq. ft.
Garage — 487 sq. ft.

Comfortable Three Bedroom Home

■ *Total living area 1,283 sq. ft.* ■ *Price Code A* ■

No. 97237

■ This plan features:

— Three bedrooms

— Two full baths

■ A covered porch

■ One floor convenience, with bedrooms grouped together

■ Spacious, a vaulted ceiling in the Great Room with a large fireplace

■ The Dining Room is open to the Great Room creating a terrific set up for entertaining

■ Efficiently arranged and including a pantry, the Kitchen directly accesses the Great Room and the Dining Room

■ The Master Suite is topped by a tray ceiling and includes a private bath and two walk-in closets

■ Roomy secondary bedrooms share a full bath in the hall

■ No materials list is available for this plan

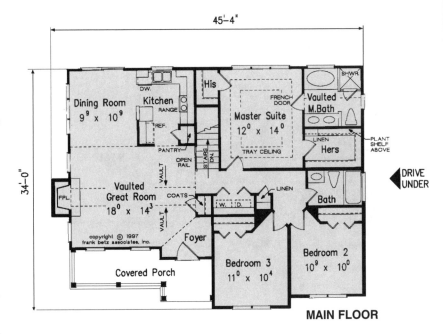

First floor — 1,283 sq. ft.
Basement — 480 sq. ft.
Garage — 470 sq. ft.

Outdoor Living Options

© 1997 Donald A. Gardner Architects, Inc.

■ *Total living area 1,609 sq. ft.* ■ *Price Code C* ■

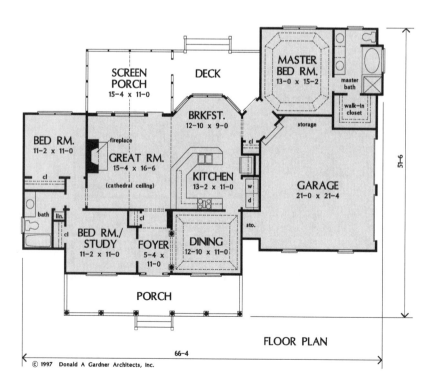

SCREEN PORCH
15-4 x 11-0

DECK

MASTER BED RM.
13-0 x 15-2

master bath

walk-in closet

storage

BED RM.
11-2 x 11-0

fireplace

BRKFST.
12-10 x 9-0

GREAT RM.
15-4 x 16-6

(cathedral ceiling)

KITCHEN
13-2 x 11-0

GARAGE
21-0 x 21-4

bath

lin.

BED RM./ STUDY
11-2 x 11-0

FOYER
5-4 x 11-0

DINING
12-10 x 11-0

sto.

PORCH

FLOOR PLAN

66-4

© 1997 Donald A Gardner Architects, Inc.

No. 96489

■ **This plan features:**

—Three bedrooms

—Two full baths

■ Living areas that are open and casual

■ Great Room crowned by a cathedral ceiling which continues out to the screened porch

■ Kitchen opens to a sunny breakfast bay and is adjacent to the formal Dining Room

■ Master suite topped by a tray ceiling and enhanced by an indulgent bath with a roomy walk-in closet

■ Two additional bedrooms sharing a full bath

Main floor —1,609 sq. ft.
Garage & storage — 500 sq. ft.

■ *Total living area 3,407 sq. ft.* ■ *Price Code F* ■

No. 97240

■ **This plan features:**

— Four bedrooms

— Three full and one half baths

■ A triple arched, columned front porch, creates a great elevation

■ The two-story Foyer is flanked by the Study and the Dining Room

■ The Kitchen is equipped with a pantry, and an island

■ The Breakfast area flows into the Family Room and has French door access to the rear yard

■ An optional basement or crawl space foundation — please specify when ordering

■ No materials list is available for this plan

First floor — 2,384 sq. ft.
Second floor — 1,023 sq. ft.
Bonus room — 228 sq. ft.
Basement — 2,384 sq. ft.
Garage — 525 sq. ft.

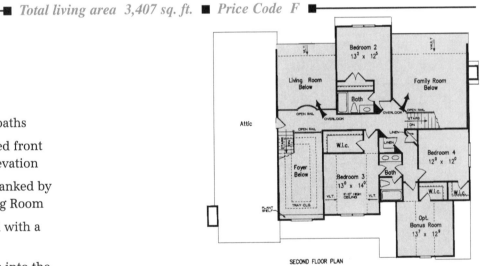

SECOND FLOOR PLAN

FIRST FLOOR PLAN

Outstanding Appeal

■ *Total living area 3,949 sq. ft.* ■ *Price Code F* ■

FIRST FLOOR PLAN

SECOND FLOOR

No. 98437

■ This plan features:

— Five bedrooms

— Four full and one half baths

■ A Butler pantry located between the Kitchen and Dining Room

■ An Island Kitchen with a walk-in pantry

■ The Breakfast room accesses the rear yard through a French door

■ The second floor Master Suite is topped by a tray ceiling

■ Three additional bedrooms with private access to full baths

■ An optional basement, slab or crawl space foundation — please specify when ordering

First floor — 2,002 sq. ft.
Second floor — 1,947 sq. ft.
Basement — 2,002 sq. ft.
Garage — 737 sq. ft.

134

Double Sided Fireplace

■ *Total living area 2,300 sq. ft.* ■ *Price Code D* ■

No. 20221

■ This plan features:

— Four bedrooms

— Two full and one half baths

■ A large Living Room with a sloped ceiling and a double sided fireplace

■ Kitchen is equipped with a boxed window above a double sink and a breakfast bar

■ A formal Dining Room directly off of the Kitchen, for ease in serving

■ A first floor Master Suite with a decorative ceiling and a private Master Bath

■ Three bedrooms on the second floor that share a full hall bath

■ No materials list is available for this plan

First floor — 1,567 sq. ft.
Second floor — 733 sq. ft.
Basement — 1,500 sq. ft.
Garage — 484 sq. ft.

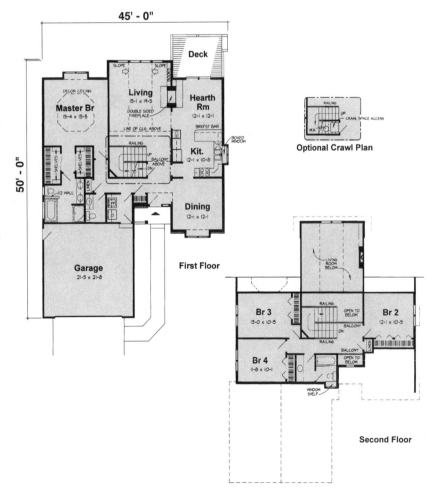

First Floor

Optional Crawl Plan

Second Floor

Especially Unique

■ Total living area 2,748 sq. ft. ■ Price Code E ■

No. 98528

■ **This plan features:**

— Four bedrooms

— Three full and one half baths

■ An arch covered entry and arched windows add flair to this home

■ From the 11-foot entry turn left into the Study/Media Room

■ The formal Dining Room is open to the Gallery, and the Living Room beyond

■ The Family Room has a built-in entertainment center

■ The Master Bedroom is isolated, and has a fireplace

■ Three additional bedrooms are on the opposite side of the home

■ No materials list is available for this plan

Main floor — 2,748 sq. ft.
Garage — 660 sq. ft.
Width — 75'-0"
Depth — 64'-5"

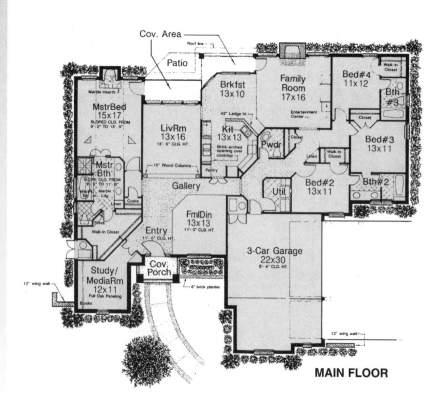

MAIN FLOOR

Enchanting Elevation

© 1997 Donald A. Gardner Architects, Inc.

Total living area 1,743 sq. ft. ■ Price Code C

No. 99837

This plan features:

— Three bedrooms

— Two full baths

■ A palladian window, a gabled dormer, and a cute front porch provide curb appeal

■ Suited for a narrow lot, this plan features a rear entry garage

■ The vaulted Great Room is highlighted by an impressive palladian window

■ The U-shaped Kitchen is adjacent to the Breakfast Room

■ Two bedrooms on the first floor share a full bath

■ The second floor Master Suite features a dormer, his-n-her closets and a private bath

First floor – 1,222 sq. ft.
Second floor – 521 sq. ft.
Garage & storage – 469 sq. ft.

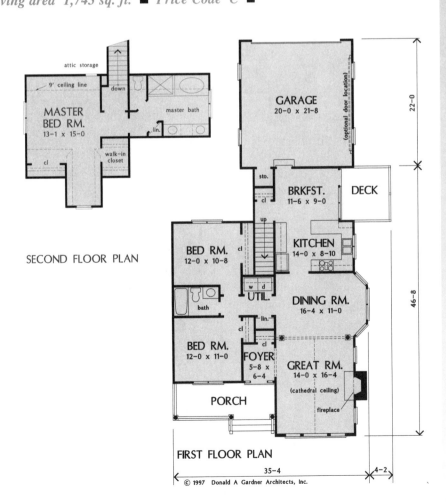

SECOND FLOOR PLAN

FIRST FLOOR PLAN

© 1997 Donald A Gardner Architects, Inc.

137

Charming Gabled Porch

■ *Total living area 1,642 sq. ft.* ■ *Price Code B* ■

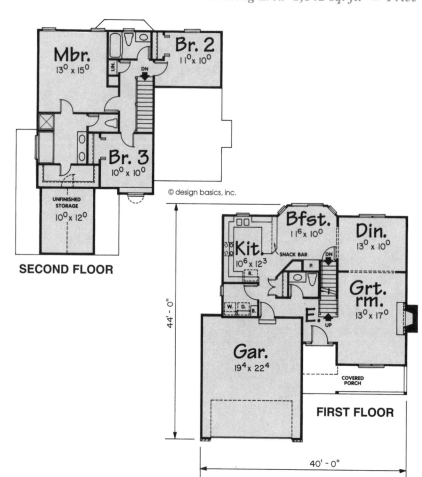

© design basics, inc.

SECOND FLOOR

Mbr.
13⁰ x 15⁰

Br. 2
11⁰ x 10⁰

Br. 3
10⁰ x 10⁰

UNFINISHED STORAGE
10⁰ x 12⁰

44' - 0"

Bfst.
11⁶ x 10⁰

Din.
13⁰ x 10⁰

Kit
10⁶ x 12³

SNACK BAR

Grt. rm.
13⁰ x 17⁰

Gar.
19⁴ x 22⁴

COVERED PORCH

FIRST FLOOR

40' - 0"

No. 94908

■ **This plan features:**

— Three bedrooms

— Two full and one half baths

■ Formal Dining Room expands into the Great Room for easy entertaining

■ Kitchen snack bar and Breakfast alcove provide two informal eating options

■ A corner Master Bedroom suite has a double vanity bath, a large walk-in closet and an Unfinished Storage area beyond

■ Two additional bedrooms share a full hall bath and linen closet

First floor — 862 sq. ft.
Second floor — 780 sq. ft.
Basement — 862 sq. ft.
Garage — 454 sq. ft.
Bonus — 132 sq. ft.

■ *Total living area 2,598 sq. ft.* ■ *Price Code D* ■

No. 99796

■ This plan features:

— Three bedrooms

— Two full and one half bath

■ A wrap-around porch and numerous Windows enhance the facade of the home

■ A classic formal Living Room with a fireplace, built-in shelves and double doors for privacy

■ Vaulted ceilings in the Dining Room, Living Room and one Bedroom

■ A corner wood stove adding a cozy touch to the Family Room

■ A built-in wetbar dividing the Family Room from the Nook area

■ An efficient U-shaped Kitchen with a built-in planning desk and an easy garage entry

■ Two additional bedrooms on the second floor sharing the use of a compartmented bath

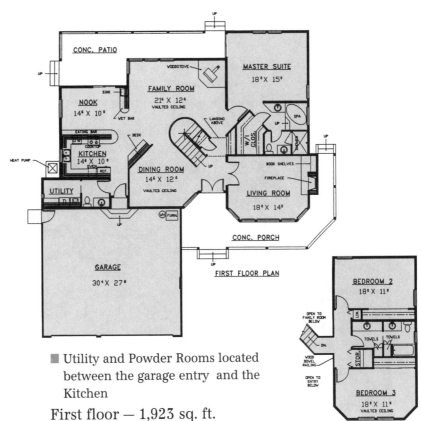

FIRST FLOOR PLAN

SECOND FLOOR PLAN

■ Utility and Powder Rooms located between the garage entry and the Kitchen

First floor — 1,923 sq. ft.
Second floor — 675 sq. ft.
Garage — 858 sq. ft.
Width — 62'-0"
Depth — 67'-0"

Unique Keeping Room

■ *Total living area 2,559 sq. ft.* ■ *Price Code D* ■

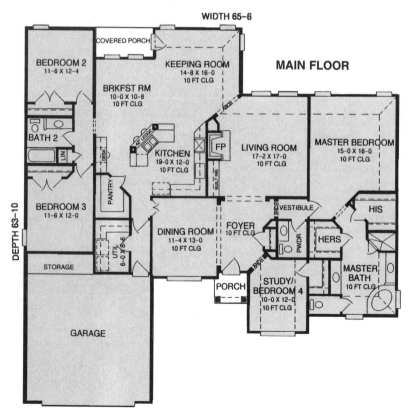

MAIN FLOOR

WIDTH 65–6

DEPTH 63-10

COVERED PORCH

BEDROOM 2
11-6 X 12-4

KEEPING ROOM
14-8 X 16-0
10 FT CLG

BRKFST RM
10-0 X 10-8
10 FT CLG

BATH 2

LIN

KITCHEN
19-0 X 12-0
10 FT CLG

FP

LIVING ROOM
17-2 X 17-0
10 FT CLG

MASTER BEDROOM
15-0 X 16-0
10 FT CLG

BUILT INS

PANTRY

BEDROOM 3
11-6 X 12-0

VESTIBULE

HIS

UTIL
6-0 X 8-6

DINING ROOM
11-4 X 13-0
10 FT CLG

FOYER
10 FT CLG

PWDR

HERS

MASTER
BATH
10 FT CLG

STORAGE

PORCH

STUDY/
BEDROOM 4
10-0 X 12-0
10 FT CLG

GARAGE

No. 93059

■ **This plan features:**

— Four bedrooms

— Two full and one half baths

■ Huge fireplace, built-ins and windows in the Living Room

■ Open, efficient Kitchen with an island counter/serving bar

■ Spacious Keeping/Breakfast Rooms adjoin the Kitchen

■ Private Master Bedroom suite with his-n-her closets and a Master Bath with two vanities and a corner whirlpool tub

■ An optional slab or crawl space foundation — please specify when ordering

■ No materials list is available for this plan

Main floor — 2,559 sq. ft.
Garage — 544 sq. ft.

■ *Total living area 2,464 sq. ft.* ■ *Price Code D* ■

No. 93209

■ This plan features:

— Four bedrooms

— Two full and one half baths

■ A wrap-around Porch adding a cozy touch to this classic style

■ A two-story Foyer area that is open to the formal Dining and Living rooms

■ A large Family Room accentuated by columns and a fireplace

■ A sunny Breakfast area with direct access to the Sun Deck, Screen Porch and Kitchen

■ A convenient Kitchen situated between the formal Dining Room and informal Breakfast Area has a Laundry Center and a Pantry

■ A private Deck highlights the Master Suite which includes a luxurious bath and a walk-in closet

An
EXCLUSIVE DESIGN
By Jannis Vann & Associates, Inc.

SECOND FLOOR

Deck
8-10 x 11-8

Master Bdrm.
12-4 x 17-6

M.Bath

Bdrm.4
13-6 x 11-6

Bth.2

Bdrm.3
13-6 x 11-6

Balcony

Open To Foyer

Bdrm.2
13-6 x 11-6

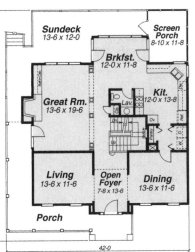

Sundeck
13-6 x 12-0

Screen Porch
8-10 x 11-8

Brkfst.
12-0 x 11-8

Kit.
12-0 x 13-8

Great Rm.
13-6 x 19-6

Lav.

Living
13-6 x 11-6

Open Foyer
7-8 x 13-6

Dining
13-6 x 11-6

Porch

42-0

FIRST FLOOR

First floor — 1,250 sq. ft.
Second floor — 1,166 sq. ft.
Finished stairs — 48 sq. ft.
Basement — 448 sq. ft.
Garage — 706 sq. ft.

Brick Detail with Arches

■ *Total living area 1,987 sq. ft.* ■ *Price Code C* ■

MAIN FLOOR

67'-0" Width
49'-0" Depth

No. 92544

■ **This plan features:**

— Four bedrooms

— Two full and one half baths

■ Front and back porches expand the living space and provide inviting access to the open layout

■ Spacious Den with a fireplace flanked by built-in shelves and double access to the rear Porch

■ Formal Dining Room with an arched window and direct access to the Kitchen

■ Efficient, U-shaped Kitchen with a snackbar counter, a bright Breakfast area and an adjoining laundry and Garage

■ Secluded Master Bedroom suite with a walk-in closet and a double vanity bath

■ Three additional bedrooms with walk-in closets, share one and half baths

■ An optional slab or crawl space foundation — please specify when ordering

Main floor — 1,987 sq. ft.
Garage/Storage — 515 sq. ft.

Great Room Heart of Home

■ *Total living area 1,087 sq. ft.* ■ *Price Code A* ■

MAIN AREA

WIDTH 35-10

No. 93015

■ **This plan features:**

— Three bedrooms

— Two full baths

■ Sheltered porch leads into the Entry with arches and a Great Room

■ Spacious Great Room with a ten foot ceiling above a wall of windows and rear yard access

■ Efficient Kitchen with a built-in pantry, a laundry closet and a Breakfast area accented by a decorative window

■ Bay of windows enhances the Master Bedroom suite with a double vanity bath and a walk-in closet

■ Two additional bedrooms with ample closets, share a full bath

■ This plan is available with a Slab foundation only

■ No materials list is available for this plan

Main floor — 1,087 sq. ft.

Attractive, Affordable Duplex

■ Total living area 1,644 sq. ft. ■ Price Code G ■

No. 24243

■ This plan features:

— Three bedrooms

— Two full and one half baths

■ A welcoming front porch

■ A formal Living and Dining Room for ease in entertaining

■ An expansive Family Room that views the efficient Kitchen

■ A large Master Suite with his-n-her closets and a private Master Bath

■ Two additional bedrooms that share a full hall bath

First floor(per unit) — 819 sq. ft.

Second floor(per unit) — 825 sq. ft.

Garage(per unit) — 470 sq. ft.

Basement(per unit) — 819 sq. ft.

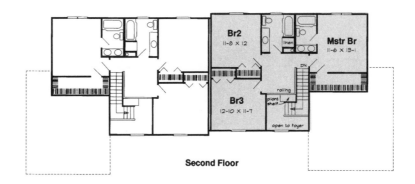

Br2
11-8 X 12

Mstr Br
11-6 X 13-1

linen

DN

Br3
12-10 X 11-7

railing
plant shelf

open to foyer

Second Floor

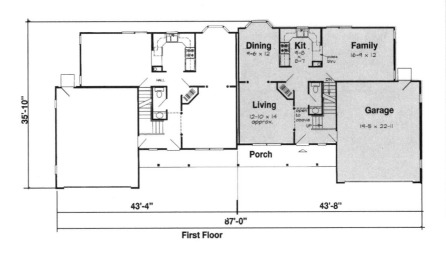

Dining
9-6 x 12

Kit
9-8
8-7

Family
16-9 x 12

pass thru

HALL

Living
12-10 x 14
approx.

open to above
UP

DN

Garage
19-5 x 22-11

35'-10"

Porch

43'-4"   43'-8"

87'-0"

First Floor

Traditional Elegance

■ *Total living area 2,995 sq. ft.* ■ *Price Code E* ■

SECOND FLOOR

BEDROOM 2
13'-6" x 11'-0"

OPEN TO
LIVING BELOW

GAME ROOM
23'-10" x 13'-6"

BATH 2

OPT. BATH

CLOSET

BALCONY

CLO.

BEDROOM 3
14'-0" x 11'-8"

OPEN TO
FOYER
BELOW

BEDROOM 4
11'-8" x 12'-4"

FIRST FLOOR PLAN

WIDTH —71'-4"
DEPTH — 57'-6"

BREAKFAST
11'-4"x8'-0"
10' CLG.

PORCH

W.I.C.

LIVING ROOM
15'-0" x 14'-10"
VOLUME CLG.

FAMILY ROOM
15'-0" x 15'-0"
10' CLG.

MASTER
BATH

F.P.

W.I.C.

KITCHEN
12'-8"x15'-4"
10' CLG.

HALL

UTIL.

MASTER BEDROOM
13'-4" x 15'-4"
10' CLG.

CLO.

FOYER

DINING ROOM
11'-4" x 11'-0"
10' CLG.

PWDR.

STOR.

STOR.

PORCH

STOR.

GARAGE

No. 93042

■ This plan features:

– Four bedrooms

– Two full and one half baths

■ Twin bay windows and an angled Garage

■ A tiled Foyer that opens to a two-story Living Room

■ An island Kitchen, with a peninsula counter and eating bar

■ A spacious Family Room that includes a focal point fireplace

■ A Master Suite with an intimate sitting area and a master bath

■ No materials list is available for this plan

First floor — 1,832 sq. ft.
Second floor — 1,163 sq. ft.
Garage — 591 sq. ft.

Perfect for a First Home

No. 92405

■**This plan features:**

– Three bedrooms

– Two full baths

■A spacious Master Suite including a separate Master Bath with a garden tub and shower

■A Dining Room and Family Room highlighted by vaulted ceilings

■An oversized patio accessible from the Master Suite, Family Room and Breakfast Room

■A well planned Kitchen measuring 12' x 11'

■No materials list available for this plan

Main area — 1,564 sq. ft.
Garage & Storage — 476 sq. ft.

■ *Total living area 1,564 sq. ft.* ■ *Price Code B* ■

MAIN FLOOR

Appealing Master Suite

No. 92239

■**This plan features:**

– Three bedrooms

– Two full baths

■Sheltered Entry into spacious Living Room with a corner fireplace and Patio access

■Efficient Kitchen with a serving counter for Dining area and nearby Utility/Garage entry

■Private Master Bedroom offers a vaulted ceiling and pampering bath with two vanities and walk-in closets and a garden window tub

■Two additional bedrooms with ample closets, share a full bath

■No materials list is available for this plan

Main floor — 1,198 sq. ft.

■ *Total living area 1,193 sq. ft.* ■ *Price Code A* ■

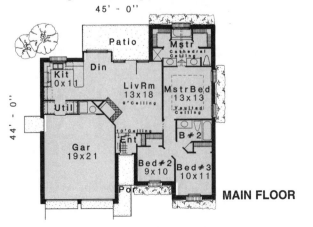

MAIN FLOOR

145

Rustic Warmth

Total living area 1,764 sq. ft. ■ Price Code B

WOOD DECK
14-0 x 10-0

DINING
10-0 x 14-2
(INCL. BAY)

KITCHEN
10-0 x 12-2
ISLAND

UTILITY

PANT.

REF.

SINK

D.W.

OVEN

S. UNIT

COATS

GARDEN TUB

WASH DRY

LIN.

WALK-IN CLOSET

BENCH

M. BEDROOM
13-6 x 13-8

OPEN RAIL

LIVING ROOM
17-2 x 14-10

FOYER

MAIN FLOOR

PORCH
26-0 x 6-0

34-0

40-0

WALK-IN CLOSET

LIN.

ATTIC STORAGE

SLOPED CEILING

BEDROOM 2
13-6 x 13-4

HALL

STORAGE

BEDROOM 3
12-8 x 15-4

FOYER (BELOW)

SLOPED CEILING

WALK-IN CLOSET

ATTIC STORAGE

SECOND FLOOR

No. 90440

■ This plan features:

— Three bedrooms

— Two full baths

■ A fireplaced Living Room with built-in bookshelves

■ A fully-equipped Kitchen with an island

■ A sunny Dining Room with glass sliders to a wood deck

■ A first floor Master Suite with walk-in closet and lavish Master Bath

■ An optional basement or crawl space foundation — please specify when ordering

First floor — 1,100 sq. ft.
Second floor — 664 sq. ft.
Basement — 1,100 sq. ft.
Garage — 1,740 sq. ft.

Plan for the Future

Total living area 1,325 sq. ft. ■ Price Code A

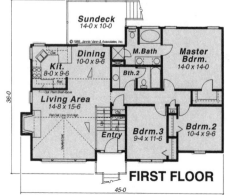

Sundeck
14-0 x 10-0

Dining
10-0 x 9-6

Kit.
8-0 x 9-6

M.Bath

Bth.2

Master Bdrm.
14-0 x 14-0

Living Area
14-8 x 15-6

Entry

Bdrm.3
9-4 x 11-6

Bdrm.2
10-4 x 9-6

36-0

45-0

FIRST FLOOR

Fut.Bth.

Future Closet

Future Playroom
15-0 x 22-8

Double Garage
22-0 x 26-0

Stor.

SECOND FLOOR

An
EXCLUSIVE DESIGN
By Jannis Vann &
Associates, Inc.

No. 93265

■ This plan features:

— Three bedrooms

— Two full baths

■ Entry leads up to Living area accented by a vaulted ceiling and arched window

■ Compact, efficient Kitchen with serving counter/snackbar, serves Dining area and Deck beyond

■ Comfortable Master Bedroom with a walk-in closet and double vanity bath with a window tub

■ Two additional bedrooms with large closets, share a full bath

■ Entry leads down to laundry, Garage and future Playroom

■ No materials list is available for this plan

Main floor — 1,269 sq. ft.
Finished stairs — 56 sq. ft.
Basement — 382 sq. ft.
Garage — 598 sq. ft.

Southern Traditional Flavor

■ *Total living area 1,567 sq. ft.* ■ *Price Code B* ■

No. 99641 ▣

■ This plan features:

— Three bedrooms

— Two full baths

■ The Living Room is enhanced by nine foot ceilings and a bookcase flanked fireplace

■ Two mullioned French doors from the Dining Room to the rear terrace

■ Laundry area serving as a Mudroom between the Garage and Kitchen

■ A Master Suite with a large walk-in closet and a compartmented Bath has a separate shower stall, whirlpool tub, double vanity and linen closet

■ Bonus area can be finished into a study or recreation room

First floor — 1,567 sq. ft.
Future bonus area — 462 sq. ft.
Basement — 1,567 sq. ft.
Garage — 504 sq. ft.

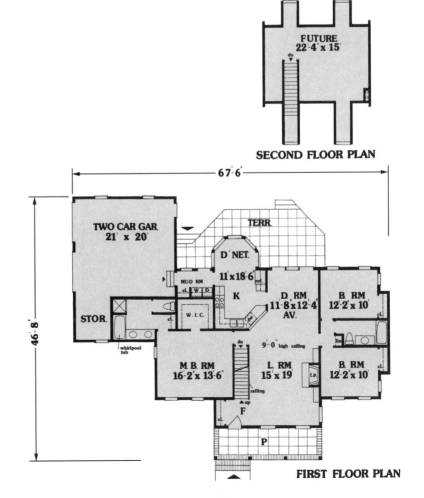

SECOND FLOOR PLAN

FIRST FLOOR PLAN

Skylight Brightens Master Bedroom

■ *Total living area 1,686 sq. ft.* ■ *Price Code B* ■

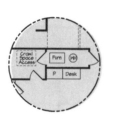

Slab/Crawl Space Option

An
EXCLUSIVE DESIGN
By Karl Kreeger

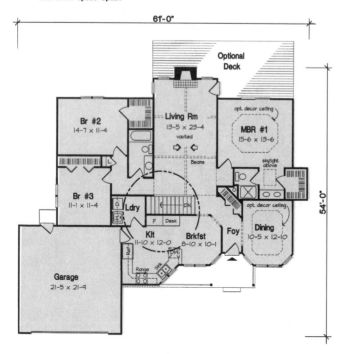

No. 34029

■ **This plan features:**

— Three bedrooms

— Two full baths

■ A covered Porch entry

■ A foyer separating the Dining Room from the Breakfast Area and Kitchen

■ A Living Room enhanced by a vaulted beam ceiling and a fireplace

■ A Master Bedroom with a decorative ceiling and a skylight in the private bath

■ An optional Deck accessible through sliding doors off the Master Bedroom

Main floor — 1,686 sq. ft.
Basement — 1,676 sq. ft.
Garage — 484 sq. ft.

Amenity-Packed Affordability

No. 92525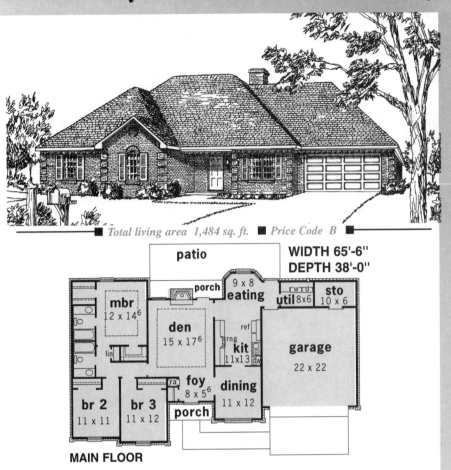

■ **This plan features:**

— Three bedrooms

— Two full baths

■ A sheltered entrance inviting your guests onward

■ A fireplace in the Den offering a focal point, while the decorative ceiling adds definition to the room

■ A well-equipped Kitchen flowing with ease into the Breakfast Bay or Dining Room

■ A Master Bedroom, having two closets and a private master bath

■ An optional slab or crawl space foundation — please specify when ordering

Main area — 1,484 sq. ft.
Garage — 544 sq. ft.

■ *Total living area 1,484 sq. ft.* ■ *Price Code B* ■

WIDTH 65'-6"
DEPTH 38'-0"

patio
porch
mbr 12 x 14⁶
eating 9 x 8
util 8x6
sto 10 x 6
den 15 x 17⁶
ref
rng
kit 11x13
garage 22 x 22
lin
foy 8 x 5⁶
dining 11 x 12
br 2 11 x 11
br 3 11 x 12
porch

MAIN FLOOR

No Wasted Space

No. 90412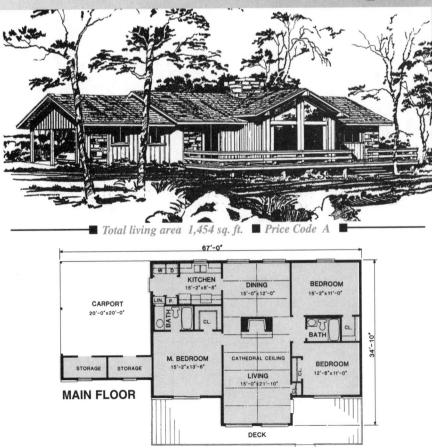

■ **This plan features:**

— Three bedrooms

— Two full baths

■ A centrally located Great Room with a cathedral ceiling, exposed wood beams and large areas of fixed glass

■ The Living and Dining areas separated by a massive stone fireplace

■ A secluded Master Suite with a walk-in closet and private Master Bath

■ An efficient Kitchen with a convenient laundry area

■ An optional basement, slab or crawl space foundation — please specify when ordering

Main area — 1,454 sq. ft.

■ *Total living area 1,454 sq. ft.* ■ *Price Code A* ■

67'-0"
KITCHEN 15'-2"x8'-8"
DINING 15'-0"x12'-0"
BEDROOM 15'-2"x11'-0"
CARPORT 20'-0"x20'-0"
LIN.
P.
BATH
CL.
BATH
CL.
34'-10"
STORAGE
STORAGE
M. BEDROOM 15'-2"x13'-6"
CATHEDRAL CEILING
LIVING 15'-0"x21'-10"
BEDROOM 12'-8"x11'-0"
CL.

MAIN FLOOR

DECK

Small Yet Sophisticated

No. 92281

■ **This plan features:**

– Three bedrooms

– Two full baths

■ Spacious Great Room highlighted by a fireplace and built-in shelving

■ Efficient, U-shaped Kitchen with ample work and storage space, sliding glass door to Covered Patio and a Dining area with a window seat

■ Spacious Master Bedroom suite enhanced by window seats, vaulted ceiling, a lavish bath and large walk-in closet

■ Two additional bedrooms share a full bath

■ Convenient Utility area and Garage entry

■ No materials list is available for this plan

Main floor — 1,360 sq. ft.
Garage — 380 sq. ft.

■ Total living area 1,360 sq. ft. ■ Price Code A ■

MAIN FLOOR

Cozy Traditional

No. 93000

■ **This plan features:**

– Three bedrooms

– Two full baths

■ An angled eating bar separating the Kitchen, Breakfast Room and Great Room, while leaving these areas open for easy entertaining

■ An efficient, well-appointed Kitchen that is convenient to both the formal Dining Room and the sunny Breakfast Room

■ A spacious Master Suite with oval tub, step-in shower, double vanity and walk-in closet

■ Two additional bedrooms with ample closet space that share a full hall bath

■ No materials list is available for this plan

Main floor — 1,862 sq. ft.
Garage — 520 sq. ft.

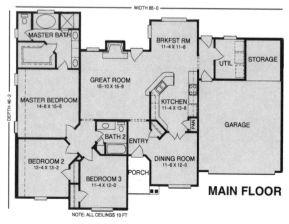

■ Total living area 1,862 sq. ft. ■ Price Code C ■

MAIN FLOOR

NOTE: ALL CEILINGS 10 FT

Enhanced by a Columned Porch

■ *Total living area 1,754 sq. ft.* ■ *Price Code C* ■

No. 92531 ✕

■ This plan features:

— Three bedrooms

— Two full baths

■ A Great Room with a fireplace and decorative ceiling

■ A large efficient Kitchen with Breakfast Area

■ A Master Bedroom with a private master bath and walk-in closet

■ A formal Dining Room conveniently located near the Kitchen

■ Two additional bedrooms with walk-in closets and use of full hall bath

■ An optional crawl space or slab foundation available — please specify when ordering

Main floor — 1,754 sq. ft.
Garage — 552 sq. ft.

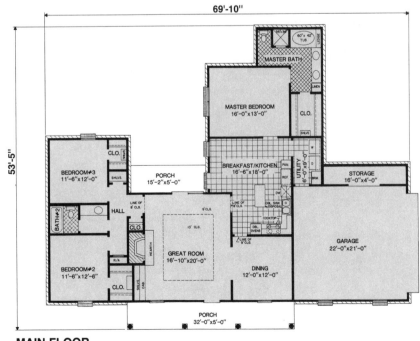

MAIN FLOOR

Regal Residence

■ *Total living area 3,039 sq. ft.* ■ *Price Code F* ■

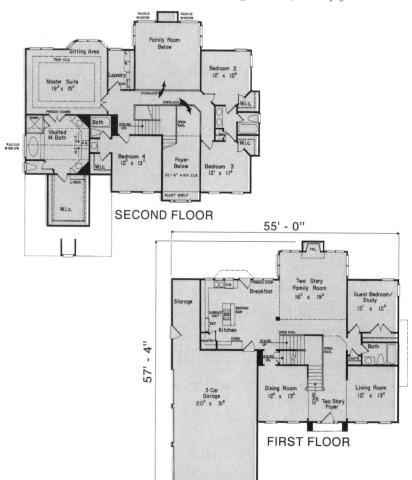

SECOND FLOOR

FIRST FLOOR

55' - 0"

57' - 4"

No. 98405

■ This plan features:

— Five bedrooms

— Four full baths

■ Keystone windows accent the exterior

■ Spacious two-story Family Room enhanced by a fireplace

■ Kitchen with a cooktop island/serving bar and a walk-in Pantry

■ First floor Guest Room/Study with roomy closet and adjoining full bath

■ Luxurious Master Suite offers a tray ceiling, Sitting Area, a huge walk-in closet and a vaulted bath

■ An optional basement or crawl space foundation — please specify when ordering

First floor — 1,488 sq. ft.
Second floor — 1,551 sq. ft.
Basement — 1,488 sq. ft.
Garage — 667 sq. ft.

A Modern Look At Colonial Styling

No. 93287

This plan features:

- Three bedrooms
- Two full and one half baths
- Brick detailing and keystones highlight elevation
- Two-story Foyer opens to formal Living and Dining rooms
- Expansive Family Room with a hearth fireplace between built-in shelves and Deck access
- U-shaped Kitchen with serving counter, Breakfast alcove, and nearby Garage entry
- Elegant Master Bedroom with a decorative ceiling, large walk-in closet and a double vanity bath
- Two additional bedrooms share a full bath, laundry and Bonus area

First floor — 987 sq. ft.
Second floor — 965 sq. ft.
Finished staircase — 72 sq. ft.
Basement — 899 sq. ft.
Bonus — 272 sq. ft.

An EXCLUSIVE DESIGN
By Jannis Vann & Associates, Inc.

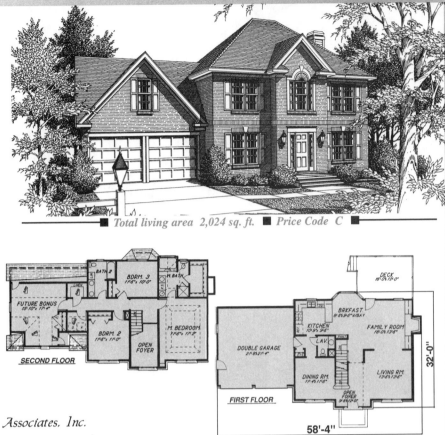

Total living area 2,024 sq. ft. ■ **Price Code C**

European Styling with a Georgian Flair

No. 92552

This plan features:

- Four bedrooms
- Two full baths
- Elegant European styling of this home has been spiced with Georgian Styling
- Arch top windows, quoins and shutters on the exterior, a columned covered front and a rear porch combine to become an eye-catching home
- Formal foyer gives access to the dining room to the left and spacious Den straight ahead
- Kitchen flows into the informal eating area and is separated from the den by an angled extended counter eating bar
- Split bedroom plan with master suite privately placed at the rear
- Three additional bedrooms share a full bath in the hall
- An optional slab or crawl space foundation — please specify when ordering

Main floor — 1,873 sq. ft.
Garage — 613 sq. ft.
Bonus — 145 sq. ft.

Total living area 1,873 sq. ft. ■ **Price Code D**

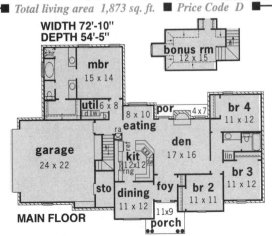

Traditional Ranch Plan

■ *Total living area 2,218 sq. ft.* ■ *Price Code D* ■

MAIN FLOOR

No. 90454

■ **This plan features:**

— Three bedrooms

— Two full baths

■ Large Foyer set between the formal Living and Dining rooms

■ Spacious Great Room adjacent to the open Kitchen /Breakfast area

■ Secluded Master Bedroom highlighted by the master bath with a garden tub, separate shower, and his-n-her vanity

■ Bay window allows bountiful natural light into the Breakfast Area

■ Two additional bedrooms sharing a full bath

■ An optional basement or crawl space foundation — please specify when ordering

Main floor — 2,218 sq. ft.
Basement — 1,658 sq. ft.
Garage — 528 sq. ft.

Style and Convenience

■ *Total living area 1,653 sq. ft.* ■ *Price Code B* ■

Main Floor

No. 92283

■ **This plan features:**

— Three bedrooms

— Two full baths

■ A sheltered Porch leads into an easy-care tile Entry

■ Spacious Living Room offers a cozy fireplace, triple window and access to Patio

■ An efficient Kitchen with a skylight, work island, Dining area, walk-in pantry and Utility/Garage entry

■ Secluded Master Bedroom highlighted by a vaulted ceiling, access to Patio and a lavish bath

■ Two additional bedrooms, one with a cathedral ceiling, share a full bath

■ No materials list is available for this plan

Main floor — 1,653 sq. ft.
Garage — 420 sq. ft.

Veranda Mirrors Two-Story Bay

■ *Total living area 4,217 sq. ft.* ■ *Price Code F* ■

No. 10780

■ This plan features:

— Four bedrooms

— Two full and one half baths

■ A huge foyer flanked by the formal Parlor and Dining Room

■ An island Kitchen with an adjoining pantry

■ A Breakfast bay and sunken Gathering Room located at the rear of the home

■ Double doors opening to the Master Suite and the book-lined Master Retreat

■ An elegant Master Bath including a raised tub and adjoining cedar closet

First floor — 2,108 sq. ft.
Second floor — 2,109 sq. ft.
Basement — 1,946 sq. ft.
Garage — 764 sq. ft.

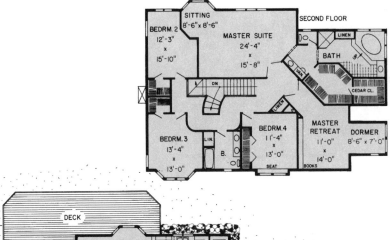

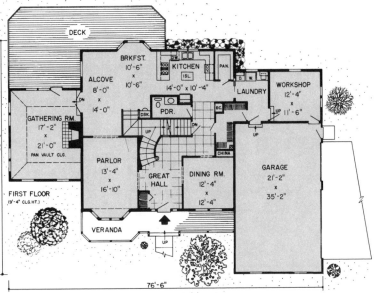

National Treasure

■ *Total living area 1,978 sq. ft.* ■ *Price Code C* ■

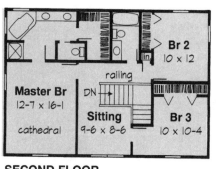

SECOND FLOOR

Master Br
12-7 x 16-1
cathedral

DN

Sitting
9-6 x 8-6

railing

Br 2
10 x 12

Br 3
10 x 10-4

crawl access

Dining

furn. w/h

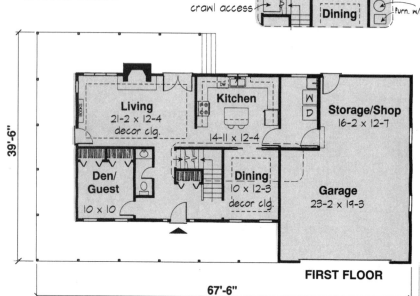

FIRST FLOOR

39'-6"

67'-6"

Living
21-2 x 12-4
decor clg.

Kitchen
14-11 x 12-4

Storage/Shop
16-2 x 12-7

W

D

Den/
Guest
10 x 10

Dining
10 x 12-3
decor clg.

Garage
23-2 x 19-3

No. 24400

■ **This plan features:**

— Three bedrooms

— Two full and one half baths

■ A wrap-around covered Porch

■ Decorative vaulted ceilings in the fireplaced Living Room

■ A large Kitchen with central island/breakfast bar

■ A sun-lit Sitting Area

First floor — 1,034 sq. ft.
Second floor — 944 sq. ft.
Basement — 944 sq. ft.
Garage & storage — 675 sq. ft.

An
EXCLUSIVE DESIGN
By Upright Design

Two-Story Farmhouse

No. 90458

This plan features:

– Three bedrooms

– Two full and one half baths

■ The wrap-around Porch gives a nostalgic appeal to this home

■ The Great Room with fireplace is accessed directly from the Foyer

■ The formal Dining Room has direct access to the efficient Kitchen

■ An island, double sink, plenty of counter/cabinet space and a built-in pantry complete the Kitchen

■ The second floor Master Suite has a five-piece, private bath and a walk-in closet

■ Two other bedrooms have walk-in closets and share a full bath

■ An optional basement or crawlspace foundation — please specify when ordering

First floor — 1,125 sq. ft.
Second floor — 1,138 sq. ft.
Basement — 1,125 sq. ft.

■ Total living area 2,263 sq. ft. ■ Price Code E ■

MAIN FLOOR PLAN

SECOND FLOOR PLAN

Arches Add Ambiance

No. 92539

This plan features:

– Four bedrooms

– Two full and one half baths

■ Arched two-story entrance highlighted by a lovely arched window

■ Expansive Den offers hearth fireplace between book shelves, raised ceiling and access to rear yard

■ Efficient Kitchen with peninsula counter, built-in pantry, Breakfast bay, Garage entry, laundry and adjoining Dining room

■ Private Master Bedroom enhanced by a large walk-in closet and plush bath

■ Three second floor bedrooms with walk-in closets share a double vanity bath

■ An optional slab or crawlspace foundation — please specify when ordering

First floor — 1,250 sq. ft.
Second floor — 783 sq. ft
Garage and Storage — 555 sq. ft.

■ Total living area 2,033 sq. ft. ■ Price Code D ■

SECOND FLOOR

FIRST FLOOR

Compact Victorian Ideal for Narrow Lot

■ Total living area 1,737 sq. ft. ■ Price Code B ■

No. 90406

■ **This plan features:**

— Three bedrooms

— Three full baths

■ A large, front Parlor with a raised hearth fireplace

■ A Dining Room with a sunny bay window

■ An efficient galley Kitchen serving the formal Dining Room and informal Breakfast Room

■ A beautiful Master Suite with two closets, an oversized tub and double vanity, plus a private sitting room with a bayed window and vaulted ceiling

■ An optional basement, slab or crawl space foundation — please specify when ordering

First floor — 954 sq. ft.
Second floor — 783 sq. ft.

FIRST FLOOR

30'-0"

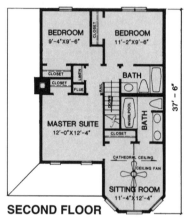

SECOND FLOOR

37'-6"

Quoin Accents Distinguish this Plan

■ Total living area 1,142 sq. ft. ■ Price Code A ■

No. 93017

■ **This plan features:**

— Three bedrooms

— Two full baths

■ A traditional brick elevation with quoin accents

■ A large Family Room with a corner fireplace and direct access to the outside

■ An arched opening leading to the Breakfast Area

■ A bay window illuminating the Breakfast Area with natural light

■ An efficiently designed, U-shaped Kitchen with ample cabinet and counter space

■ A Master Suite with a private master bath

■ Two additional bedrooms that share a full hall bath

■ No materials list is available for this plan

Main floor — 1,142 sq. ft.
Garage — 428 sq. ft.

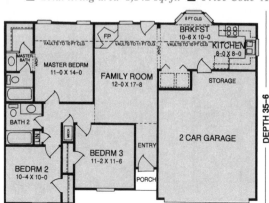

MAIN FLOOR

WIDTH 48-10

DEPTH 35-6

■ *Total living area 1,792 sq. ft.* ■ *Price Code B* ■

No. 94105

■ **This plan features:**

— Three bedrooms

— Two full and one half bath

■ Covered Entry into two-story Foyer with a dramatic landing staircase brightened by decorative window

■ Spacious Living/Dining Room combination with hearth fireplace and decorative windows

■ Hub Kitchen with built-in pantry and informal Dining area with sliding glass door to rear yard

■ First floor Master Bedroom offers a walk-in closet, dressing area and full bath

■ Two additional bedrooms on second floor share a full bath

■ No materials list is available for this plan

First floor — 1,281 sq. ft.
Second floor — 511 sq. ft.
Garage — 481 sq. ft.

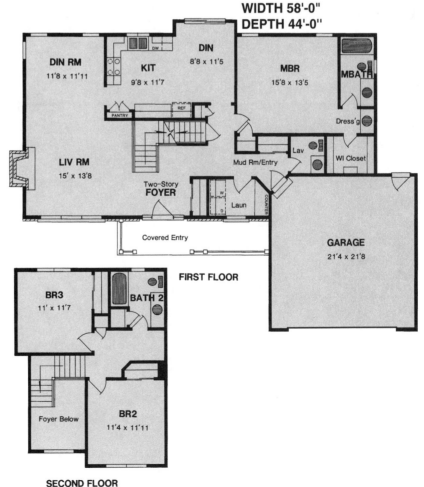

WIDTH 58'-0"
DEPTH 44'-0"

DIN RM
11'8 x 11'11

KIT
9'8 x 11'7

DIN
8'8 x 11'5

MBR
15'8 x 13'5

MBATH

DW

REF

PANTRY

Dress'g

LIV RM
15' x 13'8

Lav

WI Closet

Two-Story
FOYER

Mud Rm/Entry

Laun

COUNTER

W
D

Covered Entry

GARAGE
21'4 x 21'8

FIRST FLOOR

BR3
11' x 11'7

BATH 2

Foyer Below

BR2
11'4 x 11'11

SECOND FLOOR

Country Style For Today

■ *Total living area 2,406 sq. ft.* ■ *Price Code D* ■

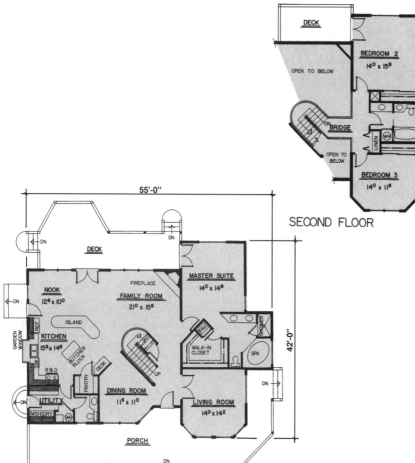

DECK

BEDROOM 2
14⁰ x 15⁸

OPEN TO BELOW

DN BRIDGE

OPEN TO BELOW

LINEN

BEDROOM 3
14⁰ x 11⁸

SECOND FLOOR

55'-0"

DECK

NOOK
12⁸ x 10⁰

FIREPLACE

FAMILY ROOM
21⁰ x 15⁶

MASTER SUITE
14⁰ x 14⁸

ISLAND

KITCHEN
15⁶ x 14⁸

BUTCHER BLOCK

WALK-IN CLOSET

SPA

42'-0"

R&O

DESK

PANTRY

DINING ROOM
11⁶ x 11⁰

LIVING ROOM
14⁰ x 14²

UTILITY

WSH DRY

PORCH

DN

FIRST FLOOR

No. 91700

■ This plan features:

— Three bedrooms

— Two full and one half baths

■ A wide wrap-around Porch for a farmhouse style

■ A spacious Living Room with double doors and a large front window

■ A garden window over the double sink in the huge, country Kitchen with two islands, one a butcher block and the other an eating bar

■ A corner fireplace in the Family Room enjoyed throughout the Nook and Kitchen, thanks to an open layout

■ A Master Suite with a spa tub, and a huge walk-in closet as well as a shower and double vanity

First floor — 1,785 sq. ft.
Second floor — 621 sq. ft.

Comfortable Design Encourages Relaxation

No. 96413

This plan features:

— Four bedrooms

— Three full bathrooms

- A wide front porch providing a warm welcome
- Center dormer lighting Foyer, as columns punctuate the entry to the Dining Room and Great Room
- Spacious Kitchen with angled countertop and open to the Breakfast Bay
- Tray ceilings adding elegance to the Dining Room and the Master Bedroom
- Master Suite, privately located, features an arrangement for physically challenged
- Two bedrooms share a third full bath with a linen closet
- Skylit Bonus Rroom is located over the Garage

Main floor — 2,349 sq. ft.
Garage — 615 sq. ft.

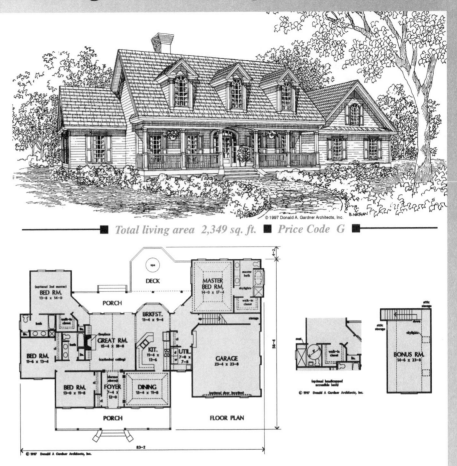

Total living area 2,349 sq. ft. ● Price Code G

© 1997 Donald A. Gardner Architects, Inc.

Exciting Three Bedroom

No. 99805

This plan features:

—Three bedrooms

—Two full baths

- A Great Room enhanced by a fireplace, cathedral ceiling, and built-in bookshelves
- A Kitchen designed for efficiency with a food preparation island and a Pantry
- A Master Suite topped by a cathedral ceiling and pampered by a luxurious bath and a walk-in closet
- Two additional bedrooms, one with a cathedral ceiling and a walk-in closet, sharing a skylit bath
- A second floor bonus room, perfect for a study or a play area
- An optional basement or crawl space foundation — please specify when ordering

Main floor — 1,787 sq. ft.
Garage & storage — 521 sq. ft.
Bonus room — 326 sq. ft.

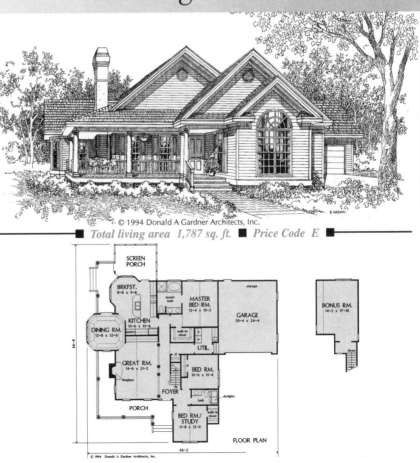

© 1994 Donald A Gardner Architects, Inc.

Total living area 1,787 sq. ft. ● Price Code E

FLOOR PLAN

161

Dressed to Impress

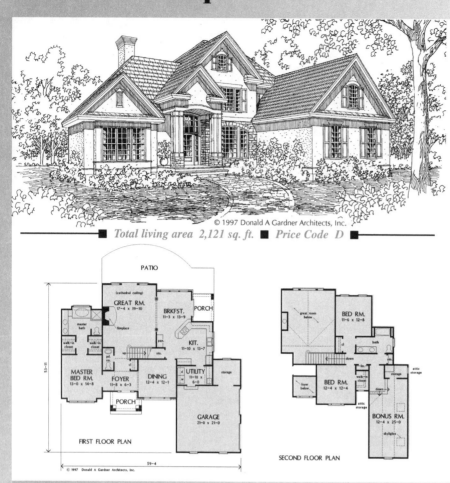

© 1997 Donald A Gardner Architects, Inc.

■ Total living area 2,121 sq. ft. ■ Price Code D ■

PATIO

GREAT RM.
(cathedral ceiling)
17-4 x 19-10

BRKFST.
11-3 x 13-9

PORCH

KIT.
11-10 x 13-7

fireplace

master bath

walk-in closet   walk-in closet

MASTER BED RM.
13-0 x 14-8

FOYER
11-8 x 6-3

DINING
12-4 x 12-1

UTILITY
11-10 x 6-0

storage

PORCH

GARAGE
21-0 x 21-0

53-11

59-4

FIRST FLOOR PLAN

© 1997 Donald A Gardner Architects, Inc.

great room below

BED RM.
11-6 x 12-8

bath

BED RM.
12-4 x 12-4

walk-in closet

storage

attic storage

foyer below

attic storage

BONUS RM.
12-4 x 25-0

skylights

SECOND FLOOR PLAN

No. 99824

■ **This plan features:**

— Three bedrooms

— Two full and one half baths

■ A stone and stucco exterior plus a dramatic entry with square columns provide impressive curb appeal

■ The Great Room has a cathedral ceiling and adjoins the Breakfast Area

■ The Kitchen is enhanced by an angled counter with stove top, a Pantry and easy access to the formal Dining Room

■ A separate Utility Room with built-in cabinets and a counter top with laundry sink add efficiency

■ Double doors lead into the Master Suite with a box bay window, two walk-in closets and a lavish bath

■ Two more bedrooms are located upstairs along with a full bath, linen closet and skylit Bonus Room

First floor — 1,572 sq. ft.
Second floor — 549 sq. ft.
Bonus — 384 sq. ft.
Garage & storage — 540 sq. ft.

French Influenced One-Story

© 1990 Donald A. Gardner Architects, Inc.

■ Total living area 2,045 sq. ft. ■ Price Code D ■

72-6

seat

DECK
25-2 x 10-0

MASTER BED RM.
13-4 x 17-8

master bath

BED RM.
11-4 x 11-8

skylights

SUN RM.
16-0 x 7-6

wet bar

skylights

BRKFST.
8-6 x 10-10

walk-in closet

storage

pantry

fireplace

GREAT RM.
18-0 x 16-2
(cathedral ceiling)

KIT.
12-0 x 10-0

UTIL.

GARAGE
21-0 x 19-6

bath

FOYER
12-4 x 5-6

vaulted clerestory

DINING
12-0 x 12-0

storage

PORCH
15-2 x 4-9

BED RM.
12-0 x 12-0

53-10

FLOOR PLAN

pantry

down

kitchen

garage

storage

ALTERNATE PLAN
FOR BASEMENT

No. 96421

■ **This plan features:**

— Three bedrooms

— Two full baths

■ Elegant details and arched windows, round columns and rich brick veneer creating curb appeal

■ Arched clerestory window in the foyer introduces natural light to a large Great Room with cathedral ceiling and built-in cabinets

■ Great room adjoins a sky lighted sun room with a wetbar which then opens onto a spacious deck.

■ Kitchen with cooking island centrally located with easy access to a large pantry and utility room

■ Large master bedrooms opening to the deck and featuring a garden tub, separate shower, and dual sink vanity

■ An optional basement or crawl space foundation — please specify when ordering

Main floor — 2,045 sq. ft.
Garage & storage — 563 sq. ft.

Cozy and Comfortable

An
EXCLUSIVE DESIGN
By Patrick Morabito,
A.I.A. Architect

■ *Total living area 1,672 sq. ft.* ■ *Price Code B* ■

No. 93306

■ **This plan features:**

— Three bedrooms

— Two full and one half baths

■ Center Foyer leads into formal Living and Dining rooms

■ Open Family Room accented by hearth fireplace

■ Efficient Kitchen with peninsula counter, nearby Laundry and Garage entry, and Dinette with access to rear yard

■ Corner Master Bedroom offers a plush bath with a double vanity and whirlpool tub

■ Two additional bedrooms with ample closets share a full bath

■ No materials list is available for this plan

First floor — 884 sq. ft.
Second floor — 788 sq. ft.
Garage — 450 sq. ft.
Basement — 884 sq. ft.

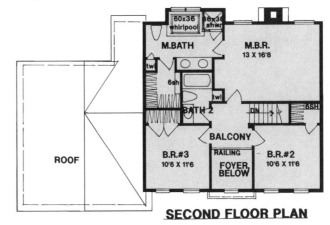

SECOND FLOOR PLAN

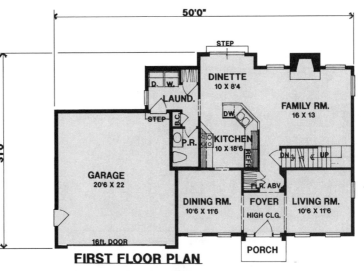

FIRST FLOOR PLAN

Grand Country Porch

■ *Total living area   2,665 sq. ft.* ■ *Price Code E* ■

No. 94615

■ This plan features:

— Four bedrooms

— Three full baths

■ Large front Porch provides shade and Southern hospitality

■ Spacious Living Room with access to Covered Porch and Patio, and a cozy fireplace between built-in shelves

■ Country Kitchen with a cooktop island, bright Breakfast bay, Utility Room and Garage entry

■ Corner Master Bedroom with a walk-in closet and private bath

■ First floor bedroom with private access to a full bath

■ Two second floor bedrooms with dormers, walk-in closets and separate vanities, share a full bath

■ An optional crawl space or slab foundation — please specify when ordering

■ No materials list is available for this plan

First floor — 1,916 sq. ft.
Second floor — 749 sq. ft.
Garage — 479 sq. ft.

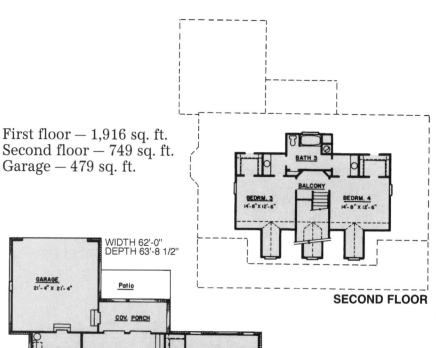

WIDTH 62'-0"
DEPTH 63'-8 1/2"

SECOND FLOOR

FIRST FLOOR

Flexibility to Expand

No. 99859

This plan features:

— Three bedrooms

— Two full and one half baths

■ Three bedroom country cottage has lots of room to expand

■ Two-story Foyer contains palladian window in a clerestory dormer

■ Efficient Kitchen opens to Breakfast area and Deck for outdoor dining

■ Columns separating the Great Room and the dining Room that have nine foot ceilings

■ Master Bedroom suite is on the first level and features a skylight above the whirlpool tub

■ An optional basement or crawl space foundation — please specify when ordering

First floor — 1,289 sq. ft.
Second floor — 542 sq. ft.
Bonus room — 393 sq. ft.
Garage & storage — 521 sq. ft.

© 1990 Donald A. Gardner, Architects, Inc.

■ *Total living area 1,831 sq. ft.* ■ *Price Code C* ■

FIRST FLOOR PLAN

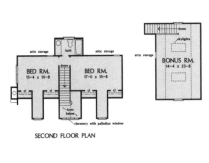

SECOND FLOOR PLAN

Traditional Two-Story Home

No. 96491

This plan features:

— Three bedrooms

— Two full and two half baths

■ Facade handsomely accented by multiple gables, keystone arches and transom windows

■ Arched clerestory window lights two-story Foyer for dramatic entrance

■ Two-story Great Room exciting with inviting fireplace, wall of windows and back Porch access

■ Great cooks will enjoy open Kitchen and easy access to Screen Porch and Dining Room

■ Private Master Bedroom suite offers two walk-in closets and deluxe bath

■ This plan comes with crawl space foundation

First floor — 1,644 sq. ft.
Second floor — 606 sq. ft.
Bonus room — 548 sq. ft.
Garage & storage — 657 sq. ft.

© 1997 Donald A. Gardner Architects, Inc.

■ *Total living area 2,250 sq. ft.* ■ *Price Code D* ■

FIRST FLOOR PLAN

SECOND FLOOR PLAN

Victorian Accents the Exterior

© 1991 Donald A. Gardner Architects, Inc.

■ *Total living area 1,865 sq. ft.* ■ *Price Code C* ■

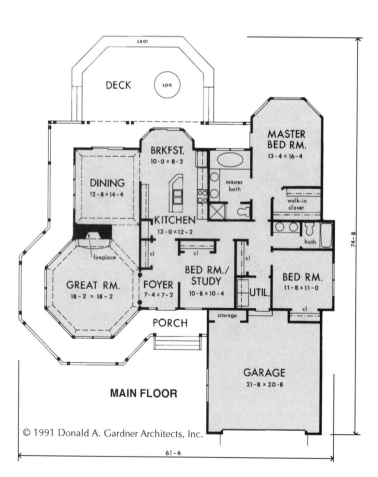

MAIN FLOOR

© 1991 Donald A. Gardner Architects, Inc.

No. 99857

■ **This plan features:**

— Three bedrooms

— Two full baths

■ The covered wrap-around porch connects to the rear deck

■ The foyer opens into the octagonal Great room that is warmed by a fireplace

■ The Dining room has a tray ceiling and convenient access to the Kitchen

■ The galley Kitchen opens into the Breakfast bay

■ The Master bedroom has a bay area in the rear, a walk in closet, and a fully appointed bath

■ Two more bedrooms complete this plan as does another full bath

Main floor — 1,865 sq. ft.
Garage — 505 sq. ft.

■ *Total living area 2,861 sq. ft.* ■ *Price Code E* ■

No. 24563

■ This plan features:

— Four bedrooms

— Two full and one half baths

■ Stone and columns accenting the wrap-around front porch

■ A formal Living Room and Dining Room adjoining with columns at their entrances

■ An island Kitchen with a double sink, plenty of cabinet and counter space and a walk-in pantry

■ A Breakfast Room flowing into the Family Room and the Kitchen

■ A corner fireplace and a built-in entertainment center in the Family Room

■ A lavish Master Suite topped by a decorative ceiling and an ultra bath

■ Three roomy, additional bedrooms sharing a full hall bath

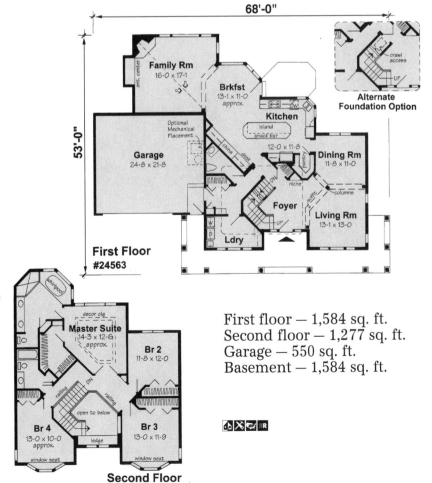

First floor — 1,584 sq. ft.
Second floor — 1,277 sq. ft.
Garage — 550 sq. ft.
Basement — 1,584 sq. ft.

Rear of Home as Attractive as Front

■ *Total living area 2,440 sq. ft.* ■ *Price Code D* ■

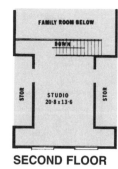

SECOND FLOOR

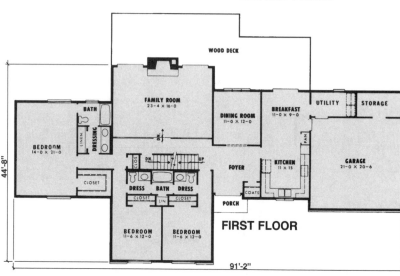

FIRST FLOOR

No. 90413

■ **This plan features:**

— Three bedrooms

— Two full and one half baths

■ A sunken Family Room with a cathedral ceiling and a stone fireplace

■ Two front bedrooms sharing a unique bath-and-a-half arrangement

■ A Master Bedroom with a compartmentalized bath, a double vanity and linen closet

■ A U-shaped Kitchen, serving the Breakfast Nook and the formal Dining Room with ease

■ A second floor with a large Studio

■ An optional basement or crawl space foundation — please specify when ordering

First floor — 2,192 sq. ft.
Second floor — 248 sq. ft.
Basement — 2,192 sq. ft.

Country Styled Home

No. 93432

■ This plan features:

- Three bedrooms
- Two full and one half baths
- ■ A country styled front Porch provides a warm welcome
- ■ The Family Room is highlighted by a fireplace and front windows
- ■ The Dining Room is separated from the U-shaped Kitchen by only an extended counter
- ■ The first floor Master Suite pampers the owners with a walk-in closet and a five-piece bath
- ■ There are two additional bedrooms with a convenient bath in the hall

First floor — 1,288 sq. ft.
Second floor — 545 sq. ft.
Garage — 540 sq. ft.

■ *Total living area 1,833 sq. ft.* ■ *Price Code C* ■

WIDTH 50'-8"
DEPTH 74'-0"

An
EXCLUSIVE DESIGN
By Greg Marquis

Great As A Mountain Retreat

No. 99815

■ This plan features:

- Three bedrooms
- Two full baths
- ■ Board and batten siding, stone, and stucco combine to give this popular plan a casual feel
- ■ User friendly Kitchen with huge pantry for ample storage and island counter
- ■ Casual family meals in sunny Breakfast bay; formal gatherings in the columned Dining area
- ■ Master Suite is topped by a deep tray ceiling, has a large walk-in closet, an extravagant private bath and direct access to back porch

Main floor — 1,912 sq. ft.
Garage — 580 sq. ft.
Bonus — 398 sq. ft.

© 1996 Donald A Gardner Architects, Inc.

■ *Total living area 1,912 sq. ft.* ■ *Price Code E* ■

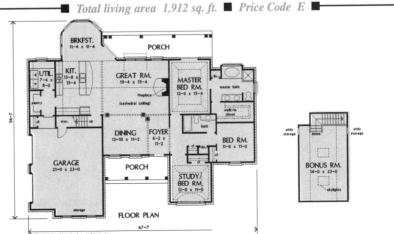

Cozy Three Bedroom

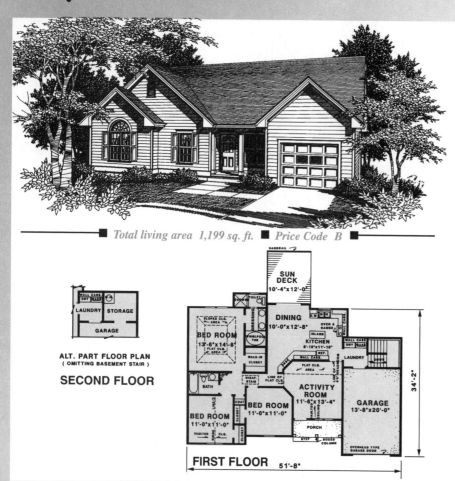

No. 94800

■ **This plan features:**

– Three bedrooms

– Two full baths

■ Covered entry leads into Activity Room highlighted by a double window and a vaulted ceiling

■ Efficient Kitchen with work island, nearby laundry and Garage entry, opens to Dining area with access to Sun Deck

■ Plush Master Bed Room offers a decorative ceiling, walk-in closet and whirlpool tub

■ Two additional bedrooms, one with a vaulted ceiling, share a full bath

■ Garage with entry into Laundry Room serving as a Mud Room

■ An optional basement, slab or crawl space foundation — please specify when ordering

Main floor — 1,199 sq. ft.
Garage — 287 sq. ft.
Basement — 1,199 sq.ft.

Total living area 1,199 sq. ft. ■ Price Code B

European Sophistication

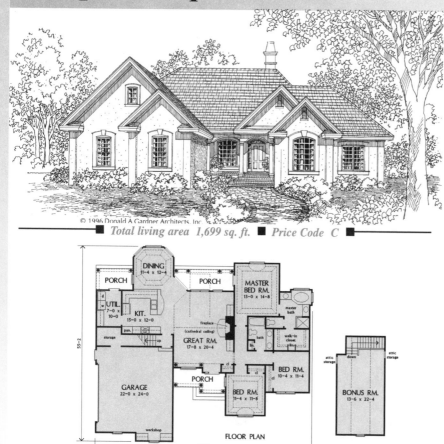

No. 99831

■ **This plan features:**

– Three bedrooms

– Two full baths

■ Keystone arches, gables, and stucco give the exterior European sophistication

■ Large Great Room with fireplace, and U-shaped Kitchen and a large utility room nearby

■ Octagonal tray ceiling dresses up the Dining Room

■ Special ceiling treatments include a cathedral ceiling in the Great Room and tray ceilings in the Master and front bedrooms

■ Indulgent master bath with a separate toilet area, a garden tub, shower and twin vanities

■ Bonus Room over the Garage adds flexibility

Main floor — 1,699 sq. ft.
Garage — 637 sq. ft.
Bonus — 386 sq. ft.

© 1996 Donald A Gardner Architects, Inc.

Total living area 1,699 sq. ft. ■ Price Code C ■

■ *Total living area 3,783 sq. ft.* ■ *Price Code F* ■

No. 92237

■ This plan features:

— Four bedrooms

— Three full and one half baths

■ A stone hearth fireplace and built-in book shelves enhance the Living Room

■ Family Room with a huge fireplace, cathedral ceiling and access to Covered Veranda

■ Spacious Kitchen with cooktop island/snackbar, built-in pantry and Breakfast Room

■ Master Bedroom with a pullman ceiling, sitting area, private Covered Patio, two walk-in closets and a whirlpool tub

■ No materials list is available for this plan

Lower level — 2,804 sq. ft.
Upper level — 979 sq. ft.
Basement — 2,804 sq. ft.
Garage — 802 sq. ft.

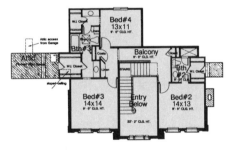

Upper Level

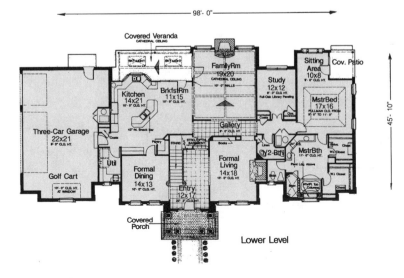

Lower Level

Home Builders on a Budget

© 1996 Donald A. Gardner Architects, Inc.

■ *Total living area 1,498 sq. ft.* ■ *Price Code B* ■

spa

DECK

MASTER
BED RM.
13-4 x 13-8

master
bath

skylights

storage

walk-in
closet

w
d

fireplace

BRKFST.
11-4 x 7-4

BED RM.
11-4 x 11-4

GREAT RM.
15-4 x 16-10
(cathedral ceiling)

cl

bath

cl

cl

KITCHEN
11-4 x 10-0

FOYER
8-2 x 6-2

cl

GARAGE
20-0 x 19-8

50-8

BED RM./
STUDY
11-4 x 10-4

PORCH

DINING RM.
11-4 x 11-4

FLOOR PLAN

59-8

© 1996 DONALD A. GARDNER ARCHITECTS, INC.

No. 99860

■ **This plan features:**

– Three bedrooms

– Two full baths

■ Down-sized Country style plan for a home builder on a budget

■ Columns punctuate open, one-level floor plan and connect Foyer with clerestory window dormers

■ Front Porch and large, rear Deck extend living space outdoors

■ Tray ceilings decorate Master Bedroom, Dining Room and Bedroom/Study

■ Private master bath features garden tub, dual vanity, separate shower and skylights

Main floor — 1,498 sq. ft.
Garage & storage — 427 sq. ft.

Four Bedroom Country Classic

No. 96408

This plan features:

- Four bedrooms
- Two full and one half baths
- Foyer open to the dining room creating a hall with a balcony over the vaulted Great Room
- Great Room opens to the deck and to the island Kitchen with convenient pantry
- Nine foot ceilings on the first floor expand volume
- Master Suite pampered by a whirlpool tub, double vanity, separate shower, and access to the deck
- Bonus room to be finished now or later

First floor — 1,499 sq. ft.
Second floor — 665 sq. ft.
Garage & storage — 567 sq. ft.
Bonus room — 380 sq. ft.

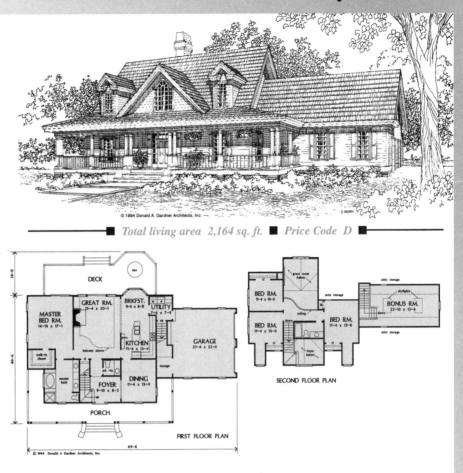

© 1994 Donald A. Gardner Architects, Inc.

Total living area 2,164 sq. ft. ■ *Price Code D*

FIRST FLOOR PLAN

SECOND FLOOR PLAN

© 1994 Donald A Gardner Architects, Inc.

Easy, Economical Building

No. 99813

This plan features:

- Three bedrooms
- Two full baths
- Many architectural elements offer efficient and economical design
- Great Room vaulted ceiling gracefully arches to include arched window dormer
- Open Kitchen with angled counter easily serves Breakfast area
- Tray ceilings enhance Dining Room, front bedroom and Master Bedroom
- Private Master Bath includes garden tub, double vanity and skylight
- An optional basement or crawl space foundation — please specify when ordering

Main floor — 1,959 sq. ft.
Bonus room — 385 sq. ft.
Garage & storage — 484 sq. ft.

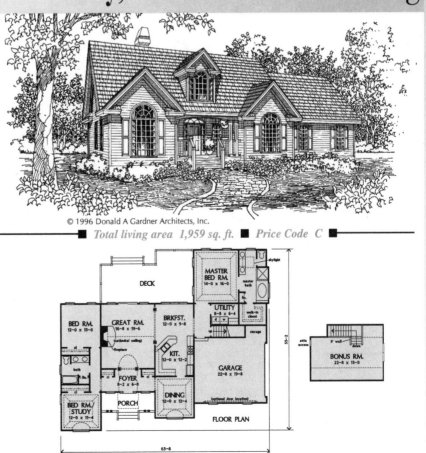

© 1996 Donald A Gardner Architects, Inc.

Total living area 1,959 sq. ft. ■ *Price Code C*

FLOOR PLAN

© 1996 Donald A Gardner Architects, Inc.

Perfect Home for Narrow Lot

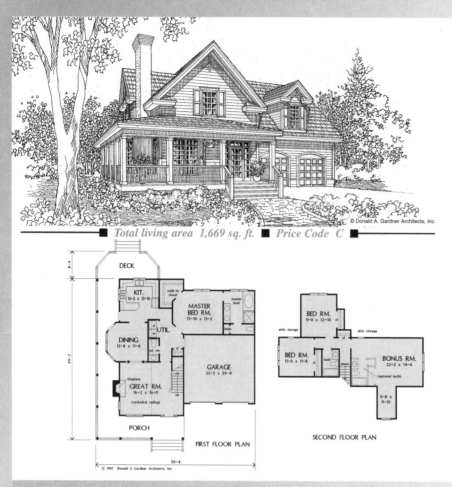

Total living area 1,669 sq. ft. ■ *Price Code C* ■

© Donald A. Gardner Architects, Inc.

FIRST FLOOR PLAN

SECOND FLOOR PLAN

© 1997 Donald A Gardner Architects, Inc.

No. 96487

■ **This plan features:**

– Three bedrooms

– Two and one half baths

■ Wraparound Porch and two-car Garage features unusual for narrow lot floor plan

■ Alcove of windows and columns add distinction to Dining Room

■ Cathedral ceiling above inviting fireplace accent spacious Great Room

■ Efficient Kitchen with peninsula counter accesses side Porch and Deck

■ Master Suite on first floor and two additional bedrooms and Bonus Room on second floor

First floor — 1,219 sq. ft.
Second floor — 450 sq. ft.
Bonus Room — 406 sq. ft.
Garage — 473 sq. ft.

Private Master Suite

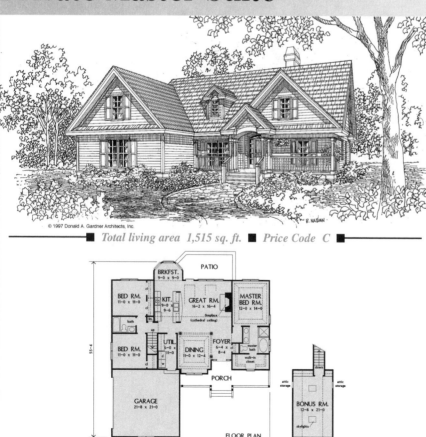

© 1997 Donald A. Gardner Architects, Inc.

B. NATHAN

Total living area 1,515 sq. ft. ■ *Price Code C* ■

FLOOR PLAN

© 1997 Donald A Gardner Architects, Inc.

No. 99835

■ **This plan features:**

– Three bedrooms

– Two full baths

■ Working at the Kitchen island focuses your view to the Great Room with it's vaulted ceiling and a fireplace

■ Clerestory dormers emanate light into the Great Room

■ Both the Dining Room and Master Bedroom are enhanced by tray ceilings

■ Skylights floods natural light into the Bonus space

■ The private Master Suite has its own bath and an expansive walk-in closet

Main floor — 1,515 sq. ft.
Bonus — 288 sq. ft.
Garage — 476 sq. ft.

Lavish Accommodations

■ *Total living area 2,733 sq. ft.* ■ *Price Code F* ■

No. 92538 ✖

■ **This plan features:**

— Four bedrooms

— Three full baths

■ A central Den with a large fireplace, built-in shelves and cabinets and a decorative ceiling

■ Columns defining the entrance to the formal Dining Room, adding a touch of elegance

■ An island Kitchen that has been well thought out and includes a walk-in Pantry

■ An informal Breakfast Room

■ A Master Bedroom with a decorative ceiling, a walk-in closet, and a luxurious master bath

■ Four additional bedrooms, each with private access to a full bath, two of which have walk-in closets

■ An optional crawl space or slab foundation — please specify when ordering

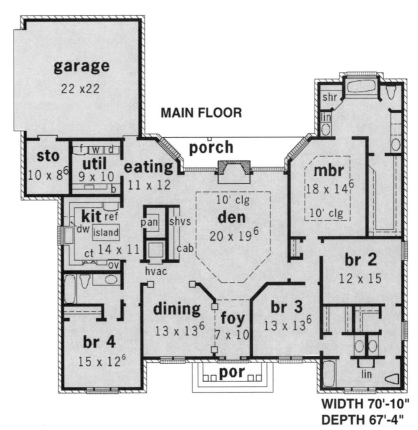

MAIN FLOOR

WIDTH 70'-10"
DEPTH 67'-4"

Main floor — 2,733 sq. ft.
Garage and storage — 569 sq. ft.

French Country Styling

■ *Total living area 2,567 sq. ft.* ■ *Price Code D* ■

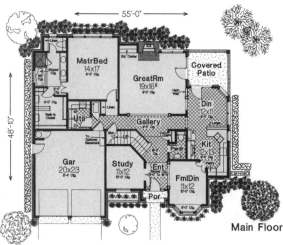

Main Floor

Main floor — 1,765 sq. ft.
Upper floor — 802 sq. ft.
Bonus room — 275 sq. ft.
Garage — 462 sq. ft.

Upper Floor

No. 98533

■ **This plan features:**

— Four bedrooms

— Two full, one half and one three-quarter baths

■ A bay window with a copper roof, a large eyebrow dormer and an arched covered entry

■ The Great Room includes a brick fireplace and a built-in entertainment center

■ An elegant formal Dining Room and angled Study are located to each side of the entry

■ Convenient Kitchen with an informal Dining Area

■ The Master Suite is located on the first floor and has a large bath

■ An optional basement or slab foundation — please specify when ordering

■ No materials list is available for this plan

No. 96478

This plan feature:

— Four bedrooms

— Three full baths

- Transom windows and gables charm the exterior

- Decorative columns and dramatic ceiling treatments highlighting the interior

- Sharing a cathedral ceiling, the Great Room and Kitchen are open to each other as well as the Breakfast Bay

- A sliding pocket door separates the Kitchen from the formal Dining Room, topped by a tray ceiling

- Master Suite also includes a tray ceiling and a luxurious bath with a skylit garden tub and a walk-in closet

- Three additional bedrooms, including on with a private bath and optional arrangement for the physically changed, are located on the opposite side of the home

Main floor — 2,203 sq. ft.

Garage & storage — 551 sq. ft.

Bonus room — 395 sq. ft.

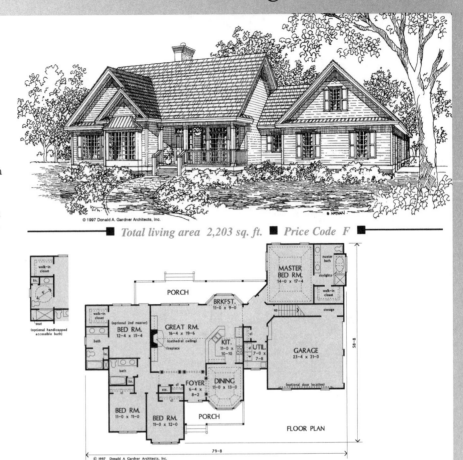

Total living area 2,203 sq. ft. ■ *Price Code F* ■

FLOOR PLAN

© 1997 Donald A Gardner Architects, Inc.

No. 99829

This plan features:

— Three bedrooms

— Two full and one half baths

- Interior columns distinguishing the inviting two-story Foyer from the Dining Room

- Spacious Great Room set off by two story windows and opening to the Kitchen and Breakfast Bay

- Nine foot ceilings adding volume and drama to the first floor

- Secluded Master Suite topped by a space amplifying tray ceiling and enhanced by a plush bath

- Two generous additional bedrooms with ample closet and storage space

- Skylit Bonus Room enjoying second floor access

First floor — 1,436 sq. ft.

Second floor — 536 sq. ft.

Garage & storage — 520 sq. ft.

Bonus room — 296 sq. ft.

Total living area 1,972 sq. ft. ■ *Price Code E* ■

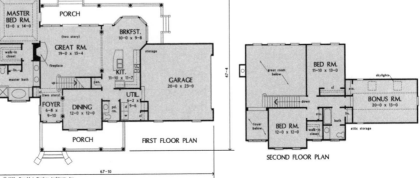

FIRST FLOOR PLAN

SECOND FLOOR PLAN

© 1995 Donald A Gardner Architects, Inc.

Exterior Shows Attention to Detail

■ *Total living area 2,165 sq. ft.* ■ *Price Code D* ■

MAIN FLOOR

Floor plan labels:
- BED ROOM 12'-0"x 11'-6"
- ACTIVITY ROOM 17'-6"x 20'-0"
- DINING ROOM 12'-0"x 13'-0"
- BED ROOM 15'-0"x 17'-0"
- SUN DECK 31'-0"x 12'-0"
- GALLERY
- BATH
- BED ROOM 12'-0"x 11'-6"
- ENTRY
- STOOP
- LAUNDRY
- KITCHEN & BREAKFAST 15'-6"x 17'-0"
- BATH
- WALK-IN CLOSET
- GARAGE 21'-6"x 21'-0"

No. 94811

■ **This plan features:**

—Three bedrooms

—Two full baths

■ Privately located Master Suite is complimented by a luxurious bath with two walk-in closets

■ Two additional bedrooms have ample closet space and share a full bath

■ The Activity Room has a sloped ceiling, large fireplace and is accented with columns

■ Access to Sun Deck from the Dining Room

■ The island Kitchen and breakfast area have access to garage for ease when bringing in groceries

Main floor — 2,165 sq. ft.
Garage — 484 sq. ft.
Basement — 2,165 sq. ft.

Tremendous Curb Appeal

© 1995 Donald A Gardner Architects, Inc.

■ *Total living area 1,246 sq. ft.* ■ *Price Code C* ■

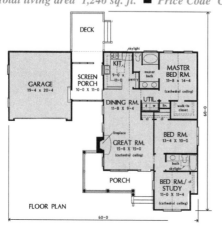

FLOOR PLAN

Floor plan labels:
- DECK
- GARAGE 19-4 x 20-4
- SCREEN PORCH 10-0 X 11-0
- KIT. 9-0 x 11-0
- skylight
- master bath
- pantry
- MASTER BED RM. 11-8 x 14-4 (cathedral ceiling)
- DINING RM. 11-8 x 9-4
- UTIL.
- walk-in closet
- GREAT RM. 15-8 X 15-0 (cathedral ceiling)
- fireplace
- BED RM. 13-4 X 10-0
- PORCH
- BED RM./ STUDY 11-0 x 11-4 (cathedral ceiling)
- bath
- skylight
- 60-0

No. 99806

■ **This plan features:**

— Three bedrooms

— Two full baths

■ Great Room topped by a cathedral ceiling and enhanced by a fireplace

■ Great Room, Dining Room and Kitchen open to each other for a feeling of spaciousness

■ Pantry, skylight and peninsula counter add to the comfort and efficiency of the Kitchen

■ Cathedral ceiling crowns the Master Suite and has these amenities; walk-in and linen closet, a luxurious private bath

■ Swing Room, bedroom or Study, topped by a cathedral ceiling

■ Skylight over full hall bath naturally illuminates the room

Main floor — 1,246 sq. ft.
Garage — 420 sq. ft.

Four Bedroom with One Floor Convenience

■ *Total living area 2,675 sq. ft.* ■ *Price Code E* ■

No. 92275

■ This plan features:

— Four bedrooms

— Three full baths

■ A distinguished brick exterior adds curb appeal

■ Formal Entry/Gallery opens to large Living Room with hearth fireplace set between windows overlooking Patio and rear yard

■ Efficient Kitchen with angled counters and serving bar easily serves Breakfast Room, Patio and formal Dining Room

■ Corner Master Bedroom enhanced by a vaulted ceiling and pampering bath with a large walk-in closet

■ Three additional bedrooms with walk-in closets have access to full baths

■ No materials list is available for this plan

Main floor — 2,675 sq. ft.
Garage — 638 sq. ft.

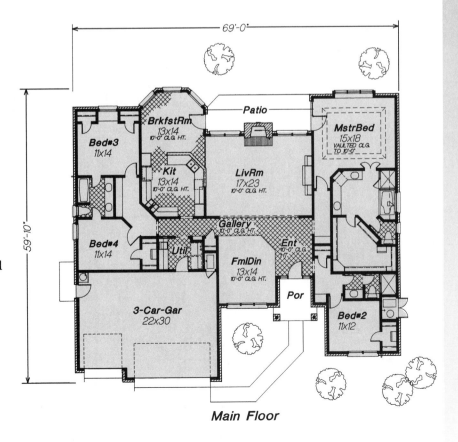

Main Floor

Modernized Traditional Ranch

■ *Total living area 2,301 sq. ft.* ■ *Price Code D* ■

UPPER GREAT ROOM

STORAGE

DN

RAIL

BATH

STORAGE

LOFT
21-4 x 12-0

VAULTED CEILING

LOFT PLAN

GARAGE
21-4 x 22-0

SCREENED PORCH
21-8 x 12-0

UTILITY

DRY | WASH

FREEZ.

STORAGE

FURN

REFG.

DW

HEARTH

FALSE BEAMS

BREAKFAST
9-8 x 9-6

RANGE

KITCHEN
11-0 x 13-0

BAR

WET BAR

S.L.

S.L.

DESK

WALK-IN
CLOSET

BEDROOM 2
12-6 x 12-0

PANTRY

GREAT ROOM
21-4 x 17-0
VAULTED CEILING

LINEN

64' - 6"

GARDEN
TUB

BATH

LR.

WALK-IN
CLOSET

MASTER BEDROOM
14-4 x 18-0

DN

UP

CLOSET

HALL

BATH

WALK-IN
CLOSET

BEDROOM 3
12-6 x 12-0

DESK

DINING ROOM
12-8 x 12-6

FOYER

HUTCH

MAIN FLOOR PLAN

PORCH

63' - 0"

No. 90444

■ This plan features:

— Three bedrooms

— Three full baths

■ A vaulted-ceiling Great Room with skylights and a fireplace

■ A double L-shaped Kitchen with an eating bar opening to a bayed Breakfast Room

■ A Master Suite with a walk-in closet, corner garden tub, separate vanities and a linen closet

■ Two additional bedrooms each with a walk-in closet and built-in desk, sharing a full hall bath

■ A loft that overlooks the Great Room which includes a vaulted ceiling and open rail balcony

■ An optional basement or crawl space foundation — please specify when ordering

Main floor — 1,996 sq. ft.
Loft — 305 sq. ft.

Charm and Personality

No. 99871

This plan features:

– Three bedrooms

– Two full baths

■ Charm and personality radiate through this country home

■ Interior columns dramatically open the Foyer and Kitchen to the spacious Great Room

■ Drama is heightened by the Great Room cathedral ceiling and fireplace

■ Master Suite with a tray ceiling combines privacy with access to the rear deck with spa, while the skylight bath has all the amenities expected in a quality home

■ Tray ceilings with round-top picture windows bring a special elegance to the Dining Room and the front swing room

■ An optional basement or crawl space foundation — please specify when ordering

Main floor — 1,655 sq. ft.
Garage — 434 sq. ft.

© 1996 Donald A. Gardner Architects, Inc.

■ *Total living area 1,655 sq. ft.* ■ *Price Code C* ■

FLOOR PLAN

© 1994 Donald A Gardner Architects, Inc.

Compact Plan

No. 99830

This plan features:

–Three bedrooms

–Two full baths

■ A Great Room topped by a cathedral ceiling, combining with the openness of the adjoining Dining Room and Kitchen, to create a spacious living area

■ A bay window enlarging the Dining Room and a palladian window allowing ample light into the Great Room

■ An efficient U-shaped Kitchen leading directly to the garage, convenient for unloading groceries

■ A Master Suite highlighted by ample closet space and a private a sky lit bath enhanced by a dual vanity and a separate tub and shower

Main floor — 1,372 sq. ft.
Garage & Storage — 537 sq. ft.

© Donald A. Gardner Architects, Inc.

■ *Total living area 1,372 sq. ft.* ■ *Price Code B* ■

FLOOR PLAN

© 1996 Donald A Gardner Architects, Inc.

Victorian Charm

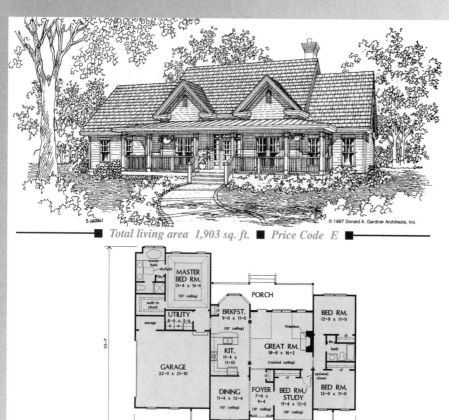

■ Total living area 1,903 sq. ft. ■ Price Code E ■

FLOOR PLAN

No. 96405

■ This plan features:

— Four bedrooms

— Two full baths

■ This home combines Victorian charm with today's lifestyle needs

■ Ceilings vaulted in Great Room and ten feet height in Foyer, Dining Room, Kitchen/Breakfast bay and Bedroom/Study

■ Secluded Master Bedroom suite features tray ceiling, walk-in closet and private, skylit bath

■ Two additional bedrooms, located in separate wing, share a full bath

■ Front and rear Porches extend living area outdoors

■ This plan comes with a crawl space foundation

Main floor — 1,903 sq. ft.
Garage & storage — 531 sq. ft.

Deck Includes Spa

■ Total living area 1,778 sq. ft. ■ Price Code E ■

No. 99873

■ This plan features:

— Three bedrooms

— Two full and one half baths

■ An exterior porch giving the home a traditional flavor

■ Great Room highlighted by a fireplace and a balcony above as well as a pass-through into the kitchen

■ Kitchen eating area with sky lights and bow windows overlooking the deck with a spa

■ Two additional bedrooms with a full bath on the second floor

■ Master Suite on the first floor and naturally illuminated by two skylights

■ An optional basement or crawl space foundation — please specify when ordering

First floor — 1,325 sq. ft.
Second floor — 453 sq. ft.

FIRST FLOOR PLAN

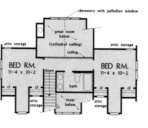

SECOND FLOOR PLAN

■ *Total living area 3,292 sq. ft.* ■ *Price Code F* ■

No. 92209

■ This plan features:

— Four bedrooms

— Three full baths

■ Entry opens to Gallery, and formal Dining and Living rooms with decorative ceilings

■ Spacious Kitchen with a work island opens to dining alcove, Family Room and Patio beyond

■ Comfortable Family Room offers vaulted ceiling above fireplace, and a wetbar

■ Corner Master Suite enhanced by a vaulted ceiling, double vanity bath and huge walk-in closet

■ Three additional bedrooms with walk-in closets have access to full baths

■ No materials list is available for this plan

Main floor — 3,292 sq. ft.
Garage — 670 sq. ft.

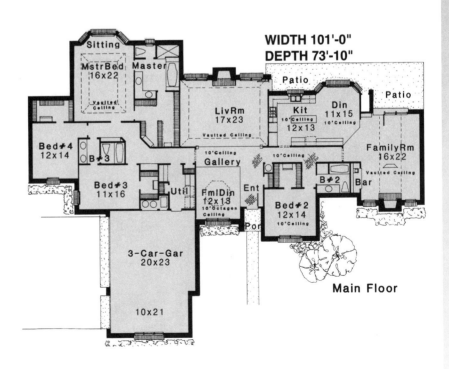

WIDTH 101'-0"
DEPTH 73'-10"

Main Floor

Fieldstone Facade and Arched Windows

■ *Total living area 1,858 sq. ft.* ■ *Price Code C* ■

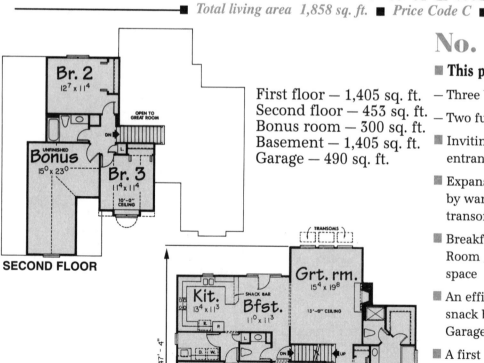

SECOND FLOOR

First floor — 1,405 sq. ft.
Second floor — 453 sq. ft.
Bonus room — 300 sq. ft.
Basement — 1,405 sq. ft.
Garage — 490 sq. ft.

FIRST FLOOR

© design basics, inc.

No. 94911

■ **This plan features:**

– Three bedrooms

– Two full and one half baths

■ Inviting Covered Porch shelters entrance

■ Expansive Great Room enhanced by warm fireplace and three transom windows

■ Breakfast area adjoins Great Room giving a feeling of more space

■ An efficient Kitchen with counter snack bar and nearby laundry and Garage entry

■ A first floor Master Bedroom with an arched window below a sloped ceiling and a double vanity bath

■ Two additional bedrooms share a Bonus area and a full bath on the second floor

No. 93413

This plan features:

— Three bedrooms

— Two full and one half baths

■ The Foyer is naturally lit by a dormer window above

■ Family Room is highlighted by two front windows and a fireplace

■ Kitchen includes an angled extended counter/snack bar and an abundance of counter/cabinet space

■ Dining Area opens to the Kitchen, for a more spacious feeling

■ The roomy Master Suite is located on the first floor and has a private five-piece bath plus a walk-in closet

■ Laundry Room doubles as a mud room from the side entrance

■ No materials list is available for this plan

First floor — 1,271 sq. ft.
Second floor — 537 sq. ft.
Basement — 1,271 sq. ft.
Garage — 555 sq. ft.

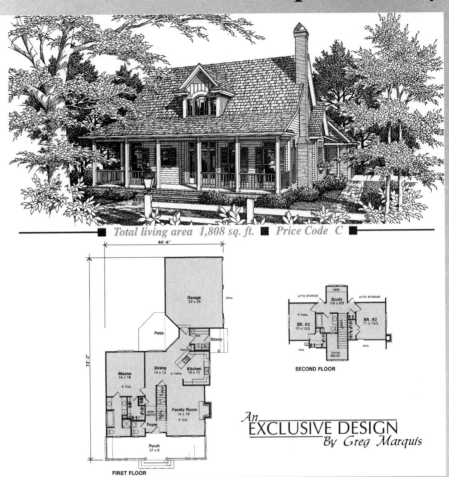

Total living area 1,808 sq. ft. ■ *Price Code C* ■

An EXCLUSIVE DESIGN *By Greg Marquis*

No. 99809

This plan features:

— Four bedrooms

— Two full baths

■ Cathedral ceiling expanding the Great room, Dining Room and Kitchen

■ A versatile bedroom or study topped by a cathedral ceiling accented by double circle-top windows

■ Master Suite complete with a cathedral ceiling, including a bath with a garden tub, linen closet and a walk-in closet

Main floor — 1,417 sq. ft.
Garage — 441 sq. ft.

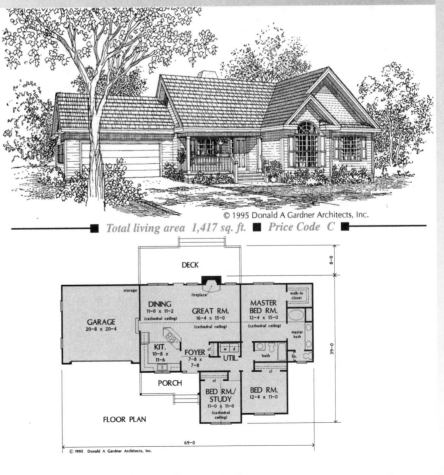

© 1995 Donald A Gardner Architects, Inc.

■ *Total living area 1,417 sq. ft.* ■ *Price Code C* ■

Covered Porches Front and Back

■ Total living area 2,301 sq. ft. ■ Price Code G ■

© 1993 Donald A. Gardner Architects, Inc.

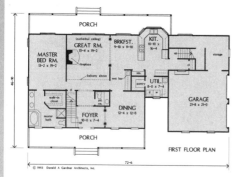

FIRST FLOOR PLAN

SECOND FLOOR PLAN

No. 96404

■ **This plan features:**

— Three bedrooms

— Two full and one half baths

■ Open floor plan plus Bonus Room great for today's family needs

■ Two-story Foyer with palladian, clerestory window and balcony overlooking Great Room

■ Great Room with cozy fireplace provides perfect gathering place

■ Columns visually separate Great Room from Breakfast area and smart, U-shaped kitchen

■ Privately located Master Bedroom accesses Porch and luxurious Master Bath with separate shower and double vanity

First floor — 1,632 sq. ft.
Second floor — 669 sq. ft.
Bonus room — 528 sq. ft.
Garage & storage — 707 sq. ft.

Cathedral Ceiling Enlarges Great Room

■ Total living area 1,699 sq. ft. ■ Price Code D ■

© 1996 Donald A Gardner Architects, Inc.

FLOOR PLAN

© 1996 Donald A Gardner Architects, Inc.

No. 99811

■ **This plan features:**

— Three bedrooms

— Two full baths

■ Two dormers add volume to the Foyer

■ Great Room, topped by a cathedral ceiling, is open to the Kitchen and Breakfast area

■ Accent columns define the Foyer, Great Room, Kitchen, and Breakfast area

■ Private Master Suite crowned in a tray ceiling and highlighted by a skylit bath

■ Front bedroom topped by a tray ceiling

Main floor — 1,699 sq. ft.
Garage — 498 sq. ft.
Bonus — 336 sq. ft.

Total living area 1,485 sq. ft. ■ *Price Code A* ■

No. 91797

■ This plan features:

— Three bedrooms

— Two full baths

■ A railed and covered wrap-around porch, adding charm to this country-styled home

■ A high vaulted ceiling in the Living Room

■ A smaller Kitchen with ample cupboard and counter space, that is augmented by a large pantry

■ An informal Family Room with access to the wood deck

■ A private Master Suite with a spa tub and a walk-in closet

■ Two family bedrooms that share a full hall bath

■ A shop and storage area in the two-car garage

Main area — 1,485 sq. ft.
Garage — 701 sq. ft.

51'-6"

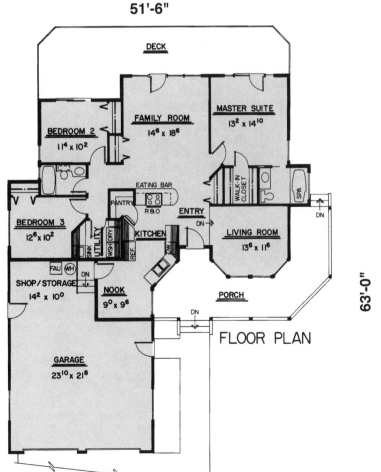

FLOOR PLAN

Split Bedroom Plan

Total living area 1,429 sq. ft. ■ **Price Code A**

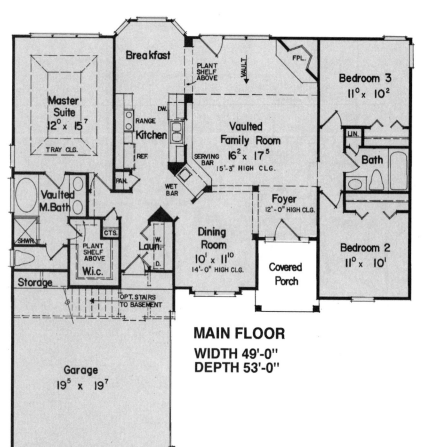

MAIN FLOOR

WIDTH 49'-0"
DEPTH 53'-0"

No. 98415

■ **This plan features:**

— Three bedrooms

— Two full baths

■ A tray ceiling adds a decorative touch the Master Bedroom

■ A full bath is located between the secondary bedrooms

■ A corner fireplace and a vaulted ceiling highlight the Family Room

■ A wetbar/serving bar in the Family Room and a built-in Pantry add to the convenience of the Kitchen

■ The Dining Room is crowned by an elegant high ceiling

■ An optional basement, crawl space or slab foundation — please specify when ordering

Main floor — 1,429 sq. ft.
Basement — 1,472 sq. ft.
Garage — 438 sq. ft.

Relaxed Country Living

No. 96402

This plan features:

— Three bedrooms

— Two full baths

■ Comfortable country home with deluxe master suite, front and back porches and dual-sided fireplace

■ Vaulted Great Room brightened by two clerestory dormers and fireplace shared with Breakfast bay

■ Dining Room and front Bedroom/Study dressed up with tray ceilings

■ Master Bedroom features vaulted ceiling, back Porch access, and luxurious bath with over-sized, walk-in closet

■ Skylit Bonus Room over Garage provides extra room for family needs

Main floor — 2,027 sq. ft.
Bonus room — 340 sq. ft.
Garage & storage — 532 sq. ft.

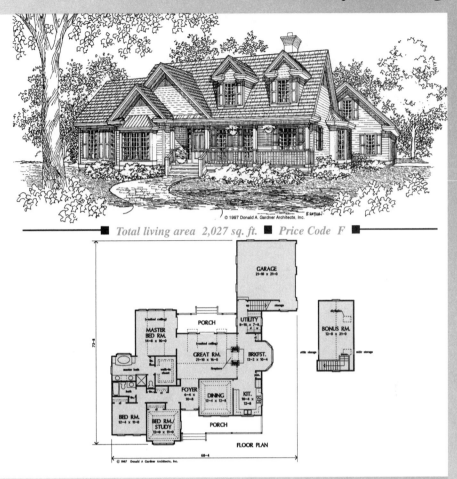

■ *Total living area 2,027 sq. ft.* ■ *Price Code F* ■

Growing Families Take Note

No. 96479

This plan features:

— Three bedrooms

— Two full baths

■ Unlimited options in the second floor bonus area

■ Columns accenting the dining room, adjacent to the Foyer

■ Great room, open to the Kitchen and Breakfast Room, enlarged by a cathedral ceiling

■ Living and entertaining space expands to the deck

■ Master Suite topped by a tray ceiling and including a walk-in closet skylit bath with garden tub and a double vanity

■ Flexible bedroom/study share a bath with another bedroom

First floor — 1,803 sq. ft.
Second floor — 80 sq. ft.
Garage & storage — 569 sq. ft.
Bonus Space — 918 sq. ft.

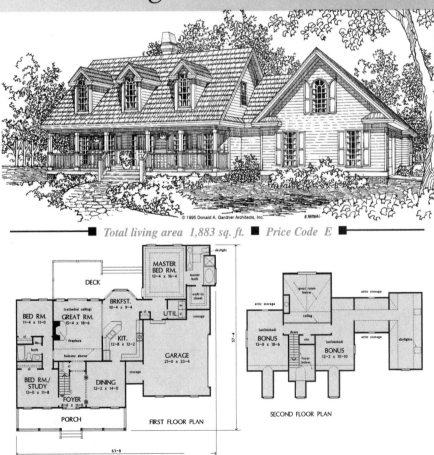

■ *Total living area 1,883 sq. ft.* ■ *Price Code E* ■

Delightful Home

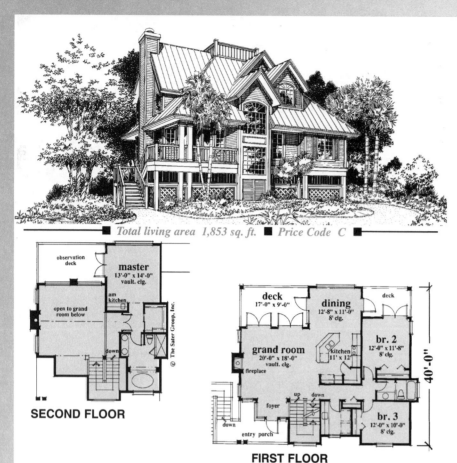

■ *Total living area 1,853 sq. ft.* ■ *Price Code C* ■

SECOND FLOOR

FIRST FLOOR

No. 94248

■ **This plan features:**

— Three bedrooms

— Two full baths

■ Grand Room with a fireplace, vaulted ceiling and double French doors to the rear deck

■ Kitchen and Dining Room open to continue the overall feel of spaciousness

■ Kitchen has a large walk-in pantry, island with a sink and dishwasher creating a perfect triangular workspace

■ Dining Room with doors to both decks, has expanses of glass looking out to the rear yard

■ Master Bedroom features a double door entry, private bath, and a morning kitchen

■ No materials list is available for this plan

First floor — 1,342 sq. ft.
Second floor — 511 sq. ft.
Garage — 1,740 sq. ft.

Appealing Farmhouse Design

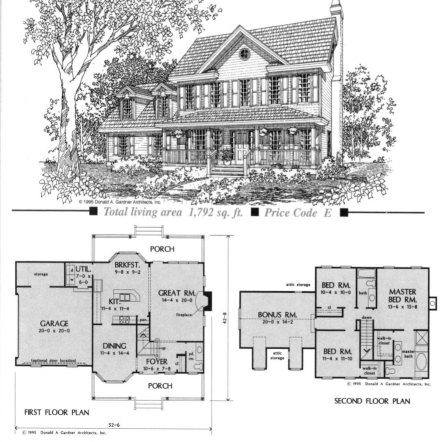

■ *Total living area 1,792 sq. ft.* ■ *Price Code E* ■

FIRST FLOOR PLAN

SECOND FLOOR PLAN

No. 99836

■ **This plan features:**

— Three bedrooms

— Two full and one half baths

■ Comfortable farmhouse features an easy to build floor plan with all the extras

■ Active families will enjoy the Great Room which is open to the Kitchen and Breakfast bay, as well as expanded living space provided by the full back porch

■ For narrower lot restrictions, the Garage can be modified to open in front

■ Second floor Master Bedroom suite contains a walk-in closet and a private bath with a garden tub and separate shower

■ Two more bedrooms on the second floor, one with a walk-in closet, share a full bath

First floor — 959 sq. f.t
Second floor — 833 sq. ft.
Bonus room — 344 sq. ft.
Garage & storage — 500 sq. ft.

■ *Total living area 1,642 sq. ft.* ■ *Price Code B* ■

No. 24717

■ **This plan features:**

— Three bedrooms

— Two full baths

■ Welcoming front Porch enhanced by graceful columns and curved windows

■ Great Room accented by a corner fireplace and outdoor access

■ Open and convenient Kitchen with a work island, angled, peninsula counter/eating bar, and nearby laundry and Garage entry

■ Secluded Master Bedroom with a large walk-in closet and luxurious bath with a dressing table

■ Two additional bedrooms with ample closets, share a double vanity bath

■ No materials list is available for this plan

Main floor — 1,642 sq. ft.
Garage — 420 sq. ft.

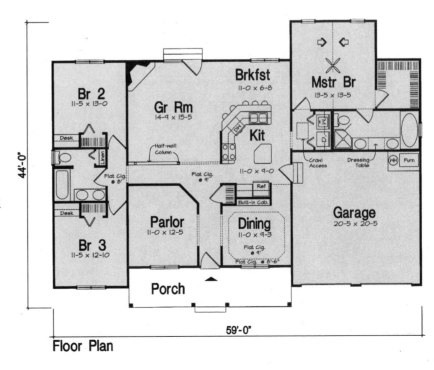

Floor Plan

Rural Farmhouse Profile

■ *Total living area 2,005 sq. ft.* ■ *Price Code C* ■

ROOF

SECOND FLOOR

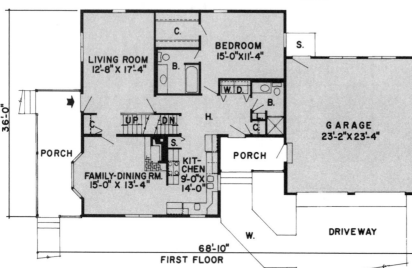

FIRST FLOOR

No. 26001

■ **This plan features:**

— Four bedrooms

— Three full baths

■ A varied gabled roof and large railed front porch

■ A Dining Room graced by a bay window and a masonry fireplace

■ A well-appointed, efficient Kitchen, with a double sink

■ A double Garage with a sheltered breezeway/porch entrance opening to the Utility Room

■ A first floor Master Suite

■ Three additional bedrooms, one with a walk-in closet, that share a full hall bath

First floor — 1,184 sq. ft.
Second floor — 821 sq. ft.
Basement — 821 sq. ft.
Garage — 576 sq. ft.

Casual Country Charmer

No. 96493

This plan features:

- Three bedrooms
- Two full baths
- Columns and arches frame the front Porch
- The open floor plan combines the Great Room, Kitchen and Dining Room
- The Kitchen offers a convenient breakfast bar for meals on the run
- The Master Suite features a private bath oasis
- Secondary bedrooms share a full bath with a dual vanity

Main floor — 1,770 sq. ft.
Bonus — 401 sq. ft.
Garage — 630 sq. ft.

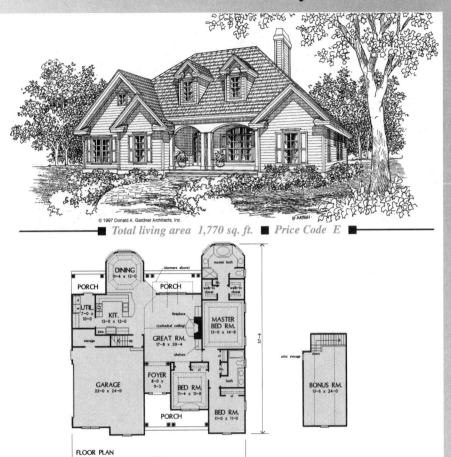

© 1997 Donald A. Gardner Architects, Inc.

Total living area 1,770 sq. ft. ■ **Price Code E**

With Room to Expand

No. 98431

This plan features:

- Three bedrooms
- Two full and one half baths
- An impressive two-story Foyer
- The Kitchen is equipped with ample cabinet and counter space
- Spacious Family Room flows from the Breakfast Bay and is highlighted by a fireplace and a French door to the rear yard
- The Master Suite is topped by a tray ceiling and is enhanced by a vaulted, five-piece master bath
- Two additional bedrooms share the full bath in the hall
- An optional basement, slab or crawl space foundation — please specify when ordering

First floor — 882 sq. ft.
Second floor — 793 sq. ft.
Bonus room — 416 sq. ft.
Basement — 882 sq. ft.
Garage — 510 sq. ft.

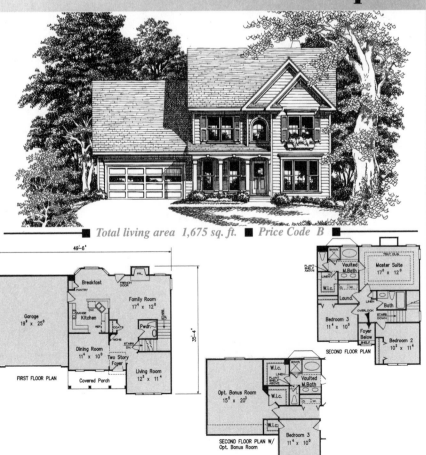

Total living area 1,675 sq. ft. ■ **Price Code B**

Whimsical Two-Story Farmhouse

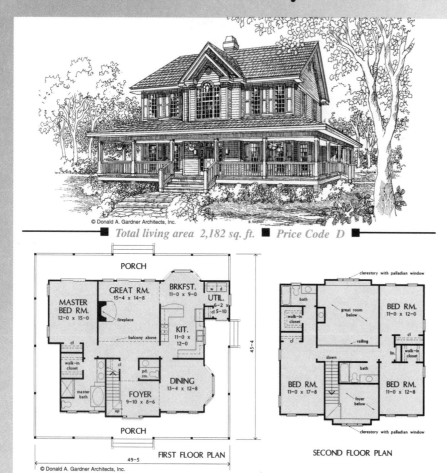

© Donald A. Gardner Architects, Inc.

B. NISSAN.

■ Total living area 2,182 sq. ft. ■ Price Code D ■

PORCH

MASTER BED RM.
12-0 x 15-0

GREAT RM.
15-4 x 14-8

BRKFST.
11-0 x 9-0

UTIL.

fireplace

balcony above

KIT.
11-0 x 12-0

walk-in closet

DINING
13-4 x 12-8

FOYER
9-10 x 8-6

PORCH

45-4

49-5

FIRST FLOOR PLAN

© Donald A. Gardner Architects, Inc.

clerestory with palladian window

bath

walk-in closet

great room below

railing

down

bath

BED RM.
11-0 x 12-0

cl

walk-in closet

BED RM.
11-0 x 17-8

foyer below

BED RM.
11-0 x 12-8

clerestory with palladian window

SECOND FLOOR PLAN

No. 96442

■ **This plan features:**

— Four bedrooms

— Two full and one half baths

■ Double gable with palladian, clerestory window and wrap-around Porch provide country appeal

■ First floor enjoys nine-foot ceilings throughout

■ Palladian windows flood two-story Foyer and Great Room with natural light

■ Both Master Bedroom and Great Room access covered, rear Porch

■ One upstairs bedroom offers a private bath and walk-in closet

First floor — 1,346 sq. ft.
Second floor — 836 sq. ft.

Details, Details, Details

■ Total living area 2,155 sq. ft. ■ Price Code C ■

54'-0"

TRAY CEILING

Master Suite
13⁰ x 17⁸

Vaulted M.Bath

RADIUS WINDOW

Vaulted Great Room
16⁰ x 18³

Vaulted Breakfast

Vaulted Keeping Room
12⁶ x 15⁰

SERVING BAR

RANGE

Kitchen

PANTRY

Lound.

W.I.c.

LINEN

Pwdr.

Two Story Foyer

Dining Room
11⁰ x 12³

Garage
19⁵ x 21⁸

46'-10"

COVERED PORCH

FIRST FLOOR PLAN

Breakfast Below

Keeping Room Below

Great Room Below

Bath

W.I.c.

Bedroom 3
12⁰ x 12⁸

Foyer Below

Bedroom 2
11⁰ x 12³

W.I.c.

Opt. Bonus Room
11⁵ x 15⁸

SECOND FLOOR PLAN

No. 98447

■ **This plan features:**

— Three bedrooms

— Two full and one half baths

■ This elevation is highlighted by stucco, stone and detailing around the arched windows

■ The two-story Foyer allows access to the Dining Room and the Great Room

■ A vaulted ceiling and a fireplace can be found in the Great Room

■ The Breakfast Room has a vaulted ceiling and flows into the Kitchen and the Keeping Room

■ Two secondary bedrooms, each with a walk-in closet, share a full hall bath

■ The Master Suite has a tray ceiling a huge walk-in closet and a compartmental bath

■ An optional basement or crawl space foundation — please specify when ordering

First floor — 1,682 sq. ft.
Second floor — 527 sq. ft.
Bonus room — 207 sq. ft.
Basement — 1,628 sq. ft.
Garage — 440 sq. ft.

Conventional and Classic Comfort

An
EXCLUSIVE DESIGN
By Patrick Morabito,
A.I.A. Architect

■ *Total living area 1,961 sq. ft.* ■ *Price Code C* ■

No. 93349

■ **This plan features:**

— Three bedrooms

— Two full and one half baths

■ Cozy Porch accesses two-story Foyer with decorative window

■ Formal Dining Room accented by a recessed window

■ Spacious Family Room crowned by a vaulted ceiling over a hearth fireplace surrounded by windows

■ Kitchen with an extended counter/eating bar and bright Dinette area with bay window

■ Convenient Laundry, Powder Room and Garage entry near Kitchen

■ Two additional bedrooms and a full bath complete second floor

■ No materials list is available for this plan

First floor — 1,454 sq. ft.
Second floor — 507 sq. ft.

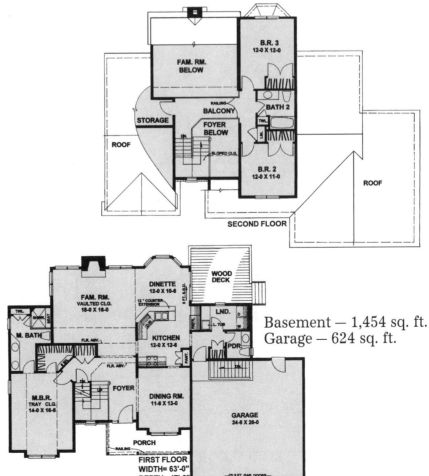

Basement — 1,454 sq. ft.
Garage — 624 sq. ft.

Southern Coastal Styling

■ *Total living area 1,589 sq. ft.* ■ *Price Code B* ■

An
EXCLUSIVE DESIGN
By United Design Associates

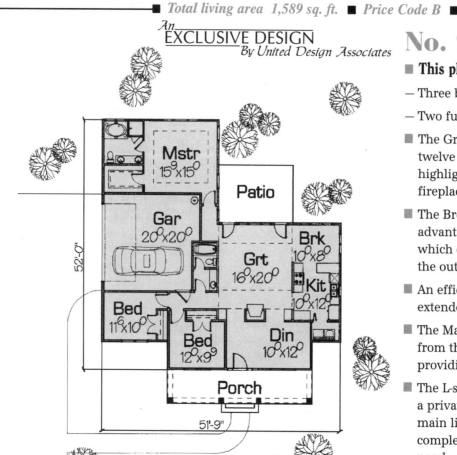

MAIN FLOOR

Mstr
15⁹x15⁰

Patio

Gar
20⁰x20⁰

Brk
10⁰x8⁰

Grt
16⁰x20⁰

Kit
10⁰x12⁰

Bed
11⁶x10⁰

Bed
12⁰x9⁹

Din
10⁰x12⁰

Porch

52'-0"

51'-9"

No. 94749

■ **This plan features:**

— Three bedrooms

— Two full baths

■ The Great room is topped by a twelve foot vaulted ceiling and is highlighted by windows plus a fireplace

■ The Breakfast room takes advantage of a corner location which offers beautiful views of the outside

■ An efficient Kitchen with extended counter/snack bar

■ The Master suite is separated from the secondary bedrooms providing privacy

■ The L-shaped layout provides for a private patio extending from the main living areas, and complements the elegant front porch

Main floor – 1,589 sq. ft.
Garage – 410 sq. ft.

No. 96457

■ **This plan features:**

– Three bedrooms

– Two full and one half baths

■ The large common area combines the Great Room and the Dining Room under a vaulted ceiling that is punctuated with skylights

■ The Kitchen/Breakfast Bay includes a peninsula counter/snack bar

■ From the Great Room extend entertaining outdoors to the covered back porch

■ The Master Suite has a generous bath and ample closet space

■ The front bedroom/study doubles as a Guest Room

■ On the second floor the loft/study makes a terrific office or play room

First floor — 1,234 sq. ft.
Second floor — 609 sq. ft.
Garage — 496 sq. ft.

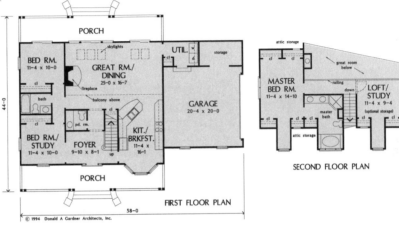

■ *Total living area 1,843 sq. ft.* ■ *Price Code E* ■

Old Fashioned With Contemporary Interior

No. 98407

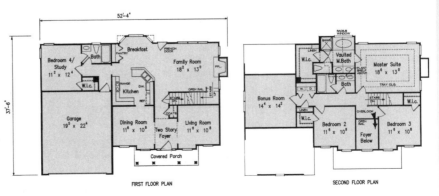

■ **This plan features:**

– Four bedrooms

– Three full baths

■ A two story Foyer is flanked by the Living Room and the Dining Room

■ The Family Room features a fireplace and a French door

■ The bayed Breakfast Nook and Pantry are adjacent to the Kitchen

■ The Master Suite with a trayed ceiling has an attached Bath with a vaulted ceiling and radius window

■ Upstairs are two additional Bedrooms, a full Bath, a laundry closet, and a Bonus room

■ An optional basement or crawl space foundation — please specify when ordering

First floor — 1,135 sq. ft.
Second floor — 917 sq. ft.
Bonus — 216 sq. ft.
Basement — 1,135 sq. ft.
Garage — 452 sq. ft.

■ *Total living area 2,052 sq. ft.* ■ *Price Code D* ■

Country Charmer

Total living area 1,438 sq. ft. ■ Price Code A

MAIN FLOOR

No. 96509

■ **This plan features:**

—Three bedrooms

—Two full baths

■ Quaint front Porch is perfect for sitting and relaxing

■ Great Room opening into Dining area and Kitchen

■ Corner deck in rear of home accessed from Kitchen and Master Suite

■ Master Suite with a private bath, walk-in closet and built-in shelves

■ Two large secondary bedrooms in the front of the home share a hall bath

■ Two-car garage located in the rear of the home

Main floor — 1,438 sq. ft.
Garage — 486 sq. ft.

Mixture of Traditional and Country Charm

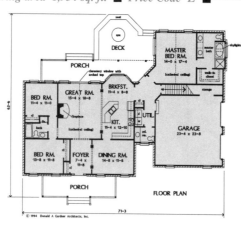

Total living area 1,954 sq. ft. ■ Price Code E

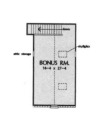

FLOOR PLAN

© 1994 Donald A. Gardner Architects, Inc.

No. 99845

■ **This plan features:**

— Three bedrooms

— Two full and one half baths

■ Stairs to the skylit bonus room located near the Kitchen and Master Suite

■ Master Suite crowned in cathedral ceilings has a skylit bath that contains a whirlpool tub and dual vanity

■ Great Room, topped by a cathedral ceiling and highlighted by a fireplace, is adjacent to the country Kitchen

■ Two additional bedrooms share a hall bath

Main floor — 1,954 sq. ft.
Garage — 649 sq. ft.
Bonus — 436 sq. ft.

Sunny Character

■ *Total living area 1,819 sq. ft.* ■ • *Price Code C* ■

No. 20158

■ **This plan features:**

— Three bedrooms

— Two full and one half baths

■ A Kitchen with easy access to
  screened Porch

■ A Master suite including walk-in
  closet and luxury bath

■ A second story balcony linking
  two bedrooms

First floor — 1,293 sq. ft
Second floor — 526 sq. ft.
Basement — 1,286 sq. ft.
Garage — 484 sq. ft.

An
EXCLUSIVE DESIGN
By Karl Kreeger

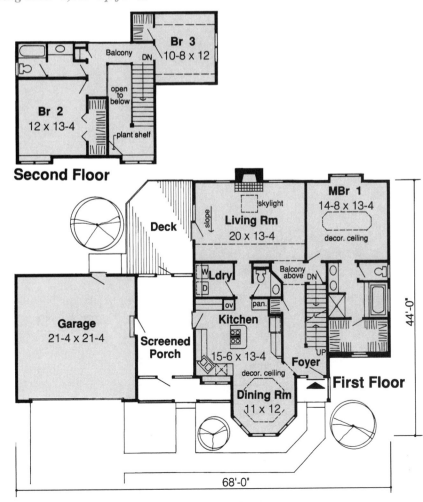

Second Floor

Br 3
10-8 x 12

Balcony DN

open
to
below

Br 2
12 x 13-4

plant shelf

First Floor

MBr 1
14-8 x 13-4

decor. ceiling

skylight

Living Rm
20 x 13-4

slope

Deck

W
D Ldry

ov

pan.

Balcony
above DN

Kitchen
15-6 x 13-4

decor. ceiling

Foyer

UP

Garage
21-4 x 21-4

Screened
Porch

Dining Rm
11 x 12

44'-0"

68'-0"

Perfect for Entertaining

© 1997 Donald A. Gardner Architects, Inc.

■ *Total living area 2,772 sq. ft.* ■ *Price Code E* ■

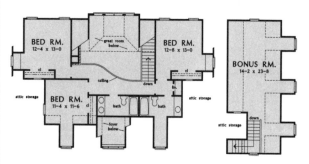

SECOND FLOOR PLAN

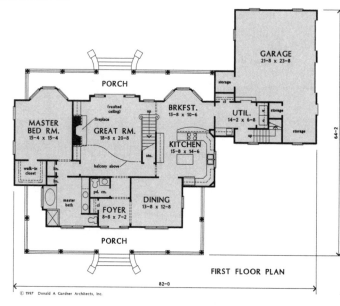

FIRST FLOOR PLAN

© 1997 Donald A Gardner Architects, Inc.

No. 96407

■ **This plan features:**

— Four bedrooms

— Three full and one half baths

■ With front dormers and wrap-around Porch, the home offers formal entertaining and casual living

■ Dramatic Great Room boasts cathedral ceiling and fireplace nestled between built-in shelves

■ French doors expand living space to full length rear Porch

■ Center island and peninsula counter create an efficient Kitchen/Breakfast Area

■ First floor Master Suite features a walk-in closet and spacious master bath

First floor — 1,831 sq. ft.
Second floor — 941 sq. ft.
Bonus room — 539 sq. ft.
Garage & storage — 684 sq. ft.

A Magnificent Manor

No. 98410

This plan features:

- Three bedrooms
- Three full baths
- The two-story Foyer is dominated by a lovely staircase
- The formal Living Room is located directly off the Foyer
- An efficient Kitchen accesses the formal Dining Room for ease in serving
- The Breakfast area is separated from the Kitchen by an extended counter/serving bar
- The two-story Family Room is highlighted by a fireplace that is framed by windows
- A tray ceiling crowns the Master Bedroom while a vaulted ceiling tops the master bath
- Two additional bedrooms share the full double vanity hall bath
- An optional basement or crawl space foundation — please specify when ordering

First floor — 1,428 sq. ft.
Second floor — 961 sq. ft.
Basement — 1,428 sq. ft.
Garage — 507 sq. ft.
Bonus — 472 sq. ft.

Total living area 2,389 sq. ft. ■ *Price Code E*

Living Room Features Exposed Beams

No. 98503

This plan features:

- Three bedrooms
- Two full baths
- A covered Porch shelters the entry to this home
- The large Living room with exposed beams includes a fireplace and built ins
- The bright Dining room is located next to the Kitchen which features a center island
- The bedroom wing features three spacious Bedrooms and two full Baths
- The two-car Garage has a handy workshop area
- No materials list is available for this plan

Main floor — 1,876 sq. ft.
Garage — 619 sq. ft.

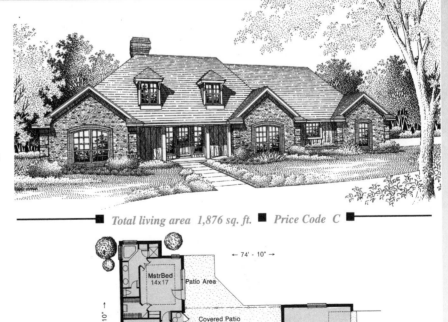

Total living area 1,876 sq. ft. ■ *Price Code C*

Bathed in Natural Light

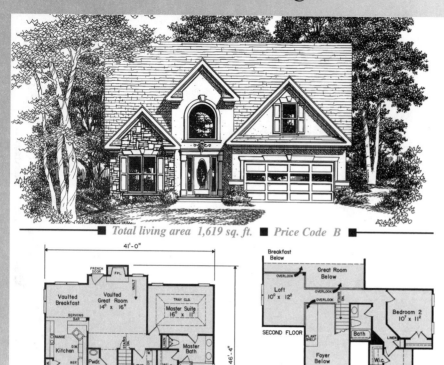

■ Total living area 1,619 sq. ft. ■ Price Code B ■

FIRST FLOOR

- Vaulted Breakfast
- FRENCH DOOR / FPL.
- Vaulted Great Room 14⁰ x 16⁰
- TRAY CLG.
- Master Suite 16⁰ x 11⁰
- SERVING BAR
- RANGE / Kitchen / D.W.
- Master Bath
- PAN. / REF.
- Pwdr.
- Laun. / W.i.c. / SHWR.
- Vaulted Dining Room 10⁰ x 12⁰
- COATS
- Two Story Foyer
- STAIRS UP
- Garage 19⁵ x 19⁰
- 41'-0"
- 46'-4"

SECOND FLOOR

- Breakfast Below
- Great Room Below
- OVERLOOK
- Loft 10⁰ x 12²
- OVERLOOK
- OVERLOOK
- Bedroom 2 10⁷ x 11²
- PLANT SHELF
- Bath
- LINEN
- Foyer Below
- W.i.c.
- Bedroom 3 10⁰ x 16⁰

Optional Bedroom
- Opt. Bedroom 4 10⁰ x 10⁰

No. 98416 ✕

■ **This plan features:**

– Three bedrooms

– Two full and one half baths

■ A high arched window illuminates the Foyer and adds style to the exterior of the home

■ Vaulted ceilings in the formal Dining Room, Breakfast Room and Great Room create volume

■ The Master Suite is crowned with a decorative tray ceiling

■ The Master Bath has a double vanity, oval tub, separate shower and a walk-in closet

■ The Loft, with the option of becoming a fourth bedroom, highlights the second floor

■ An optional basement or crawl space foundation — please specify when ordering

First floor — 1,133 sq. ft.
Second floor — 486 sq. ft.
Basement — 1,133 sq. ft.
Bonus — 134 sq. ft.
Garage — 406 sq. ft.

Family-Sized Accommodations

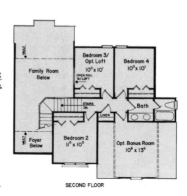

■ Total living area 1,874 sq. ft. ■ Price Code C ■

FIRST FLOOR

- 54'-6"
- FPL.
- TRAY CLG.
- Master Suite 13⁰ x 16⁰
- Vaulted Family Room 15⁰ x 17⁴
- FRENCH DOOR
- DW / Kitchen / Laund.
- Breakfast
- ISLAND / RANGE
- Storage
- OPEN RAIL
- PAN.
- REF.
- Vaulted M.Bath
- RAD. WDW.
- PLANT SHELF ABOVE
- Pwdr.
- LINEN
- Vaulted Foyer
- STAIRS UP
- Dining Room 11⁰ x 13⁰
- Garage 19⁵ x 19⁰
- W.i.c.
- Covered Porch
- 42'-4"

SECOND FLOOR

- Bedroom 3/ Opt. Loft 10⁰ x 10'
- Bedroom 4 10⁰ x 10'
- Family Room Below
- OPEN RAIL W/ LOFT
- STAIRS DN
- Bath
- LINEN
- Foyer Below
- Bedroom 2 11⁰ x 10⁰
- Opt. Bonus Room 10⁰ x 13⁰

No. 98454 ✕

■ **This plan features:**

– Four bedrooms

– Two full and one half baths

■ This home has been designed for today's hectic lifestyle

■ The spacious feeling provided by a vaulted ceiling in Foyer carries into Family Room

■ A fireplace is nestled by an alcove of windows in Family Room which invites cozy gatherings

■ An angled Kitchen with a work island and a pantry easily serves the Breakfast area and the Dining Room

■ The Master Bedroom is accented by a tray ceiling, a lavish bath and a walk-in closet

■ On second floor find three additional bedrooms that share a double vanity bath and an optional Bonus Room

■ An optional basement, slab or crawl space foundation — please specify when ordering

First floor — 1,320 sq. ft.
Second floor — 554 sq. ft.
Bonus room — 155 sq. ft.
Garage — 406 sq. ft.
Basement — 1,320 sq. ft.

An Old-Fashioned Country Feel

■ Total living area 2,091 sq. ft. ■ Price Code C ■

No. 93212

■ This plan features:

— Three bedrooms

— Two full and one half baths

■ Living Room with a cozy fireplace

■ A formal Dining Room with a bay window and direct access to the Sun Deck

■ U-shaped Kitchen efficiently arranged with ample work space

■ Master Suite with an elegant private bath complete with jacuzzi and a step-in shower

■ A future Bonus Room to finish, tailored to your needs

■ An optional basement, crawl space or slab foundation — please specify when ordering

■ No materials list is available for this plan

First floor — 1,362 sq. ft.
Second floor — 729 sq. ft.
Bonus room — 384 sq. ft.
Basement — 988 sq. ft.
Garage — 559 sq. ft.

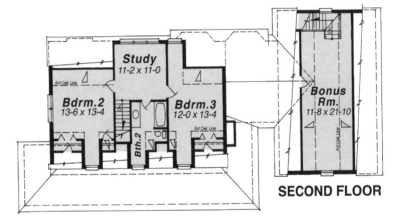

Study 11-2 x 11-0

Bdrm.2 13-6 x 13-4

Bdrm.3 12-0 x 13-4

Bonus Rm. 11-8 x 21-10

SECOND FLOOR

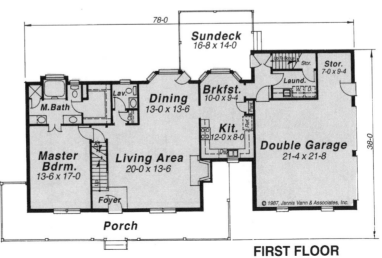

Sundeck 16-8 x 14-0

Brkfst. 10-0 x 9-4

Stor. 7-0 x 9-4

Laund.

Dining 13-0 x 13-6

M.Bath

Lav.

Kit. 12-0 x 8-0

Double Garage 21-4 x 21-8

Master Bdrm. 13-6 x 17-0

Living Area 20-0 x 13-6

Foyer

Porch

78-0

38-0

© 1987, Jannis Vann & Associates, Inc.

FIRST FLOOR

An **EXCLUSIVE DESIGN** *By Jannis Vann & Associates, Inc.*

A Unique Look

■ *Total living area 1,714 sq. ft.* ■ *Price Code B* ■

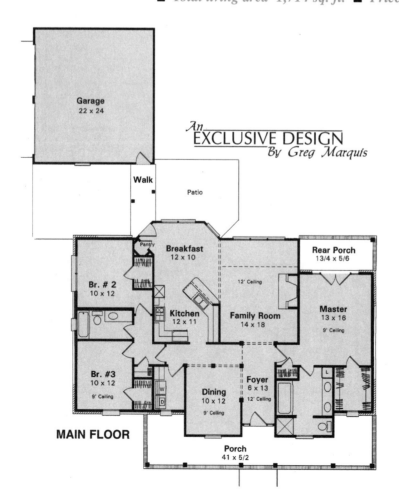

An EXCLUSIVE DESIGN
By Greg Marquis

MAIN FLOOR

Garage 22 x 24

Walk

Patio

Pant'y

Breakfast 12 x 10

Rear Porch 13/4 x 5/6

Br. # 2 10 x 12

12' Ceiling

Kitchen 12 x 11

Family Room 14 x 18

Master 13 x 16

9' Ceiling

Br. #3 10 x 12

9' Ceiling

Foyer 6 x 13

Dining 10 x 12

12' Ceiling

9' Ceiling

Porch 41 x 5/2

No. 93415

■ **This plan features:**

— Three bedrooms

— Two full baths

■ The covered front porch leads into the foyer that has a 12-foot ceiling

■ The Dining room is punctuated by columns

■ The Family room also has a 12-foot ceiling, plus a fireplace

■ The Master bedrooms has a 9-foot ceiling, and two closets

■ Two additional bedrooms on the other side of the home

■ A covered walkway leads to a two-car garage in the rear

■ No materials list is available for this plan

Main floor — 1,714 sq. ft.
Garage — 528 sq. ft.
Width — 55'-0"
Depth — 40'-0"

Exciting Ceilings Add Appeal

No. 96452

■ This plan features:

- Three bedrooms
- Two full baths
- ■ Open design enhanced by cathedral and tray ceilings above arched windows
- ■ Foyer with columns defining Great Room with central fireplace and Deck access
- ■ Cooktop island in Kitchen provides great cooks with convenience and company
- ■ Ultimate Master Suite offers walk-in closet, tray ceiling and whirlpool bath
- ■ Front Bedroom/Study offers multiple uses with tray ceiling and arched window

Main floor — 1,475 sq. ft.
Garage & storage — 478 sq. ft.

■ *Total living area 1,475 sq. ft.* ■ *Price Code B* ■

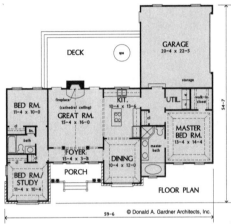

FLOOR PLAN

© Donald A. Gardner Architects, Inc.

Distinguished Look

No. 98429

■ This plan features:

- Three bedrooms
- Two full and one half baths
- ■ The Family Room, Breakfast Room and the Kitchen are presented in an open layout
- ■ A fireplace in the Family Room provides a warm atmosphere
- ■ The plush Master Suite pampers the owner and features a trapezoid glass above the tub
- ■ Two additional bedrooms share the use of the double vanity bath in the hall
- ■ An optional basement, slab or crawl space foundation — please specify when ordering

First floor — 1,028 sq. ft.
Second floor — 878 sq. ft.
Bonus room — 315 sq. ft.
Garage — 497 sq. ft.

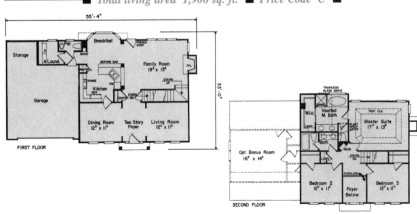

■ *Total living area 1,906 sq. ft.* ■ *Price Code C* ■

FIRST FLOOR

SECOND FLOOR

Easy Living Plan

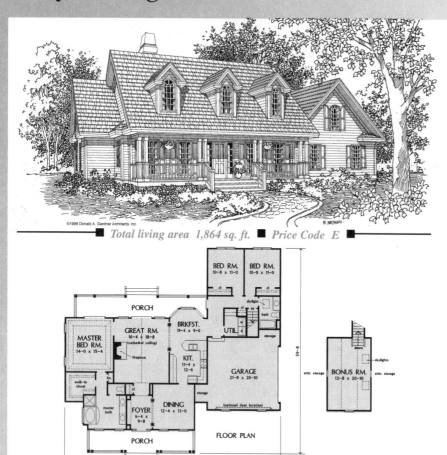

©1996 Donald A. Gardner Architects, Inc.

B. NATHAN

Total living area 1,864 sq. ft. ■ Price Code E

FLOOR PLAN

© 1996 Donald A Gardner Architects, Inc.

No. 96468

■ This plan features:

— Three bedrooms

— Two full baths

■ Sunlit Foyer flows easily into the generous Great Room

■ Great Room crowned in a cathedral ceiling and accented by a fireplace

■ Accent columns define the open Kitchen and Breakfast Bay

■ Master Bedroom topped by a tray ceiling and highlighted by a well-appointed Master Bath

■ Two additional bedrooms, sharing a skylit bath in the hall, create the children's wing

Main floor—1,864 sq. ft.
Bonus room—319 sq. ft.
Garage—503 sq. ft.

Open Plan is Full of Air & Light

Total living area 1,505 sq. ft. ■ Price Code B

FIRST FLOOR PLAN

copyright © 1994 frank betz associates, inc.

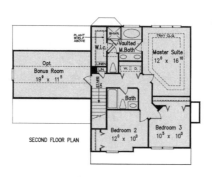

SECOND FLOOR PLAN

No. 98463

■ This plan features:

—Three bedrooms

—Two full and one half baths

■ Foyer open to the Family Room and highlighted by a fireplace

■ Dining Room with a sliding glass door to rear yard adjoins Family Room

■ Kitchen and Nook in an efficient open layout

■ Second floor Master Suite topped by tray ceiling over the bedroom and a vaulted ceiling over the lavish bath

■ Two additional bedrooms sharing a full bath in the hall

■ An optional basement or crawl space foundation — please specify when ordering

■ No materials list is available for this plan

First floor — 767 sq. ft.
Second floor — 738 sq. ft.
Bonus room — 240 sq. ft.
Basement — 767 sq. ft.
Garage — 480 sq. ft.

Country Charm

■ *Total living area 2,377 sq. ft.* ■ *Price Code D* ■

No. 94943 ✕

■ This plan features:

— Four bedrooms

— Two full and one half baths

■ A charming front porch and well-proportioned gables

■ The Media Room offers versatility for entertaining

■ The bayed breakfast area includes direct access to the rear yard

■ An island in the Kitchen which opens up to the Breakfast Room

■ Three secondary bedrooms share a compartmentalized bath

■ An elegant balcony overlooks the two story entry and reveals a French Door to the Master Suite

■ A whirlpool bath and a walk-in closet highlight the Master Suite

First floor – 1,206 sq. ft.
Second floor – 1,171 sq. ft.
Basement – 1,206 sq. ft.
Garage – 521 sq. ft.

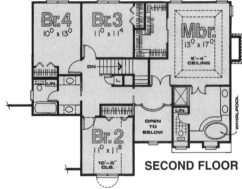

SECOND FLOOR

FIRST FLOOR

Welcoming Wrap-Around Porch

Total living area 2,594 sq. ft. ■ **Price Code D** ■

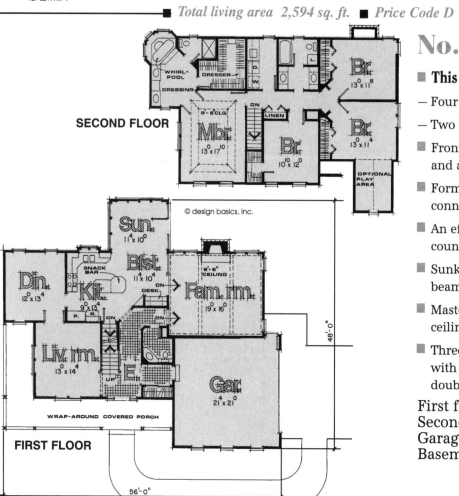

SECOND FLOOR

WHIRL-POOL

DRESSING

DRESSER

9'-8"CLG.

Mbr.
13⁰x17⁰

LINEN

DN

Br.
10¹⁰x12⁰

Br.
13⁰x11⁸

Br.
13⁰x11⁴

OPTIONAL PLAY AREA

© design basics, inc.

Sun.
11⁴x10⁰

Dn.
12⁰x13⁴

SNACK BAR

Kit.
9⁰x13⁰

P. R.

Bfst.
11⁴x10⁴

DESK

DN

8'-6"
CEILING

Fam. rm.
19⁰x16⁰

DN

Liv. rm.
13⁰x14⁰

UP

Gar.
21⁴x21⁴

48'-0"

WRAP-AROUND COVERED PORCH

FIRST FLOOR

56'-0"

No. 94932

- **This plan features:**

– Four bedrooms

– Two full and one half baths

■ Front porch expands living space and accesses easy-care tile Entry

■ Formal Living and Dining rooms connected by French doors

■ An efficient Kitchen with serving counter/snackbar

■ Sunken Family Room with beamed ceiling and fireplace

■ Master Bedroom with decorative ceiling and French doors

■ Three additional bedrooms, one with an optional play area, share a double vanity bath

First floor — 1,322 sq. ft.
Second floor — 1,272 sq. ft.
Garage — 468 sq. ft.
Basement — 1,322 sq. ft.

Sense of Spaciousness

No. 96456

■ This plan features:

— Three bedrooms

— Two full and one half baths

■ Creative use of natural lighting gives a feeling of spaciousness to this country home

■ Traffic flows easily from the bright Foyer into the Great Room which has a vaulted ceiling and skylights

■ The open floor plan is efficient for Kitchen/Breakfast area and the Dining Room

■ Master Bedroom suite features a walk-in closet and a private bath with whirlpool tub

■ Two second floor bedrooms with storage access share a full bath

First floor — 1,180 sq. ft.
Second floor — 459 sq. ft.
Bonus room — 385 sq. ft.
Garage & storage — 533 sq. ft.

©1994 Donald A. Gardner Architects, Inc.

■ *Total living area 1,639 sq. ft.* ■ *Price Code D* ■

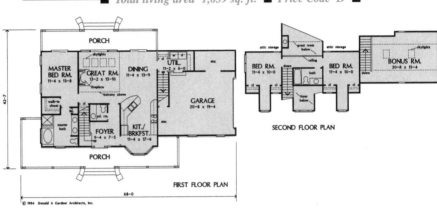

SECOND FLOOR PLAN

FIRST FLOOR PLAN

© 1994 Donald A Gardner Architects, Inc.

Small, Yet Lavishly Appointed

No. 98425

■ This plan features:

— Three bedrooms

— Two full and one half baths

■ The Dining Room, Living Room, Foyer and Master Bath all topped by high ceilings

■ Master Bedroom includes a decorative tray ceiling and a walk-in closet

■ Kitchen open to the Breakfast Room enhanced by a serving bar and a pantry

■ Living Room with a large fireplace and a French door to the rear yard

■ Master Suite located on opposite side from secondary bedrooms, allowing for privacy

■ An optional basement or crawl space foundation — please specify when ordering

Main floor — 1,845 sq. ft.
Bonus — 409 sq. ft.
Basement — 1,845 sq. ft.
Garage — 529 sq. ft.

MAIN FLOOR

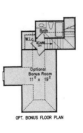

OPT. BONUS FLOOR PLAN

■ *Total living area 1,845 sq. ft.* ■ *Price Code C* ■

Columned Keystone Arched Entry

Total living area 2,256 sq. ft. ■ Price Code E

Main floor

No. 96503

■ **This plan features:**

— Three bedrooms

— Two full baths

■ Keystone arches and arched transoms above the windows

■ Formal Dining Room and Study flank the Foyer

■ Fireplace in Great Room

■ Efficient Kitchen with a peninsula counter and bayed Nook

■ A step ceiling in the Master Suite and interesting master bath with a triangular area for the oval bath tub

■ The secondary bedrooms share a full bath in the hall.

Main floor — 2,256 sq. ft.
Garage — 514 sq. ft.

High Ceilings Add Volume

Total living area 1,715 sq. ft. ■ Price Code B

MAIN FLOOR

No. 98456

■ **This plan features:**

— Three bedrooms

— Two full baths

■ A covered entry gives way to a 14-foot high ceiling in the Foyer

■ An arched opening greets you in the Great Room that also has a vaulted ceiling and a fireplace

■ The Dining Room is brightened by triple windows with transoms above

■ The Kitchen is a gourmet's delight and is open to the Breakfast nook

■ The Master Suite is sweet with a tray ceiling, vaulted Sitting Area and private bath

■ Two bedrooms on the opposite side of the home share a bath in the hall

■ An optional basement, slab or crawl space foundation — please specify when ordering

Main floor — 1,715 sq. ft.
Basement — 1,715 sq. ft.
Garage — 450 sq. ft.

Multiple Porches Provide Added Interest

■ *Total living area 3,149 sq. ft.* ■ *Price Code E* ■

No. 94622

■ **This plan features:**

— Four bedrooms

— Three full and one half baths

■ Great Room with large fireplace and French doors to Porch and Deck

■ Country-size Kitchen with cooktop work island, walk-in pantry and Breakfast Area with Porch access

■ Pampering Master Bedroom offers a decorative ceiling, sitting area, Porch and Deck access, a huge walk-in closet and lavish bath

■ Three second floor bedrooms with walk-in closets have private access to a full bath

■ An optional crawl space or slab foundation — please specify when ordering

■ No materials list is available for this plan

First floor — 2,033 sq. ft.
Second floor — 1,116 sq. ft.

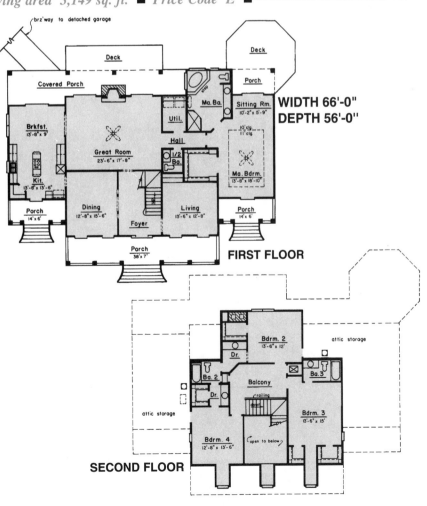

brz'way to detached garage

Deck

Deck

Covered Porch

Porch

Ma. Ba.

Sitting Rm.
10'-2" x 5'-9"

WIDTH 66'-0"
DEPTH 56'-0"

Brkfst.
13'-8" x 9'

Util.

Hall

10' clg
11' clg

Great Room
23'-6" x 17'-8"

1/2
Ba.

Kit.
13'-8" x 13'-6"

Ma. Bdrm.
13'-8" x 18'-10"

Porch
14' x 6'

Dining
12'-8" x 15'-6"

Living
13'-6" x 12'-6"

Porch
14' x 6'

Foyer

Porch
38' x 7'

FIRST FLOOR

Bdrm. 2
13'-6" x 12'

attic storage

Dr.

Ba. 2

Balcony

Ba. 3

Dr.

railing

attic storage

Bdrm. 3
13'-6" x 15'

Bdrm. 4
12'-8" x 13'-6"

open to below

SECOND FLOOR

Convenient and Efficient Ranch

An **EXCLUSIVE DESIGN**
By Patrick Morabito,
A.I.A. Architect

■ *Total living area 1,810 sq. ft.* ■ *Price Code C* ■

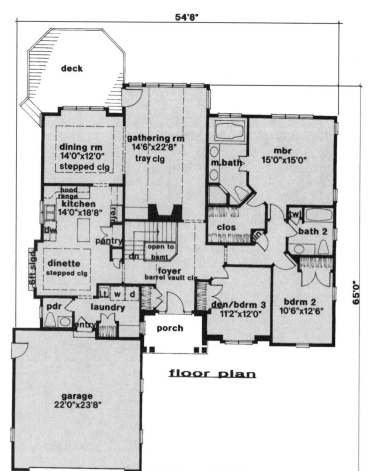

No. 93311

■ This plan features:

— Three bedrooms

— Two full and one half baths

■ A barrel vault ceiling in the Foyer

■ A stepped ceiling in both the Dinette and the formal Dining Room

■ An expansive Gathering Room with a large focal point fireplace and access to the wood deck

■ An efficient Kitchen that includes a work island and a built-in pantry

■ A luxurious Master Suite with a private bath that includes a separate tub and step-in shower

■ Two additional bedrooms that share a full hall bath

■ No materials list is available for this plan

Main floor — 1,810 sq. ft.
Garage — 528 sq. ft.

Easy Living Plan

No. 98406

This plan features:

- Three bedrooms
- Two full and one half baths
- Kitchen, Breakfast Bay, and Family Room blend into a spacious open living area
- Convenient Laundry Center is tucked into the rear of the Kitchen
- Luxurious Master Suite is topped by a tray ceiling while a vaulted ceiling is in the bath
- Two roomy secondary bedrooms share the full bath in the hall
- An optional basement, slab or crawl space foundation — please specify when ordering

First floor — 828 sq. ft.
Second floor — 772 sq. ft.
Basement — 828 sq. ft.
Garage — 473 sq. ft.

■ *Total living area 1,600 sq. ft.* ■ *Price Code B* ■

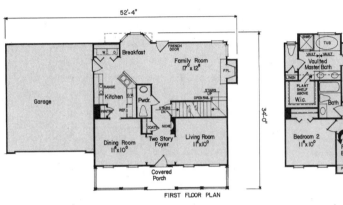

FIRST FLOOR PLAN

SECOND FLOOR PLAN

Attractive Exterior

No. 98512

This plan features:

- Three bedrooms
- Two full baths
- In the gallery, columns separate the space into the Great Room and the Dining Room
- Access to backyard covered patio from bayed Breakfast Nook
- The large Kitchen is a chef's dream with lots of counter space and a pantry
- The Master Bedroom is removed from traffic areas and contains a luxurious Master Bath
- A hall connects the two secondary bedrooms which share a full skylit bath
- No materials list is available for this plan

Main floor — 2,167 sq. ft.
Garage — 690 sq. ft.

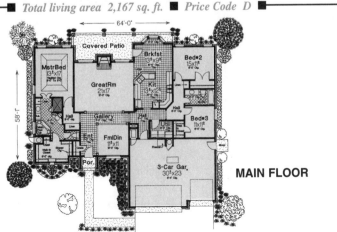

■ *Total living area 2,167 sq. ft.* ■ *Price Code D* ■

MAIN FLOOR

Celebrate the Outdoors

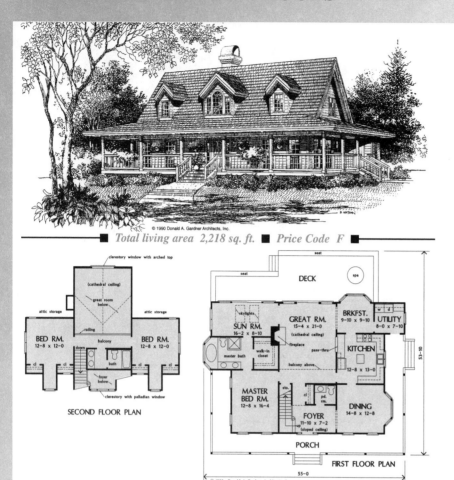

© 1990 Donald A. Gardner Architects, Inc.

Total living area 2,218 sq. ft. ● **Price Code F**

SECOND FLOOR PLAN

© 1992 Donald A Gardner Architects, Inc.

FIRST FLOOR PLAN

No. 96423

■ This plan features:

— Three bedrooms

— Two full and one half baths

■ Country classic celebrating the outdoors with a wrap-around Porch, Sun Room and spacious rear Deck

■ Palladian window in front, a grand arched window in the rear and skylights in the Sun Room letting the sun shine in

■ Second floor balcony overlooking the generous Great Room with a cathedral ceiling and clerestory

■ Large country Kitchen with a pass-through to the Great Room and a center island for easy food preparation

■ Private Master Suite with access to the Sun Room through a luxurious master bath

■ An optional basement or crawl space foundation — please specify when ordering

First floor — 1,651 sq. ft.
Second floor — 567 sq. ft.

Grace with an Elegant Front Porch

Total living area 1,750 sq. ft. ● **Price Code B**

FIRST FLOOR

OPT. BONUS ROOM

SECOND FLOOR

No. 98462

■ This plan features:

— Three bedrooms

— Two full and one half baths

■ The two-story Foyer accesses the Dining Room, Living Room and Family Room with ease

■ The Kitchen opens to the Breakfast Area and in turn the Breakfast Area is open to the Family Room

■ The Family Room is enhanced by a fireplace

■ A work island adds counter space to the Kitchen

■ The Master Suite with a private bath is topped by a vaulted ceiling

■ The front secondary bedroom is highlighted by a window seat

■ An optional basement, slab or crawl space foundation — please specify when ordering

■ No materials list is available for this plan

First floor — 926 sq. ft.
Second floor — 824 sq. ft.
Bonus room — 282 sq. ft.
Basement — 926 sq. ft.
Garage — 440 sq. ft.

Decorative Detailing Adds Charm

■ *Total living area 1,441 sq. ft.* ■ *Price Code A* ■

No. 34005

■ This plan features:

— Three bedrooms

— One full and one three quarter baths

■ A Living Room with a cozy fireplace and sloped ceiling

■ An efficient Kitchen equipped with a plant shelf easily accessible to the Dining Room

■ A Master Bedroom with a decorative ceiling and a private bath

■ A second bath equipped with a washer and dryer

Main area — 1,441 sq. ft.
Garage — 672 sq. ft.
Basement — 769 sq. ft.

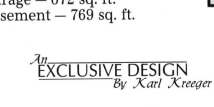

An
EXCLUSIVE DESIGN
By Karl Kreeger

52'-0"

Patio

slope → ← slope

plant shelf →

Kitchen
11-8 x 11-4

Living Rm
15-4 x 18

decor. ceiling

MBr 1
13-4 x 13-11

lin.

W

D

DN

UP

Dining
11-8 x 13

decor. ceiling

38'-0"

lin.

Br 3
10-6 x 11-8

Br 2
11-7 x 11-8

Floor Plan

Isolated Master Suite

■ *Total living area 2,473 sq. ft.* ■ *Price Code D* ■

STUDIO
13-0×20-0

BALCONY   **DOWN**
OPEN RAIL

LIVING AREA BELOW

SECOND FLOOR

WIDTH 91'-8"
DEPTH 45'-8"

BEDROOM
12-0×12-0   **BEDROOM**
12-0×12-0

BEDROOM
14-0×20-6

BATH   **CLOSET**   **CLOSET**
BATH
LINEN   CLOS   DOWN   UP

DINING
11-0×12-6   **KITCHEN**
11-0×14-0   **GARAGE**
20-0×20-6

PLANTER

CLOSET   OPEN RAIL   OPEN RAIL   ENTRY   **BREAKFAST**
11-0×10-0

CLOS   **UTILITY**
10-0×6-0   **STORAGE**
10-0×6-0

FIRST FLOOR

SUNKEN LIVING AREA
24-6×18-0

No. 90420 ✖

■ **This plan features:**

— Three bedrooms

— Two full baths

■ A spacious, sunken Living Room with a cathedral ceiling

■ An isolated Master Suite with a private bath and walk-in closet

■ Two additional bedrooms with a unique bath-and-a-half and ample storage space

■ An efficient U-shaped Kitchen with a double sink, ample cabinets, counter space and a Breakfast area

■ A second floor Studio overlooking the Living Room

■ An optional basement, slab or crawl space foundation — please specify when ordering

First floor — 2,213 sq. ft.
Second floor — 260 sq. ft.
Basement — 2,213 sq. ft.
Garage — 422 sq. ft.

Attractive Ceiling Treatments and Open Layout

No. 96506

■ This plan features:

— Three bedrooms

— Two full and one half baths

■ Great Room and Master Suite with step-up ceiling treatments

■ A cozy fireplace providing warm focal point in the Great Room

■ Open layout between Kitchen, Dining and Great Room lending a more spacious feeling

■ Five-piece, private bath and walk-in closet pampering Master Suite

■ Two additional bedrooms located at opposite end of home share the full bath in the hall

Main floor — 1,654 sq. ft.
Garage — 480 sq. ft.

■ *Total living area 1,654 sq. ft.* ■ *Price Code B* ■

MAIN FLOOR

With All the Amenities

No. 98430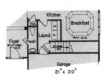

■ This plan features:

— Three bedrooms

— Two full and one half baths

■ A sixteen-foot high ceiling over the Foyer

■ Arched openings highlight the hallway accessing the Great Room which is further enhanced by a fireplace

■ A French door to the rear yard and decorative columns at its arched entrance

■ Another vaulted ceiling topping the Dining Room, convenient to both the Living Room and the Kitchen

■ An expansive kitchen features a center work island, a built-in pantry and a Breakfast Area defined by a tray ceiling

■ A Master Suite also has a tray ceiling treatment and includes a lavish private bath and a huge walk-in closet

■ Secondary bedrooms have private access to a full bath

■ An optional basement, slab or crawl space foundation — please specify when ordering

Main floor – 1,884 sq. ft.
Basement – 1,908 sq. ft.
Garage – 495 sq. ft.

■ *Total living area 1,884 sq. ft.* ■ *Price Code C* ■

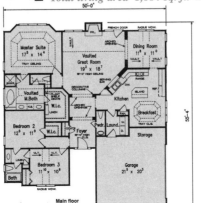

Main floor

Executive Home

© 1994 Donald A. Gardner Architects, Inc.

No. 96449

■ This home features:

— Three bedrooms

— Two full baths

■ Exciting roof lines and brick detailing fit in the finest neighborhood

■ Open kitchen assures great cooks lots of company

■ Large Deck easily accessible for Breakfast area, Great Room and Master Bedroom

■ Great Room also offers cathedral ceiling above arched windows and fireplace nestled between built-ins

■ Private Master Suite features walk-in closet and plush bath with twin vanities, shower and corner window tub

Main floor — 2,211 sq. ft.
Bonus room — 408 sq. ft.
Garage & storage — 700 sq. ft.

■ Total living area 2,211 sq. ft. ■ Price Code F ■

FLOOR PLAN

Three Bedroom Ranch

No. 98414

■ This plan features:

— Three bedrooms

— Two full baths

■ Formal Dining Room enhanced by a plant shelf and a side window

■ Wetbar located between the Kitchen and the Dining Room

■ Built-in pantry, a double sink and a snack bar highlight the Kitchen

■ Breakfast Room containing a radius window and a French door to the rear yard

■ Large cozy fireplace framed by windows in the Great Room

■ Master Suite with a vaulted ceiling over the sitting area, a master bath and a walk-in closet

■ Two additional bedrooms sharing the full bath in the hall

■ An optional basement or crawl space foundation — please specify when ordering

Main floor — 1,575 sq. ft.
Garage — 459 sq. ft.
Basement — 1,658 sq. ft.

■ Total living area 1,575 sq. ft. ■ Price Code B ■

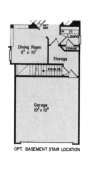

MAIN FLOOR

OPT. BASEMENT STAIR LOCATION

Quoins and Keystones Accent Stucco

■ *Total living area 3,840 sq. ft.* ■ *Price Code F* ■

No. 93247

■ **This plan features:**

— Three bedrooms

— Two full and four half baths

■ Living Room with a vaulted ceiling, Sundeck access and an inviting fireplace

■ Elegant Dining Room with decorative ceiling and corner built-ins

■ Kitchen with cooktop serving counter and Breakfast area

■ Palatial Master Bedroom with a fireplace, private Deck and a spectacular bath

■ Second floor offers three additional bedrooms, one and a half baths, Storage and space for future expansion

■ No materials list available

First floor — 2,656 sq. ft.
Second floor — 1,184 sq. ft.
Bonus — 508 sq. ft.
Basement — 2,642 sq. ft.
Garage — 528 sq. ft.

Elegant Brick Two-Story

■ *Total living area 2,398 sq. ft.* ■ *Price Code D* ■

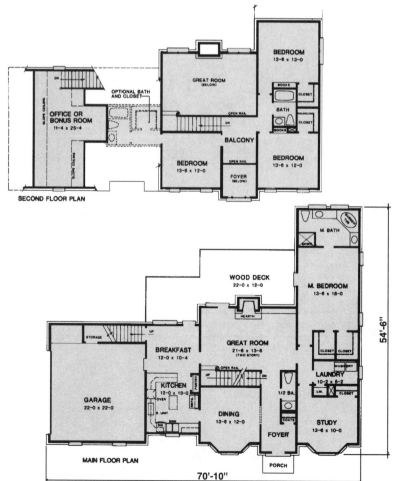

SECOND FLOOR PLAN

OFFICE OR BONUS ROOM
11-4 x 25-4

OPTIONAL BATH AND CLOSET

GREAT ROOM (BELOW)

BEDROOM
13-6 x 13-0

BOOKS

CLOSET

BATH

OPEN RAIL

CLOSET

BALCONY

BOOKS

BEDROOM
13-6 x 12-0

OPEN RAIL

BEDROOM
13-6 x 12-0

FOYER (BELOW)

MAIN FLOOR PLAN

GARAGE
22-0 x 22-0

STORAGE

BREAKFAST
12-0 x 10-4

WOOD DECK
22-0 x 12-0

M. BEDROOM
13-6 x 18-0

M. BATH

HEARTH

GREAT ROOM
21-6 x 13-6
(TWO STORY)

KITCHEN
12-0 x 13-0

OPEN RAIL

CLOSET CLOSET

LAUNDRY
10-2 x 5-2

DINING
13-6 x 12-0

1/2 BA.

STUDY
13-6 x 10-0

FOYER

COATS

PORCH

54'-6"

70'-10"

No. 90450 ✖

■ **This plan features:**

— Four bedrooms

— Two or three full and one half baths

■ A two-story Great Room with a fireplace and access to a deck

■ Master Suite with two walk-in closets and a private master bath

■ A large island Kitchen serving the formal Dining Room and the sunny Breakfast Nook with ease

■ Three additional bedrooms, two with walk-in closets, sharing a full hall bath

■ An optional Bonus Room with a private entrance from below

■ An optional basement or crawl space foundation — please specify when ordering

First floor — 1,637 sq. ft.
Second floor — 761 sq. ft.
Bonus — 453 sq. ft.

Farmhouse Charm

No. 96462

■ This plan features:

— Three bedrooms

— Two full and one half baths

■ Nine foot ceilings and vaulted ceilings in Great Room and Master Bedroom add spaciousness

■ Dining Room accented by columns and accesses Deck for outdoor living

■ Efficient Kitchen features peninsula counter with serving bar for Breakfast area

■ Master Suite includes a luxurious bath with walk-in closet, garden tub, shower and dual vanity

■ Two upstairs bedrooms. one with walk-in closet, share full bath with skylight

First floor — 1,380 sq. ft.
Second floor — 466 sq. ft.
Bonus room — 326 sq. ft.
Garage — 523 sq. ft.

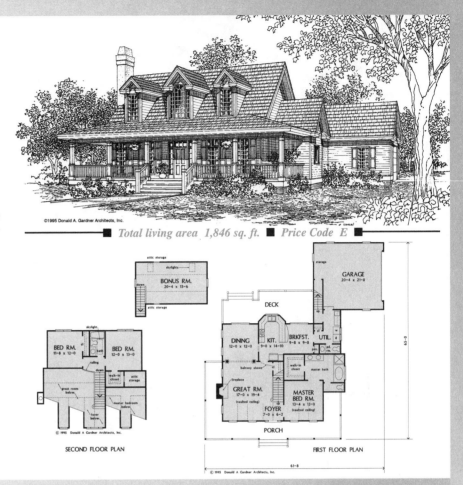

Total living area 1,846 sq. ft. ■ *Price Code E* ■

©1995 Donald A. Gardner Architects, Inc.

SECOND FLOOR PLAN

FIRST FLOOR PLAN

Spacious Elegance

No. 98455

■ This plan features:

— Four bedrooms

— Three full baths

■ This appealing home has gables a hip roof, and keystone window accents

■ The two-story Foyer with palladian window illuminates a lovely staircase and the Dining Room entry way

■ The Family Room has a vaulted ceiling and an inviting fireplace

■ Vaulted ceiling and a radius window highlight the Breakfast area and the efficient Kitchen

■ The Master Bedroom suite boasts a tray ceiling, luxurious bath and a walk-in closet

■ An optional basement or crawl space foundation — please specify when ordering

First floor — 1,761 sq. ft.
Second floor — 588 sq. ft.
Bonus Room — 267 sq. ft.
Garage — 435 sq. ft.
Basement — 1,761 sq. ft.

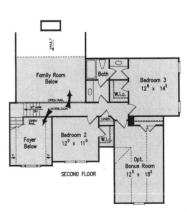

Total living area 2,349 sq. ft. ■ *Price Code E* ■

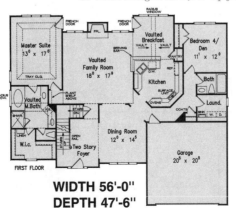

FIRST FLOOR

SECOND FLOOR

WIDTH 56'-0"
DEPTH 47'-6"

221

Split Bedroom Plan

■ Total living area 2,051 sq. ft. ■ Price Code D ■

No. 98427

■ **This plan features:**

— Three bedrooms

— Two full baths

■ Dining Room is crowned by a tray ceiling

■ Living Room/Den privatized by double doors at its entrance, and is enhanced by a bay window

■ The Kitchen includes a walk-in pantry and a corner double sink

■ The vaulted Breakfast Room flows naturally from the Kitchen

■ The Master Suite is topped by a tray ceiling, and contains a compartmental bath plus two walk-in closets

■ Two roomy additional bedrooms share a full bath in the hall

■ An optional basement, slab or crawl space foundation — please specify when ordering

Main floor — 2,051 sq. ft.
Basement — 2,051 sq. ft.
Garage — 441 sq. ft.

WIDTH 56'-0"
DEPTH 60'-6"

MAIN FLOOR

Beautiful Stucco & Stone

■ Total living area 1,913 sq. ft. ■ Price Code C ■

No. 98445

■ **This plan features:**

— Three bedrooms

— Two full and one half baths

■ This home is accented by keystone arches and a turret styled roof

■ The vaulted Family Room is highlighted by a fireplace and French doors to the rear yard

■ The Dining Room adjoins the Family Room which has access to the covered porch and the Kitchen

■ The Master Bedroom is crowned by a tray ceiling, while Master Bath has a vaulted ceiling

■ A Balcony overlooks the Family Room and Foyer below

■ An optional basement, slab or crawl space foundation — please specify when ordering

■ No materials list is available for this plan

First floor — 1,398 sq. ft.
Second floor — 515 sq. ft.
Basement — 1,398 sq. ft.
Garage — 421 sq. ft.
Bonus — 282 sq. ft.

FIRST FLOOR PLAN

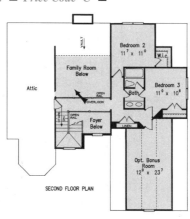

SECOND FLOOR PLAN

Colonial Home with All the Comforts

■ *Total living area 2,224 sq. ft.* ■ *Price Code D* ■

No. 34705

■ **This plan features:**

— Four bedrooms

— Two full and one half baths

■ A formal Living Room and Dining Room flanking a spacious entry

■ Family areas flowing together into an open space at the rear of the home

■ An island Kitchen with a built-in pantry centrally located for easy service to the Dining Room and Breakfast area

■ A Master Suite including large closets and double vanities in the bath

First floor — 1,090 sq. ft.
Second floor — 1,134 sq. ft.
Basement — 1,090 sq. ft.
Garage — 576 sq. ft.

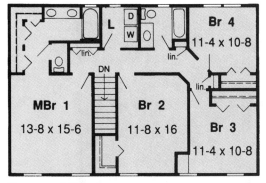

Br 4
11-4 x 10-8

MBr 1
13-8 x 15-6

Br 2
11-8 x 16

Br 3
11-4 x 10-8

Second Floor

Basement Option

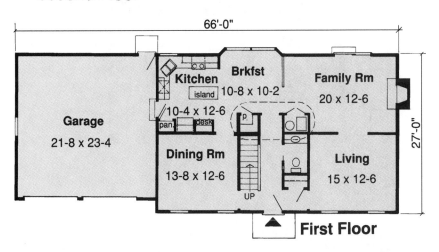

66'-0"

Kitchen

Brkfst
island 10-8 x 10-2

Family Rm
20 x 12-6

10-4 x 12-6

pan. desk

Garage
21-8 x 23-4

Dining Rm
13-8 x 12-6

Living
15 x 12-6

27'-0"

UP

First Floor

223

Easy Everyday Living and Entertaining

■ *Total living area 1,664 sq. ft.* ■ *Price Code B* ■

No. 92238

■ **This plan features:**

— Three bedrooms

— Two full baths

■ Front entrance accented by segmented arches, sidelight and transom windows

■ Open Living Room with focal point fireplace, wetbar and access to Patio

■ Dining area open to both the Living Room and the Kitchen

■ Efficient Kitchen with a cooktop island, walk-in pantry and Utility area with a Garage entry

■ Large walk-in closet, double vanity bath and access to Patio featured in the Master Bedroom suite

■ No materials list is available for this plan

Main floor — 1,664 sq. ft.
Basement — 1,600 sq. ft.
Garage — 440 sq. ft.

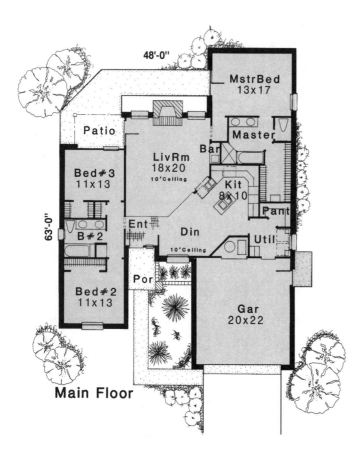

Main Floor

Expansive Living Room

No. 98434

This plan features:

—Three bedrooms

—Two full baths

■ Vaulted ceiling crowns spacious Living Room highlighted by a fireplace

■ Built-in pantry and direct access from the garage adding to the conveniences of the Kitchen

■ Walk-in closet and a private five piece bath topped by a vaulted ceiling in the Master Bedroom suite

■ Proximity to the full bath in the hall from the secondary bedrooms

■ An optional basement, slab or crawl space foundation — please specify when ordering

Main floor — 1,346 sq. ft.
Garage — 385 sq. ft.
Basement — 1,358 sq. ft.

■ *Total living area 1,346 sq. ft.* ■ *Price Code A* ■

European Flair

No. 98460

This plan features:

– Three bedrooms

– Two full baths

■ Large fireplace serving as an attractive focal point for the vaulted Family Room

■ Decorative column defining the elegant Dining Room

■ Kitchen including a serving bar for the Family Room and a Breakfast area

■ Master Suite topped by a tray ceiling over the bedroom and a vaulted ceiling over the five piece Master Bath

■ Optional bonus room for future expansion

■ An optional basement or crawl space foundation — please specify when ordering

■ No materials list is available for this plan

Main floor — 1,544 sq. ft.
Bonus room — 284 sq. ft.
Garage — 440 sq. ft.
Basement — 1,544 sq. ft.

■ *Total living area 1,544 sq. ft.* ■ *Price Code B* ■

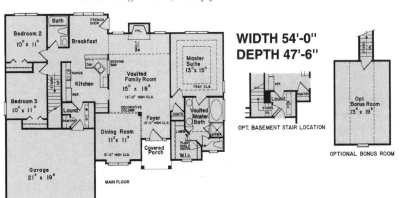

WIDTH 54'-0"
DEPTH 47'-6"

High Ceilings and Arched Windows

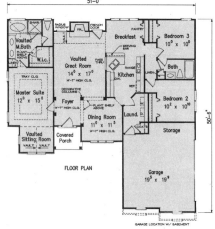

Total living area 1,502 sq. ft. ■ Price Code B

FLOOR PLAN

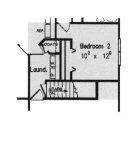

GARAGE LOCATION W/ BASEMENT

No. 98441

■ **This plan features:**

—Three bedrooms

—Two full baths

■ Natural illumination streaming into the Dining Room and Sitting area of the Master Suite through large arched windows

■ Kitchen with convenient pass through to the Great Room and a serving bar for the Breakfast Room

■ Great Room topped by a vaulted ceiling accented by a fireplace and a French door

■ Decorative columns accenting the entrance of the Dining Room

■ Tray ceiling over the Master Suite and a vaulted ceiling over the sitting room and the master bath

■ An optional basement or crawl space foundation — please specify when ordering

■ No materials list is available for this plan

Main floor — 1,502 sq. ft.
Garage — 448 sq. ft.
Basement — 1,555 sq. ft.

Sunny Two-story Foyer

© 1994 Donald A. Gardner Architects, Inc.

Total living area 1,823 sq. ft. ■ Price Code C

SECOND FLOOR PLAN

FIRST FLOOR PLAN

No. 96476

■ **This plan features:**

— Three bedrooms

— Two full and one half baths

■ The two-story Foyer off the formal Dining Room sets an elegant mood in this one-and-a-half story, dormered home

■ The Great Room and Breakfast Area are both topped by a vaulted ceiling

■ The screened porch has a relaxing atmosphere

■ The Master Suite on the first floor includes a cathedral ceiling and an elegant bath with whirlpool tub and separate shower

■ There is plenty of attic and garage storage space available

First floor — 1,335 sq. ft.
Second floor — 488 sq. ft.
Garage & Storage — 465 sq. ft.

Total living area 2,387 sq. ft. ■ *Price Code E* ■

No. 92546 ✖

■ This plan features:

— Four bedrooms

— Two full and one half baths

■ Dining Room accented by an arched window and pillars

■ Decorative ceiling crowns the Den which contains a hearth fireplace, built-in shelves and large double window

■ Kitchen with a peninsula serving counter and Breakfast area, adjoining the Utility Room and Garage

■ Master Bedroom Suite with a decorative ceiling, two vanities and a large walk-in closet

■ Three additional bedrooms with double closets share a full bath

■ An optional slab or crawl space foundation — please specify when ordering

Main floor — 2,387 sq. ft.
Garage — 505 sq. ft.

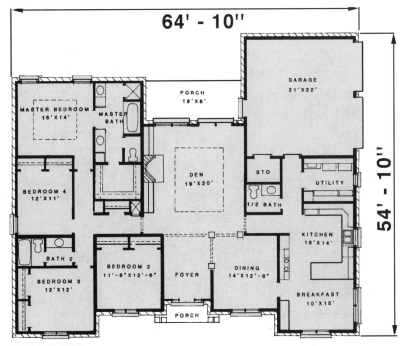

MAIN FLOOR

Outdoor-Lovers' Delight

■ *Total living area 1,540 sq. ft.* ■ *Price Code B* ■

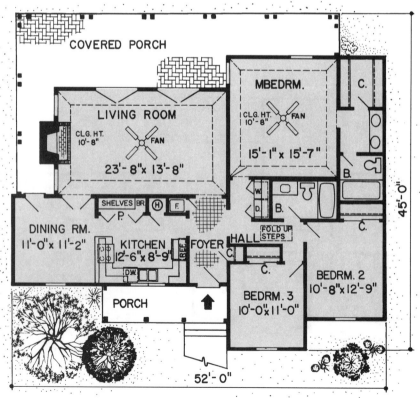

MAIN AREA

No. 10748 ✕

■ **This plan features:**

— Three bedrooms

— Two full baths

■ A roomy Kitchen and Dining Room

■ A massive Living Room with a fireplace and access to the wrap-around porch via double French doors

■ An elegant Master Suite and two additional spacious bedrooms closely located to the laundry area

Main Area — 1,540 sq. ft.
Porches — 530 sq. ft.

One Floor Convenience

No. 98443

■ This plan features:

— Three bedrooms

— Two full baths

■ Vaulted Foyer blending with the vaulted Great Room giving a larger feeling to the home

■ Formal Dining Room opening into the Great Room allowing for a terrific living area in which to entertain

■ Kitchen including a serving bar and easy flow into the Breakfast Room

■ Master Suite topped by a decorative tray ceiling and a vaulted ceiling in the Master Bath

■ Two additional bedrooms sharing the full bath in the hall

■ An optional slab or crawl space foundation — please specify when ordering

■ No materials list is available for this plan

Main floor — 1,359 sq. ft.
Garage — 439 sq. ft.

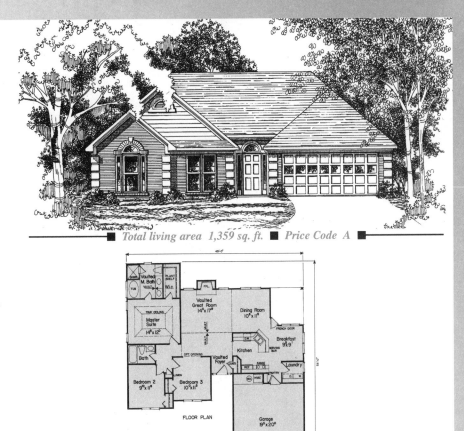

■ *Total living area 1,359 sq. ft.* ■ *Price Code A* ■

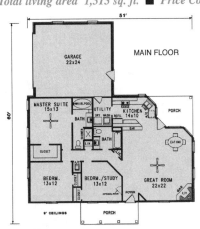

Cozy Three Bedroom

No. 96522

■ This plan features:

— Three bedrooms

— Two full baths

■ The triple arched front Porch adds to the curb appeal of the home

■ The expansive Great Room is accented by a cozy gas fireplace

■ The efficient Kitchen includes an eating bar that separates it from the Great Room

■ The Master Bedroom is highlighted by a walk-in closet and a whirlpool bath

■ Two secondary bedrooms share use of the full hall bath

■ The rear porch extends dining to the outdoors

■ An optional crawl space or slab foundation — please specify when ordering

Main floor — 1,515 sq. ft.
Garage — 528 sq. ft.

■ *Total living area 1,515 sq. ft.* ■ *Price Code B* ■

Brick Abounds

No. 98522

■ **This plan features:**

— Three bedrooms

— Two full baths

■ The covered front Porch opens into the entry that has a 10-foot ceiling and a coat closet

■ The large Living Room is distinguished by a fireplace and a front window wall

■ The Dining Room features a 10-foot ceiling and access to the rear covered Patio

■ The Kitchen is angled and has a pantry, and a cooktop island

■ The Master Bedroom is located in the rear for privacy and boasts a triangular walk-in closet, plus a private bath

■ Two more bedrooms each have large closets and share a hallway bath

■ This home has a two-car Garage that is accessed through the Utility Room

■ No materials list is available for this plan

Main floor — 1,528 sq. ft.
Garage — 440 sq. ft.

Total living area 1,528 sq. ft. ■ *Price Code B* ■

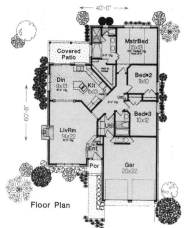

Floor Plan

Outstanding Four Bedroom

No. 98435

■ **This plan features:**

— Four bedrooms

— Two full baths

■ Radius window highlighting the exterior and the formal Dining Room

■ High ceiling topping the Foyer for a grand first impression

■ Vaulted ceiling enhances the Great Room accented by a fireplace framed by windows to either side

■ Arched opening to the Kitchen from the Great Room

■ Breakfast Room topped by a vaulted ceiling and enhanced by an elegant French door to the rear yard

■ Tray ceiling and a five piece compartmental bath gives luxurious presence to the Master Suite

■ Three additional bedrooms share a full, double vanity bath in the hall

■ An optional basement or crawl space foundation — please specify when ordering

Main floor — 1,945 sq. ft.

Total living area 1,945 sq. ft. ■ *Price Code C* ■

Bay Windows and a Terrific Front Porch

■ *Total living area 1,778 sq. ft.* ■ *Price Code B* ■

No. 93261

■ **This plan features:**

— Three bedrooms

— Two full baths

■ A Country style front Porch

■ An expansive living area that includes a fireplace

■ A Master Suite with a private master bath and a walk-in closet, as well as a bay window view of the front yard

■ An efficient Kitchen that serves the sunny Breakfast Area and the Dining Room with equal ease

■ A built-in Pantry and a desk add to the conveniences in the Breakfast Area

■ Two additional bedrooms that share the full hall bath

■ A convenient main floor Laundry Room

An EXCLUSIVE DESIGN
*By Jannis Vann &
Associates, Inc.*

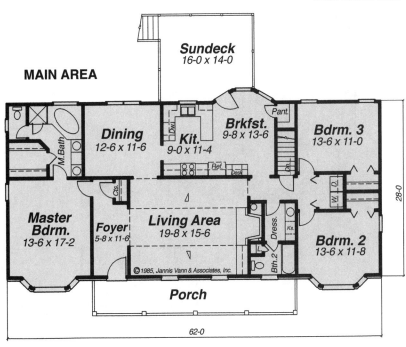

Main area — 1,778 sq. ft.
Basement — 1,008 sq. ft.
Garage — 728 sq. ft.

Elegant Presence

■ *Total living area 2,980 sq. ft.* ■ *Price Code E* ■

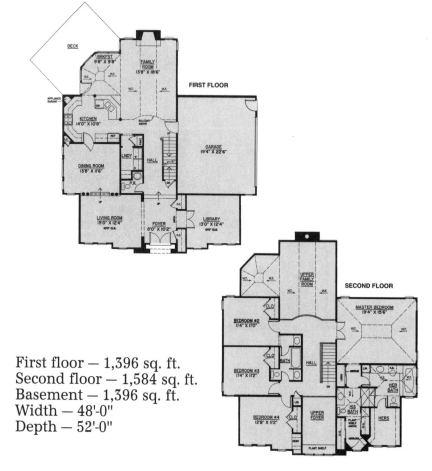

First floor — 1,396 sq. ft.
Second floor — 1,584 sq. ft.
Basement — 1,396 sq. ft.
Width — 48'-0"
Depth — 52'-0"

No. 98231

■ **This plan features:**

— Four bedrooms

— Two full, one three-quarter and one half baths

■ A double-door entrance into the grand Foyer, and an attached double-door entry accesses the Library

■ The Living Room is to the left of the Foyer and steps up into the Dining Room

■ A vaulted ceiling crowns the Family Room and the Breakfast Room

■ The Master Suite is topped by a vaulted ceiling and includes a his-n-her bath

■ An optional basement or slab foundation — please specify when ordering

■ No material list is available for this plan

© 1995 Donald A Gardner Architects, Inc.

Total living area 1,879 sq. ft. ■ **Price Code C**

No. 99807

■ This plan features:

— Three bedrooms

— Two full baths

■ Great Room crowned with a cathedral ceiling and accented by columns and a fireplace

■ Tray ceilings and arched picture windows accent front bedroom and the Dining Room

■ Secluded Master Suite highlighted by a tray ceiling and contains a bath with skylight, a garden tub and spacious walk-in closet

■ Two additional bedrooms share a full bath

■ An optional crawl space or basement foundation — please specify when ordering

Main floor — 1,879 sq. ft.
Bonus — 360 sq. ft.
Garage — 485 sq. ft.

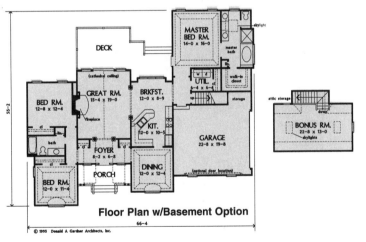

Floor Plan w/Basement Option

© 1995 Donald A Gardner Architects, Inc.

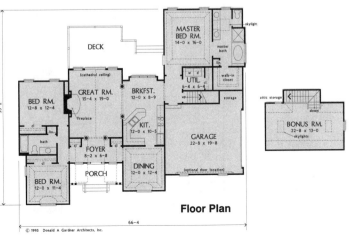

Floor Plan

© 1995 Donald A Gardner Architects, Inc.

233

Traditional Elegance

■ *Total living area 3,813 sq. ft.* ■ *Price Code F* ■

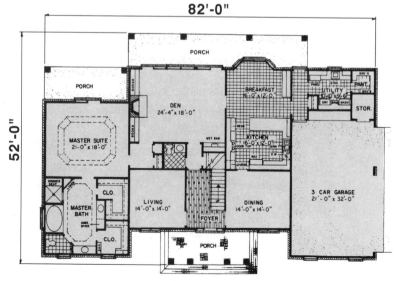

CHILDRENS DEN
18'-8" x 12'-0"

BEDROOM 3
14'-0" x 12'-0"

CLO.

34'-0"

HALL

CLO.

CLO.

BEDROOM 4
14'-4" x 12'-0"

OPEN TO FOYER

BEDROOM 2
16'-4" x 12'-0"

40'-8"

SECOND FLOOR PLAN

82'-0"

52'-0"

PORCH

PORCH

MASTER SUITE
21'-0" x 18'-0"

DEN
24'-4" x 18'-0"

BREAKFAST
16'-0" x 12'-0"

UTILITY

PANT.

STOR.

WET BAR

KITCHEN
16'-0" x 12'-0"

MASTER BATH

CLO.

LIVING
14'-0" x 14'-0"

FOYER

DINING
14'-0" x 14'-0"

3 CAR GARAGE
21'-0" x 32'-0"

CLO.

PORCH

FIRST FLOOR PLAN

No. 92504

■ **This plan features:**

— Four bedrooms

— Three full and one half baths

■ A elegant entrance leading into a two-story Foyer

■ Floor-to-ceiling windows in the formal Living and Dining rooms

■ A spacious Den with a hearth fireplace, built-in book shelves, a wetbar and a wall of windows

■ A Kitchen equipped with a bright Breakfast Area and a walk-in Pantry

■ A grand Master Suite with decorative ceilings, a private Porch and two walk-in closets

■ An optional crawl space or slab foundation — please specify when ordering

First floor — 2,553 sq. ft.
Second floor — 1,260 sq. ft.
Garage — 714 sq. ft.

234

■ *Total living area 1,475 sq. ft.* ■ *Price Code A* ■

No. 93416

■ **This plan features:**

— Three bedrooms

— Two full baths

■ Timely floor plan easily supports a busy family's lifestyle

■ Generous center island Kitchen facilitates quick meal preparation

■ Family room has a corner fireplace

■ Bedroom wing contains three bedrooms

■ Deck connects home to garage

■ No materials list is available for this plan

Main floor — 1,475 sq. ft.
Garage & Storage — 455 sq. ft

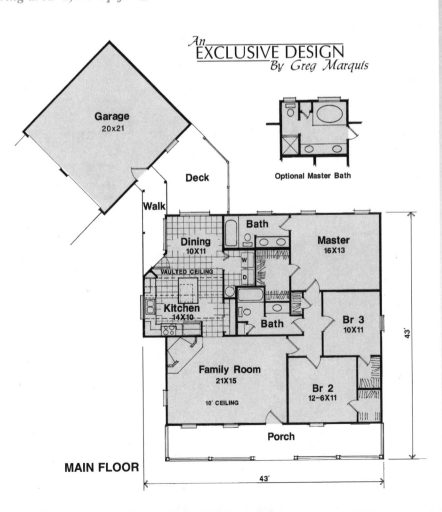

An
EXCLUSIVE DESIGN
By Greg Marquis

Optional Master Bath

MAIN FLOOR

Champagne Style on a Soda-Pop Budget

■ *Total living area 988 sq. ft.* ■ *Price Code A* ■

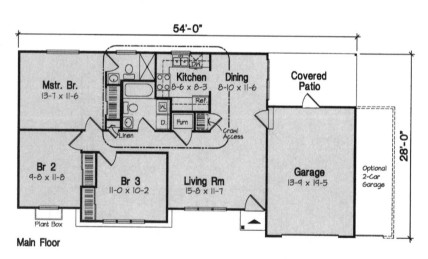

54'-0"

Mstr. Br.
13-7 x 11-6

Kitchen
8-6 x 8-3

Dining
8-10 x 11-6

Covered
Patio

Br 2
9-8 x 11-8

Br 3
11-0 x 10-2

Living Rm
15-8 x 11-7

Garage
13-9 x 19-5

Linen

Crawl
Access

Fum

D.

W

Ref.

Plant Box

Optional
2-Car
Garage

28'-0"

Main Floor

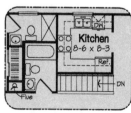

Kitchen
8-6 x 8-3

Ref.

DN

Flue

Optional Basement Plan

An
EXCLUSIVE DESIGN
By Marshall Associates

No. 24302

■ **This plan features:**

— Three bedrooms

— One full and one three-quarter baths

■ Multiple gables, circle-top windows, and a unique exterior setting this delightful Ranch apart in any neighborhood

■ Living and Dining rooms flowing together to create a very roomy feeling

■ Sliding doors leading from the Dining Room to a covered Patio

■ A Master Bedroom with a private bath

Main floor — 988 sq. ft.
Basement — 988 sq. ft.
Garage — 280 sq. ft
Optional 2-car garage — 384 sq. ft.

■ *Total living area 2,562 sq. ft.* ■ *Price Code D* ■

No. 90439

■ This plan features:

— Three bedrooms

— Two full and one half baths

■ A spacious Family Room including a fireplace flanked by bookshelves

■ A sunny Breakfast Bay and adjoining country Kitchen with a peninsula counter

■ An expansive Master Suite spanning the width of the house including built-in shelves, walk-in closet, and a private bath

■ Two bedrooms tucked into the gables at the front of the house

■ An optional basement or crawl space foundation — please specify when ordering

First floor — 1,366 sq. ft.
Second floor — 1,196 sq. ft.
Basement — 1,250 sq. ft.
Garage — 484 sq. ft.

SECOND FLOOR

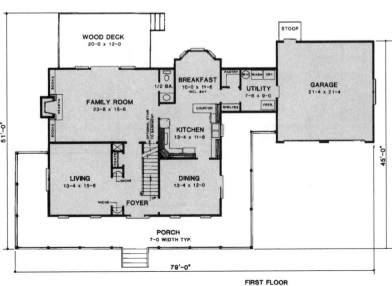

FIRST FLOOR

Elegance And A Relaxed Lifestyle

© 1994 Donald A. Gardner Architects, Inc.

B. NATHAN

■ *Total living area 2,435 sq. ft.* ■ *Price Code D* ■

SECOND FLOOR PLAN

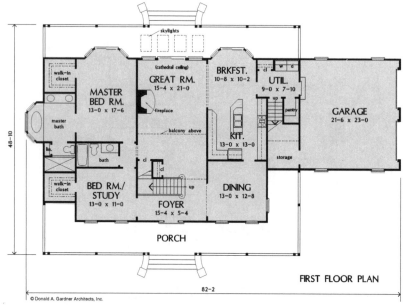

FIRST FLOOR PLAN

No. 99895

■ This plan features:

— Four bedrooms

— Three full baths

■ This family home has combined elegance with a relaxed lifestyle in an open plan full of surprises

■ Open two-level Foyer has a palladian window which visually ties in the formal Dining Area to the expansive Great Room

■ Windows all around, including bays in Master Bedroom and Breakfast Area provide natural light, while nine-foot ceilings create volume

■ Master Bedroom features a whirlpool tub, separate shower and his-n-her vanities

First floor — 1,841 sq. ft.
Second floor — 594 sq. ft.
Bonus room — 411 sq. ft.
Garage & storage — 596 sq. ft.

© Donald A. Gardner Architects, Inc.

Country Estate Home

Total living area 3,480 sq. ft. ■ *Price Code F* ■

No. 98508

■ This plan features:

— Four bedrooms

— Three full and one half baths

■ Formal Living and Dining rooms gracefully defined with columns and decorative windows

■ Wood plank flooring and a massive fireplace accent the Great Room

■ Hub Kitchen with brick pavers and extended serving counter

■ Private Master Bedroom offers a Private Lanai and plush dressing area

■ Three second floor bedrooms with walk-in closets and private access to a full bath

■ No materials list is available for this plan

Main floor — 2,441 sq. ft.
Upper floor — 1,039 sq. ft.
Bonus — 271 sq. ft.
Garage — 660 sq. ft.

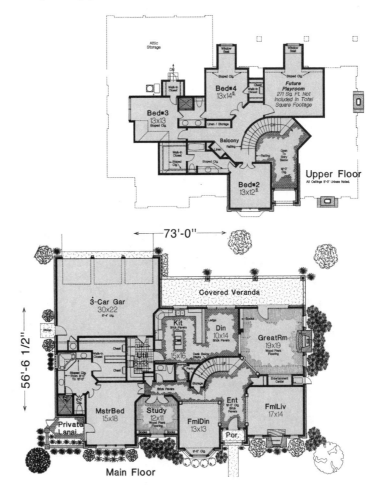

A Warm Welcome

Total living area 2,042 sq. ft. ■ *Price Code C* ■

No. 94984

■ **This plan features:**

— Three bedrooms

— Two full and one half baths

■ The quaint covered Porch has a front railing

■ The Entry opens into the formal Dining room

■ The L-shaped Kitchen with a center island opens into the Breakfast bay

■ The large Family room features rear wall fireplace and windows

■ The Master bedroom has a private bath and a large walk-in closet

■ Two additional bedrooms share a full bath

Main floor — 2,042 sq. ft.
Garage — 506 sq. ft.

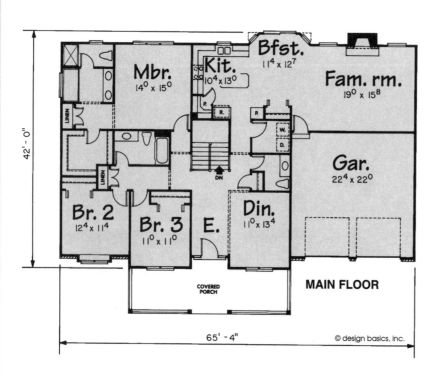

MAIN FLOOR

© design basics, inc.

A Dash of Country

■ *Total living area 1,489 sq. ft.* ■ *Price Code A* ■

No. 97241

■ **This plan features:**

— Four bedrooms

— Two full and one half baths

■ The covered front porch gives this home a dash of country flavoring

■ Wide open spaces are created by the Living Room and the Dining Room

■ An impressive two-story ceiling is over the Living Room

■ The Kitchen has a corner sink and a pantry cupboard

■ Three additional bedrooms on the second floor share a full bath

■ An optional basement, slab or crawl space foundation — please specify when ordering

■ No materials list is available for this plan

First floor – 906 sq. ft.
Second floor – 583 sq. ft.

Basement – 906 sq. ft.
Garage – 460 sq. ft.

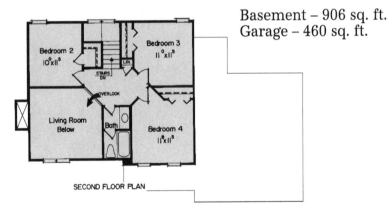

SECOND FLOOR PLAN

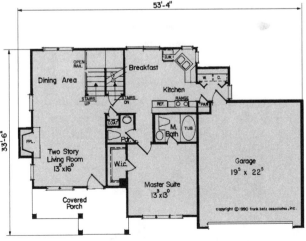

FIRST FLOOR PLAN

A Home with Tremendous Appeal

■ *Total living area 3,512 sq. ft.* ■ *Price Code F* ■

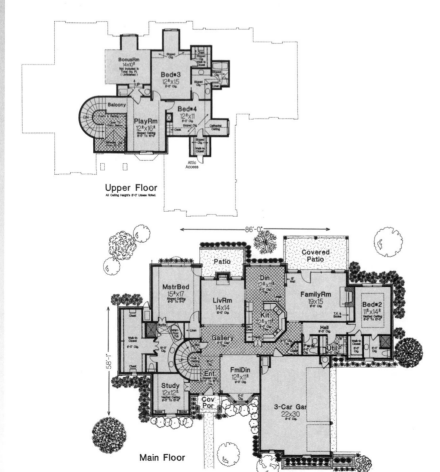

Upper Floor

Main Floor

No. 98535

■ **This plan features:**

— Four bedrooms

— Three full and one half baths

■ A circular stairway in the entry

■ The formal Dining Room has a bay window

■ A private Study with a double-door entry

■ Formal Living Room has a fireplace and elegant columns

■ The Family Room boasts a brick fireplace and built-ins

■ An angled Kitchen contains a built-in pantry and ovens

■ The Master Suite occupies one wing of the house

■ No materials list is available for this plan

Main floor — 2,658 sq. ft.
Upper floor — 854 sq. ft.
Garage — 660 sq. ft.

Country Cottage Charm

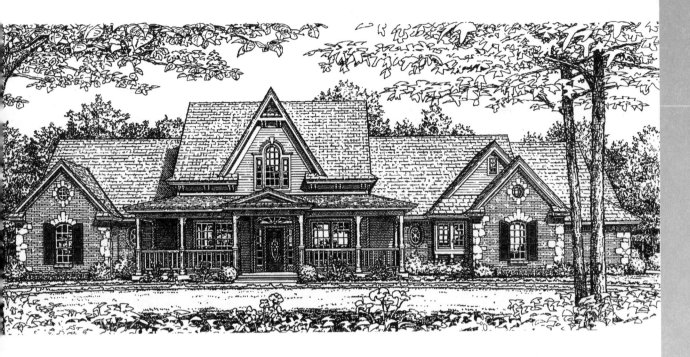

■ *Total living area 3,423 sq. ft.* ■ *Price Code F* ■

No. 98536

■ This plan features:

— Four bedrooms

— Two full and one half baths

■ Vaulted Master Bedroom has a private skylit bath

■ Three more bedrooms have walk-in closets and share a full bath

■ A Loft and Bonus Room above the Living Room

■ Family Room has built-in book shelves, a fireplace, and overlooks the covered Verandah

■ The huge three-car Garage has a separate Shop Area

■ An optional slab or a crawl space foundation — please specify when ordering

■ No materials list is available for this plan

Main floor — 2,787 sq. ft.
Upper floor — 636 sq. ft.
Garage — 832 sq. ft.

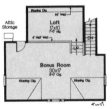

Upper Floor
Optional Bonus Room & Loft

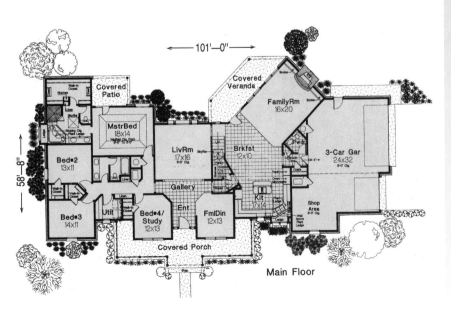

Main Floor

Backyard Views

Total living area 1,746 sq. ft. ■ *Price Code B* ■

No. 92655

■ This plan features:

– Three bedrooms

– Two full baths

■ Front Porch accesses open Foyer, and spacious Dining Room and Great Room with sloped ceilings

■ Corner fireplace, windows and atrium door to Patio enhance Great Room

■ Convenient Kitchen with a pantry, peninsula serving counter for bright Breakfast area and nearby Laundry/Garage entry

■ Luxurious bath, walk-in closet and backyard view offered in Master Bedroom

■ No materials list is available for this plan

Main floor — 1,746 sq. ft.
Garage — 480 sq. ft.
Basement — 1,697 sq. ft.

Patio

Breakfast
10'10" x 12'

Great Room
16'2" x 18'4"

Master Bedroom
15' x 12'10"

Bath

walk-in closet

Kitchen
11'8" x 14' 4"

Dining Room
11' x 9'2"

Foyer

Hall

Bath

Laun.

Porch

Bedroom
11' x 12'6"

Bedroom
12'6"x 11'11"

WIDTH: 65' - 10"
DEPTH: 56' - 0"

MAIN FLOOR

Two-car Garage
22' x 20'8"

■ *Total living area 4,082 sq. ft.* ■ *Price Code F* ■

No. 98538

■ This plan features:

— Four bedrooms

— Three full and one half baths

■ A decorative dormer, a bay window and an eyebrow arched window make a pleasing facade

■ The cozy Study has its own fireplace and a bay window

■ The large formal Living Room has a fireplace and built-in bookcases

■ The huge island Kitchen is open to the Breakfast Bay and the Family Room

■ The Master Suite includes a large bath with a unique closet

■ Three more bedrooms located at the other end of the home each have private access to a full bath

■ No materials list is available for this plan

Main floor — 4,082 sq. ft.
Garage — 720 sq. ft.

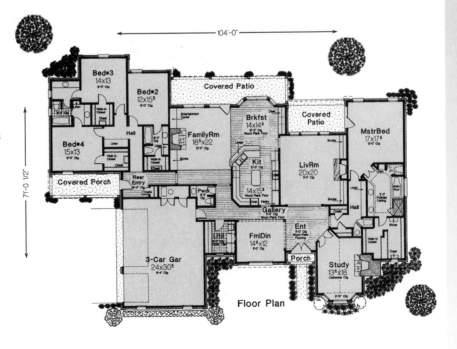

Floor Plan

Triple Arched Front Porch

■ *Total living area 1,466 sq. ft.* ■ *Price Code A* ■

SECOND FLOOR PLAN

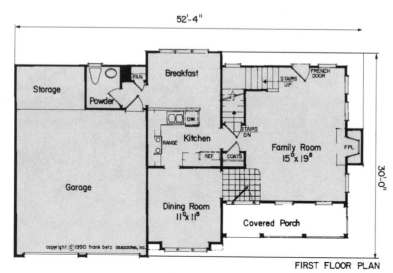

FIRST FLOOR PLAN

No. 97247

■ **This plan features:**

— Three bedrooms

— Two full and one half baths

■ A front porch with three arches

■ The Family Room is accented by a fireplace and a French door

■ The Kitchen is located between both of the eating areas

■ The Master Suite is topped by a tray ceiling and includes a vaulted ceiling over the Master Bath

■ Additional bedrooms share the full bath located between them

■ An optional basement or crawl space foundation — please specify when ordering

■ No materials list is available for this plan

First floor – 763 sq. ft.
Second floor – 703 sq. ft.
Basement – 763 sq. ft.
Garage – 497 sq. ft.

■ *Total living area 828 sq. ft.* ■ *Price Code A* ■

No. 93422

■ This plan features:

— Two bedrooms

— One full bath

■ A cozy, covered porch leads to the Kitchen and Dining Area

■ An L-Shaped Kitchen includes a double sink with a generous window above it

■ The Dining area overlooks the Porch through the front room

■ The Family Room includes a mood enhancing fireplace

■ A first floor bedroom is located across the hall from a full bath

■ A secondary bedroom is located on the second floor

■ No materials list is available for this plan

First floor 660 sq. ft.
Second floor – 168 sq. ft.

An
EXCLUSIVE DESIGN
By Greg Marquis

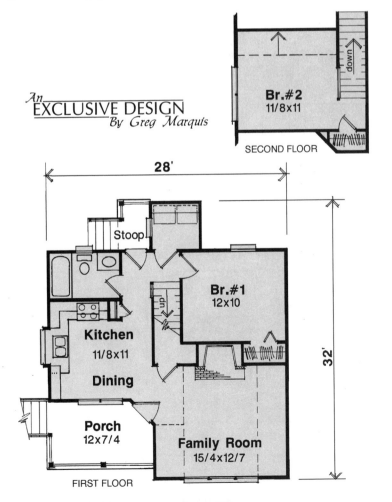

Perfect for the Growing Family

©1993 Donald A. Gardner Architects, Inc.

B. NATHAN

■ *Total living area 2,144 sq. ft.* ■ *Price Code D* ■

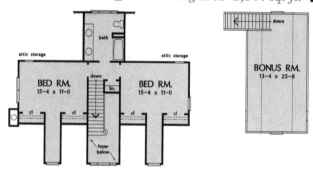

SECOND FLOOR PLAN

BONUS RM.
13-4 x 25-8

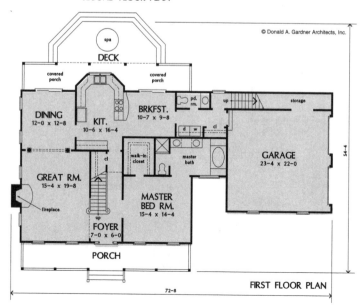

FIRST FLOOR PLAN

No. 96446

■ This plan features:

— Three bedrooms

— Two full and one half baths

■ Natural light fills the two-story foyer through a palladian window in dormer above

■ Dining Room and Great Room adjoin for entertaining possibilities

■ U-shaped Kitchen with a curved counter opens to a large Breakfast Area

■ Master Suite, situated downstairs for privacy with generous walk-in closet, double vanity, separate shower and a whirlpool tub

■ An optional basement or crawl space foundation — please specify when ordering

First floor — 1,484 sq. ft.
Second floor — 660 sq. ft.
Bonus room — 389 sq. ft.
Garage — 600 sq. ft.

Victorian Touches Disguise Modern Design

■ *Total living area 1,992 sq. ft.* ■ *Price Code C* ■

No. 90616 ⚒

■ This plan features:

— Three bedrooms

— Two full and one half baths

■ A Master Suite with a high ceiling, an arched window, a private bath, and a tower sitting room with an adjoining roof deck

■ Two additional bedrooms that share a full hall bath

■ A Living Room accentuated by a brick fireplace

■ A well-equipped Kitchen with a built-in pantry and peninsula counter

■ A sky-lit Family Room with a built-in entertainment center

First floor — 1,146 sq. ft.
Second floor — 846 sq. ft.
Basement — 967 sq. ft.
Garage — 447 sq. ft.

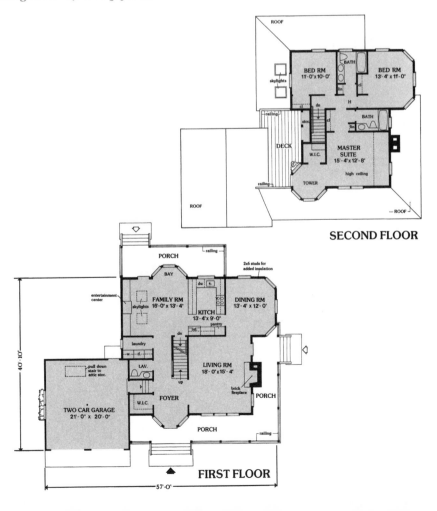

SECOND FLOOR

FIRST FLOOR

Expansive Inside and Out

Total living area 2,115 sq. ft. ▪ **Price Code C**

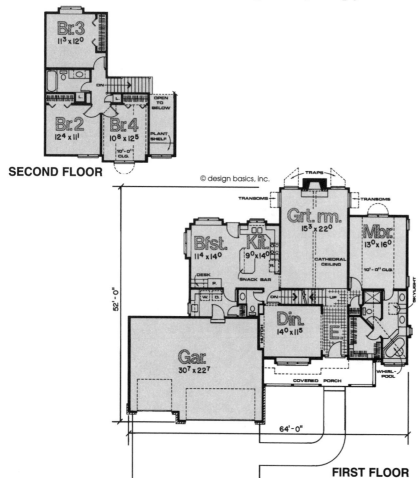

SECOND FLOOR

© design basics, inc.

FIRST FLOOR

No. 94996

▪ **This plan features:**

— Four bedrooms

— Two full and one half baths

▪ Dramatic Entry opens to Dining Room with built-in hutch, and the Great Room with a fireplace set between decorative windows

▪ Convenient Kitchen has an island snack bar, Breakfast area, built-in desk and a pantry

▪ Master Bedroom wing with arched window, skylit dressing area, whirlpool tub and a walk-in closet

▪ Three second floor bedrooms, one with an arched window, share a full bath

First floor — 1,505 sq. ft.
Second floor — 610 sq. ft.
Basement — 1,505 sq. ft.
Garage — 693 sq. ft.

A Whisper of Victorian Styling

■ Total living area 3,198 sq. ft. ■ Price Code E ■

No. 93333

■ This plan features:

— Four bedrooms

— Two full and one half baths

■ Formal Living Room features wrap-around windows and direct access to the front Porch

■ An elegant, formal Dining Room accented by a stepped ceiling

■ Efficient Kitchen is equipped with a cooktop island/eating bar and a double sink

■ A bright, all-purpose Sun Room with glass on four sides adjoining an expansive Deck

■ A private Master Suite with a decorative ceiling and a luxurious bath with a raised, atrium tub, oversized walk-in shower, two vanities and an oversized walk-in closet

■ Three additional bedrooms sharing a full, hall bath with double vanity

■ No materials list is available for this plan

First floor — 1,743 sq. ft.
Second floor — 1,455 sq. ft.

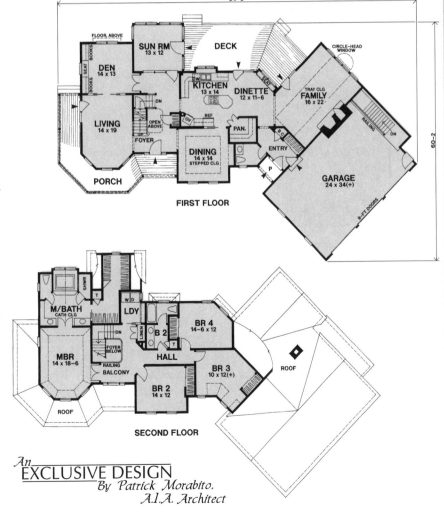

An EXCLUSIVE DESIGN
By Patrick Morabito,
A.I.A. Architect

Old-Fashioned Country Porch

■ Total living area 1,668 sq. ft. ■ Price Code B ■

No. 93219

■ **This plan features:**

— Three bedrooms

— Two full and one half baths

■ A Traditional front Porch, with matching dormers above and a garage hidden below, leading into an open, contemporary layout

■ A Living Area with a cozy fireplace visible from the Dining Room for warm entertaining

■ An efficient U-shaped Kitchen featuring a corner, double sink and pass-thru to the Dining Room

■ A convenient half bath with a laundry center on the first floor

■ A spacious, first floor Master Suite with a lavish bath including a double vanity, walk-in closet and an oval, corner window tub

■ Two large bedrooms with dormer windows sharing a full hall bath

An
EXCLUSIVE DESIGN
By Jannis Vann & Associates, Inc.

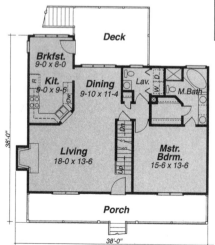

SECOND FLOOR

Bdrm. 2
15-8 x 13-4

Bdrm. 3
15-6 x 11-0

Bath

FIRST FLOOR

Deck

Brkfst.
9-0 x 8-0

Kit.
9-0 x 9-6

Dining
9-10 x 11-4

Lav.

W. D.

M. Bath

Living
18-0 x 13-6

Mstr.
Bdrm.
15-6 x 13-6

Porch

38'-0"

First floor — 1,057 sq. ft.
Second floor — 611 sq. ft.
Basement — 511 sq. ft.
Garage — 546 sq. ft.

Executive Features

Total living area 3,063 sq. ft. ■ *Price Code H* ■

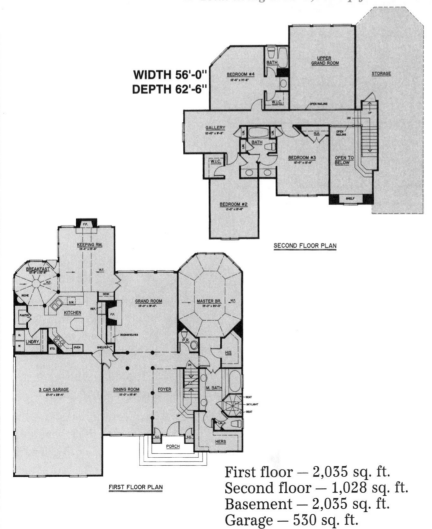

WIDTH 56'-0"
DEPTH 62'-6"

SECOND FLOOR PLAN

FIRST FLOOR PLAN

First floor — 2,035 sq. ft.
Second floor — 1,028 sq. ft.
Basement — 2,035 sq. ft.
Garage — 530 sq. ft.

No. 98211 ✖

■ **This plan features:**

— Four bedrooms

— Three full and one half baths

■ High volume ceilings

■ An extended staircase highlights the Foyer as columns define the Dining Room and the Grand Room

■ A massive glass exterior rear wall and high ceiling in the Master Suite

■ His-n-her walk-in closets and a five-piece lavish bath highlight the master bath

■ The island Kitchen, Keeping Room and Breakfast Room create an open living space

■ A fireplace accents both the Keeping Room and the two-story Grand Room

■ An optional basement or crawl space foundation — please specify when ordering

■ No materials list is available for this plan

Three Bedroom Traditional Country Cape

■ Total living area 1,494 sq. ft. ■ Price Code A ■

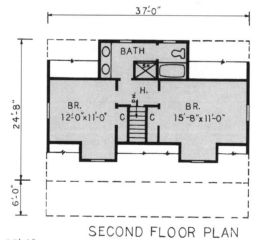

SECOND FLOOR PLAN

37'-0"

24'-8"

6'-0"

BATH

BR.
12'-0"x11'-0"

BR.
15'-8"x11'-0"

H.

C   C

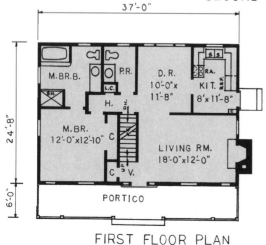

FIRST FLOOR PLAN

37'-0"

24'-8"

6'-0"

M.BR.B.   P.R.

L.C.

D.R.
10'-0"x
11'-8"

KIT.
8'x11'-8"

REF.

R.A.

H.

M.BR.
12'-0"x12'-10"   C

LIVING RM.
18'-0"x12'-0"

C   V.

PORTICO

No. 99022

■ This plan features:

— Three bedrooms

— Two full and one half baths

■ Entry area with a coat closet

■ An ample Living Room with a fireplace

■ A Dining Room with a view of the rear yard and located conveniently close to the Kitchen and Living Room

■ A U-shaped Kitchen with a double sink, ample cabinet and counter space and a side door to the outside

■ A first floor Master Suite with a private Master Bath

■ Two additional, second floor bedrooms that share a full, double vanity bath with a separate shower

First floor — 913 sq. ft.
Second floor — 581 sq. ft.

Rustic Exterior; Complete Home

■ Total living area 1,328 sq. ft. ■ Price Code A ■

No. 34600

■ **This plan features:**

— Three bedrooms

— Two full baths

■ A two-story, fireplaced Living Room with exposed beams adds to the rustic charm

■ An efficient, modern Kitchen with ample work and storage space

■ Two first floor bedrooms with individual closet space share a full bath

■ A Master Bedroom secluded on the second floor with its own full bath

■ A welcoming front Porch adding to the living space

First floor — 1,013 sq. ft.
Second floor — 315 sq. ft.
Basement — 1,013 sq. ft.

Crawl Space / Slab Plan

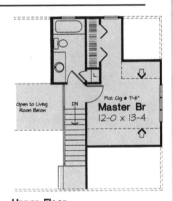

Open to Living Room Below

Flat Clg @ 7'-6"

Master Br
12-0 x 13-4

Upper Floor

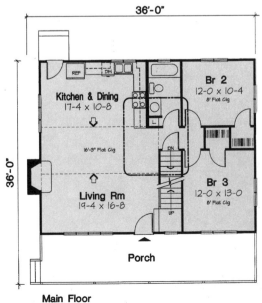

36'-0"

36'-0"

Kitchen & Dining
17-4 x 10-8

16'-3" Flat Clg

Living Rm
19-4 x 16-8

Br 2
12-0 x 10-4
8' Flat Clg

Br 3
12-0 x 13-0
8' Flat Clg

REF

DW

UP

DN

Porch

Main Floor

Cozy Cottage

■ *Total living area 1,028 sq. ft.* ■ *Price Code A* ■

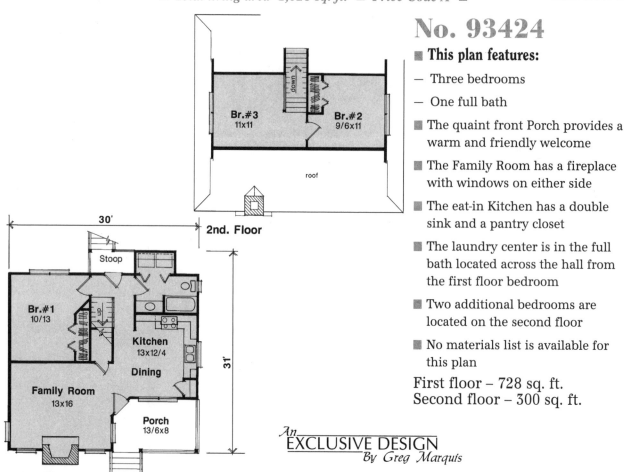

2nd. Floor

Br.#3
11x11

Br.#2
9/6x11

down

roof

30'

Stoop

Br.#1
10/13

UP

Kitchen
13x12/4

Dining

Family Room
13x16

Porch
13/6x8

31'

1st. Floor

No. 93424

■ **This plan features:**

— Three bedrooms

— One full bath

■ The quaint front Porch provides a
warm and friendly welcome

■ The Family Room has a fireplace
with windows on either side

■ The eat-in Kitchen has a double
sink and a pantry closet

■ The laundry center is in the full
bath located across the hall from
the first floor bedroom

■ Two additional bedrooms are
located on the second floor

■ No materials list is available for
this plan

First floor – 728 sq. ft.
Second floor – 300 sq. ft.

An
EXCLUSIVE DESIGN
By Greg Marquis

©1994 Donald A. Gardner Architects, Inc.

■ Total living area 1,537 sq. ft. ■ Price Code D ■

No. 96454

■ This plan features:

— Three bedrooms

— Two full baths

■ Tray, cathedral, and nine-foot ceilings throughout the home provide vertical drama

■ An open layout creates expansive living areas

■ A smart Kitchen with a curved counter serving both the Great Room and the Dining area

■ Bedrooms are separated to give the master suite complete privacy

■ A dual vanity, whirlpool tub, and separate shower in the bath

Main floor — 1,537 sq. ft.
Garage & storage — 434 sq. ft.

GARAGE
20-0 x 20-8

DECK

spa

UTIL.

d
w

lin.

cl

cl

cl

BED RM.
13-4 x 10-4

master bath

fireplace

KIT.
10-4 x 13-6

walk-in
closet

GREAT RM.
15-4 x 16-0
(cathedral ceiling)

bath

BED RM.
13-4 x 10-4

MASTER
BED RM.
11-4 x 15-0

FOYER
15-4 x 3-8

DINING
10-4 x 12-0

55-0

59-2

FLOOR PLAN

© 1994 Donald A Gardner Architects, Inc.

A Grand Presence

■ *Total living area 3,620 sq. ft.* ■ *Price Code J* ■

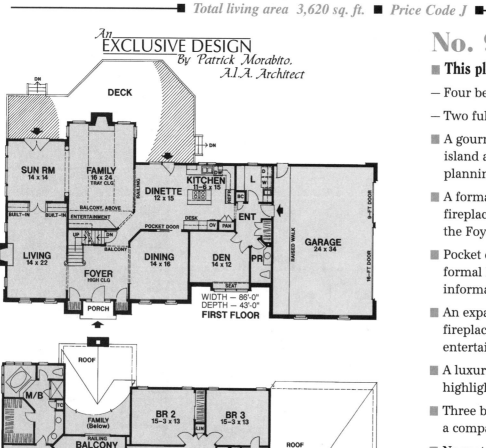

An EXCLUSIVE DESIGN
*By Patrick Morabito,
A.I.A. Architect*

WIDTH — 86'-0"
DEPTH — 43'-0"
FIRST FLOOR

SECOND FLOOR

No. 93330

■ This plan features:

— Four bedrooms

— Two full and one half baths

■ A gourmet Kitchen with a cooktop island and built-in pantry and planning desk

■ A formal Living Room with a fireplace that can be seen from the Foyer

■ Pocket doors that separate the formal Dining Room from the informal Dinette area

■ An expansive Family Room with a fireplace and a built-in entertainment center

■ A luxuriant Master Bath that highlights the Master Suite

■ Three bedrooms that share use of a compartmented full hall bath

■ No materials list is available for this plan

First floor — 2,093 sq. ft.
Second floor — 1,527 sq. ft.
Basement — 2,093 sq. ft.
Garage — 816 sq. ft.

Fireplace-Equipped Family Room

■ Total living area 1,505 sq. ft. ■ Price Code B ■

No. 24326

■ This plan features:

— Four bedrooms

— One full, one three-quarter and one half baths

■ A lovely front Porch shading the entrance

■ A spacious Living Room that opens into the Dining Area which flows into the efficient Kitchen

■ A Family Room equipped with a cozy fireplace and sliding glass doors to a patio

■ A Master Suite with a large walk-in closet and a private bath with a step-in shower

■ Three additional bedrooms that share a full hall bath

First floor — 692 sq. ft.
Second floor — 813 sq. ft.
Basement — 699 sq. ft.
Garage — 484 sq. ft.

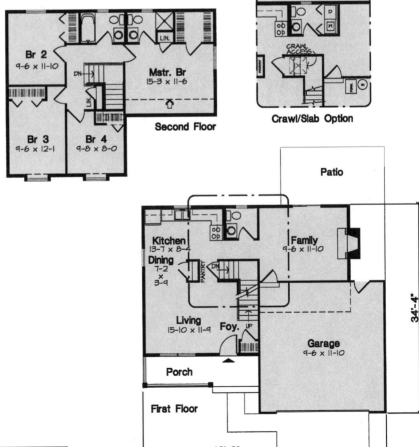

An
EXCLUSIVE DESIGN
By Marshall Associates

That Old Fashioned Feeling

Total living area 1,492 sq. ft. ■ Price Code A

No. 97250

■ This plan features:

— Three bedrooms

— Two full and one half baths

■ A wrapping front porch

■ Decorative columns define the Great Room

■ The U-shaped Kitchen includes a built-in pantry

■ The Master Suite is topped by a vaulted ceiling

■ Two additional spacious bedrooms share the full hall bath

■ An optional basement, slab or crawl space foundation — please specify when ordering

■ No materials list is available for this plan

First floor – 757 sq. ft.
Second floor – 735 sq. ft.
Basement – 757 sq. ft.
Garage – 447 sq. ft.

■ *Total living area 3,902 sq. ft.* ■ *Price Code G* ■

No. 98524

■ This plan features:

— Four bedrooms

— Three full and one half baths

■ French doors introduce Study and columns define the Gallery and formal areas

■ The expansive Family Room with an inviting fireplace and a cathedral ceiling opens to the Kitchen

■ The Kitchen features a cooktop island, butler's Pantry, Breakfast Area and Patio access

■ The first floor Master Bedroom offers a private Patio, vaulted ceiling, twin vanities and a walk-in closet

■ No materials list is available for this plan

■ An optional basement or slab foundation — please specify when ordering

First floor — 2,036 sq. ft.
Second floor — 866 sq. ft.
Garage — 720 sq. ft.

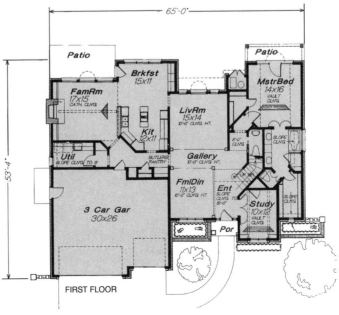

Unique Gazebo Shaped Nook

■ *Total living area 1,664 sq. ft.* ■ *Price Code B* ■

No. 98742

■ **This plan features:**

— Three bedrooms

— Two full baths

■ Covered porch and rear deck

■ Vaulted ceiling in the Nook with bay windows and natural illumination

■ A uniquely-designed Kitchen with a walk-in pantry, access to formal the Dining area and Nook

■ A focal point fireplace with windows on either side in the Living Room

■ A large walk-in closet, linen closet and a full private Bath highlight the Master Suite

■ Two additional bedrooms that share a full compartmented Bath

■ Utility/Mud Room located between the Garage and Kitchen

■ No materials list is available for this plan

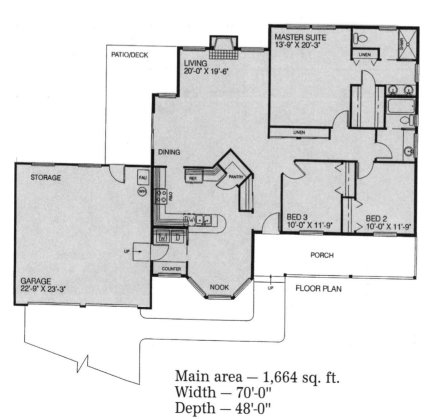

Main area — 1,664 sq. ft.
Width — 70'-0"
Depth — 48'-0"

Total living area 2,095 sq. ft. ■ **Price Code D**

No. 90622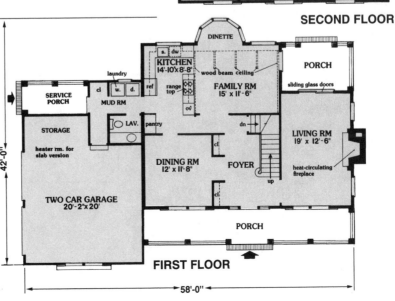

■ This plan features:

— Four bedrooms

— Two full and one half baths

■ A wood beam ceiling in the spacious Family Room

■ An efficient, island Kitchen with a sunny bay window dinette

■ A formal Living Room with a heat-circulating fireplace

■ A large Master Suite with a walk-in closet and a private Master Bath

■ Three additional bedrooms sharing a full hall bath

First floor — 1,082 sq. ft.
Second floor — 1,013 sq. ft.
Garage — 481 sq. ft.

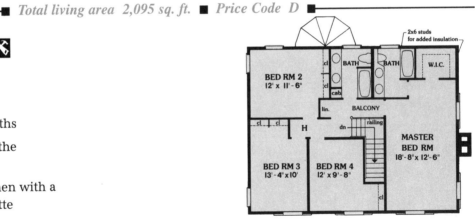

SECOND FLOOR

- BED RM 2 12' x 11'-6"
- BATH
- BATH
- W.I.C.
- 2x6 studs for added insulation
- cab.
- lin.
- BALCONY
- H
- dn railing
- MASTER BED RM 18'-8" x 12'-6"
- BED RM 3 13'-4" x 10'
- BED RM 4 12' x 9'-8"

FIRST FLOOR

- SERVICE PORCH
- STORAGE
- heater rm. for slab version
- TWO CAR GARAGE 20'-2" x 20'
- MUD RM
- laundry w. d.
- LAV.
- ref
- KITCHEN 14'-10" x 8'-8"
- s. dw
- range top
- ov
- pantry
- DINETTE
- wood beam ceiling
- FAMILY RM 15' x 11'-6"
- PORCH
- sliding glass doors
- dn
- LIVING RM 19' x 12'-6"
- heat-circulating fireplace
- DINING RM 12' x 11'-8"
- FOYER
- up
- PORCH
- 42'-0"
- 58'-0"

Elegant and Inviting

■ *Total living area 2,744 sq. ft.* ■ *Price Code F* ■

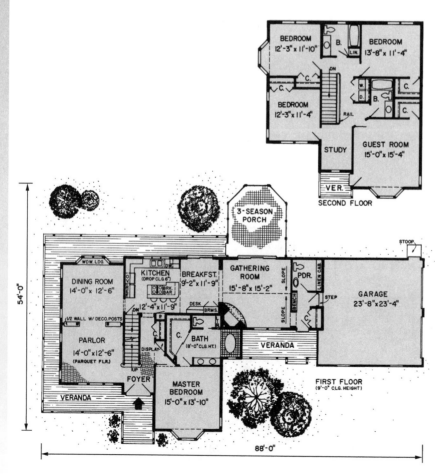

No. 10689

■ This plan features:

— Five bedrooms

— Three full and one half baths

■ Wrap-around verandas and a three-season porch

■ An elegant Parlor with a parquet floor and a formal Dining Room separated by a half-wall

■ An adjoining Kitchen with a Breakfast bar and Nook

■ A Gathering Room with a fireplace, soaring ceilings and access to the 3-Season Porch

First floor — 1,580 sq. ft.
Second floor — 1,164 sq. ft.
Basement — 1,329 sq. ft.
Garage — 576 sq. ft.

■ *Total living area 2,445 sq. ft.* ■ *Price Code E* ■

No. 98511

■ This plan features:

– Four bedrooms

– Three full and one half baths

■ Entertaining in grand style in the formal Living Room, the Dining Room, or under the covered patio in the backyard

■ A Family Room crowned in a cathedral ceiling, enhanced by a center fireplace and built-in book shelves

■ An efficient Kitchen highlighted by a wall oven, plentiful counter space and a pantry

■ A Master Bedroom with a sitting area, huge walk in closet, private bath and access to a covered lanai

■ A secondary bedroom wing containing three additional bedrooms with ample closet space and two full baths

■ No materials list is available for this plan

Main floor — 2,445 sq. ft.
Garage — 630 sq. ft.

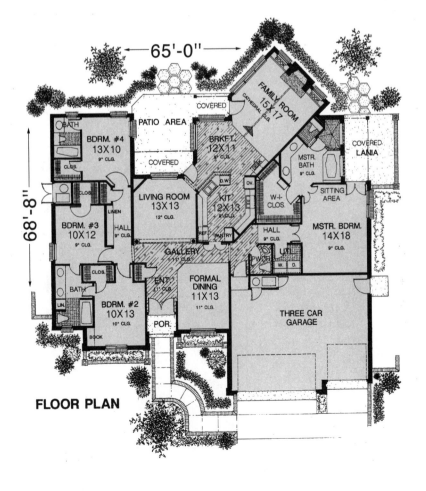

FLOOR PLAN

Elegant Ceiling Treatments

■ *Total living area 1,692 sq. ft.* ■ *Price Code B* ■

No. 97254

■ **This plan features:**

— Three bedrooms

— Two full baths

■ A wrapping front porch with six keystone arches

■ The Kitchen flows into the Breakfast Room

■ A vaulted ceiling highlights the Great Room

■ The Master Suite includes a tray ceiling

■ Two bedrooms are located on the other side of the house

■ An optional basement or crawl space foundation — please specify when ordering

■ No materials list is available for this plan

Main floor – 1,692 sq. ft.
Bonus room – 358 sq. ft.
Basement – 1,705 sq. ft.
Garage – 472 sq. ft.

OPTIONAL BONUS ROOM PLAN

Opt. Bonus
12⁵ x 20⁹

OPEN RAIL

FLOOR PLAN

GARAGE LOCATION W/ BASEMENT

54'-0"

56'-6"

Vaulted M.Bath

W.i.c.

LINEN

RADIUS WINDOW

RADIUS WINDOW

SHWR

Master Suite
15⁰ x 13²
TRAY CLG.

Vaulted Great Room
15⁰ x 20⁰
14'-6" CLG. HT.

Breakfast

Bedroom 3
11³ x 11⁰

Serving Bar

Kitchen

Bath

PANTRY

REF.

LINEN

DECORATIVE COLUMN

ARCHED OPG.

Sitting Room

Foyer
14'-6" CLG. HT.

Dining Room
11⁰ x 12⁴
12'-0" CLG. HT.

Bedroom 2
11⁰ x 11⁰

Laund.

STAIRS TO OPT. BSMT.

Covered Porch

Garage
20⁵ x 22²

copyright © 1997 frank betz associates, inc.

Stately Colonial Home

━━ *Total living area 2,959 sq. ft.* ■ *Price Code G* ■ ━━

No. 98534

■ This plan features:

— Four bedrooms

— Three full and one half baths

■ Stately columns and lovely arched windows

■ The Entry is highlighted by a palladian window, a plant shelf and an angled staircase

■ The formal Living and Dining Rooms located off the Entry for ease in entertaining

■ Great Room has a fireplace and opens to Kitchen/Breakfast area and the Patio

■ The Master Bedroom wing offers Patio access, a luxurious bath and a walk-in closet

■ No materials list is available for this plan

First floor — 1,848 sq. ft.
Second floor — 1,111 sq. ft.
Garage & shop — 722 sq. ft.

WIDTH 73'-4"
DEPTH 44'-1"

SECOND FLOOR

FIRST FLOOR

A Modern Slant On A Country Theme

■ *Total living area 1,648 sq. ft.* ■ *Price Code B* ■

No. 96513

■ **This plan features:**

— Three bedrooms

— Two full and one half baths

■ Country styled front Porch highlighting exterior which is enhanced by dormer windows

■ Modern open floor plan for a more spacious feeling

■ Great Room accented by a quaint, corner fireplace and a ceiling fan

■ Dining Room flowing from the Great Room for easy entertaining

■ Kitchen graced by natural light from attractive bay window and a convenient snack bar for meals on the go

■ Master Suite secluded in separate wing for total privacy

■ Two additional bedrooms sharing full bath in the hall

Main floor — 1,648 sq. ft.
Garage — 479 sq. ft.

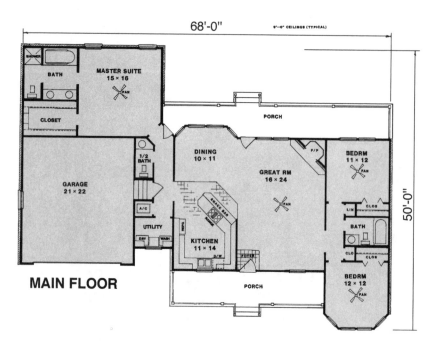

MAIN FLOOR

Arched Windows Accent Sophisticated Design

— Total living area 2,551 sq. ft. ■ Price Code F ■—

No. 92509 ✖

■ This plan features:

— Four bedrooms

— Two full and one half baths

■ Graceful columns and full-length windows highlight front Porch

■ Spacious Great Room with decorative ceiling over hearth fireplace between built-in cabinets

■ Kitchen with peninsula counter and breakfast alcove

■ Secluded Master Bedroom offers access to back Porch, and has a decorative ceiling and plush bath

■ Three additional bedrooms with loads of closets space share double vanity bath

■ An optional crawl space or slab foundation — please specify when ordering

Main area — 2,551 sq. ft.
Garage — 532 sq. ft.

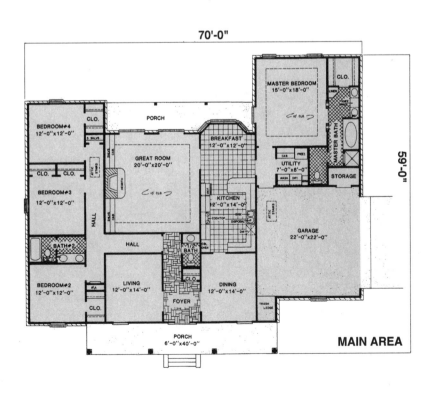

Sunny Dormer Brightens Foyer

© 1996 Donald A Gardner Architects, Inc.

■ *Total living area 1,386 sq. ft.* ■ *Price Code C* ■

No. 99812

■ **This plan features:**

— Three bedrooms

— Two full baths

■ Today's comforts with cost effective construction

■ Open Great Room, Dining Room and Kitchen topped by a cathedral ceiling emphasizing spaciousness

■ Adjoining Deck provides extra living or entertaining space

■ The Master Bedroom is crowned by a cathedral ceiling and pampered by a private Bath with a garden tub, a dual vanity and a walk-in closet

■ Skylit Bonus Room above the Garage offers flexibility and opportunity for growth

Main floor — 1,386 sq. ft.
Bonus room — 314 sq. ft.
Garage — 517 sq. ft.

DECK

DINING
9-10 x 11-0
(cathedral ceiling)

GREAT RM.
15-10 x 16-10
(cathedral ceiling)

fireplace

MASTER
BED RM.
12-4 x 13-6
(cathedral ceiling)

walk-in closet

master bath

bath

KIT.
9-10 x 11-8

FOYER
9-6 x 5-6

storage

PORCH

BED RM.
11-0 x 11-0

GARAGE
22-0 x 20-8

BED RM.
11-0 x 11-0
(cathedral ceiling)

FLOOR PLAN

54-10

© 1996 Donald A Gardner Architects, Inc.

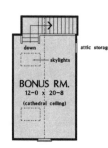

down

skylights

attic storage

BONUS RM.
12-0 x 20-8
(cathedral ceiling)

Windows Create Horizontal Space

© 1997 Donald A. Gardner Architects, Inc.

B. NATHAN

■ *Total living area 1,695 sq. ft.* ■ *Price Code D* ■

No. 96488

■ **This plan features:**

— Three bedrooms

— Two full and one half bath

■ Formal Foyer punctuated by elegant interior columns leading to a spacious Great Room

■ Great Room with a fireplace crowned in a cathedral ceiling

■ Octagonal Dining Room flowing from the Great Room and Kitchen

■ Kitchen defined by columns, a pantry and an angled countertop with a liberal Breakfast Bar

■ Master Suite with double door entry, cathedral ceiling, patio access, and lavish bath

■ Two additional bedrooms sharing a hall bath

■ Bonus space above the garage providing extra room for storage and expansion

Main floor — 1,695 sq. ft.
Bonus room — 287 sq. ft.
Garage & storage — 527 sq. ft.

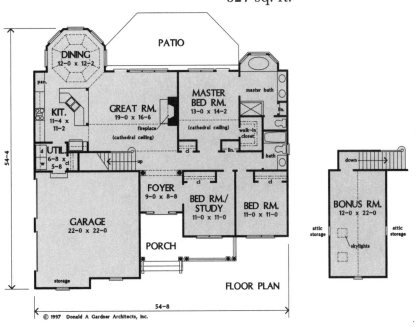

© 1997 Donald A Gardner Architects, Inc.

Maximum Privacy

■ *Total living area 2,201 sq. ft.* ■ *Price Code D* ■

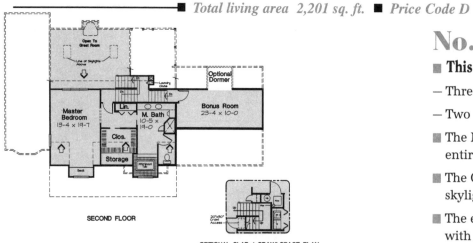

SECOND FLOOR

OPTIONAL SLAB / CRAWLSPACE PLAN

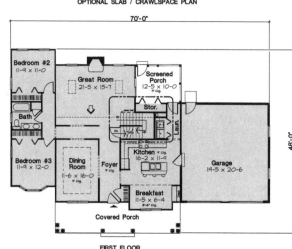

FIRST FLOOR

No. 24726

■ **This plan features:**

— Three bedrooms

— Two full baths

■ The Master Suite encompasses the entire second floor

■ The Great Room is enhanced by skylights and a cozy fireplace

■ The efficient Kitchen is equipped with a work island

■ The formal Dining Room is directly across from the Foyer

■ A screened Porch off the Great Room adds to the living space

■ No materials list is available for this plan

First floor — 1,525 sq. ft.
Second floor — 676 sq. ft.
Bonus — 288 sq. ft.
Basement — 1,510 sq. ft.
Garage — 614 sq. ft.

Delightful Detailing

■ *Total living area 2,622 sq. ft.* ■ *Price Code F* ■

No. 98426

■ This plan features:

— Three bedrooms

— Two full and one half baths

■ The vaulted ceiling extends from the Foyer into the Living Room

■ The Dining Room is delineated by columns with a plant shelf above

■ Family Room has a vaulted ceiling, and a fireplace with radius windows on either side

■ The Kitchen equipped with an island serving bar, a desk, a wall oven, a Pantry and a Breakfast Bay

■ The Master Suite is highlighted by a Sitting Room, a walk-in closet and a private bath with a vaulted ceiling

■ An optional Bonus Room over the Garage

■ An optional basement or crawl space foundation — please specify when ordering

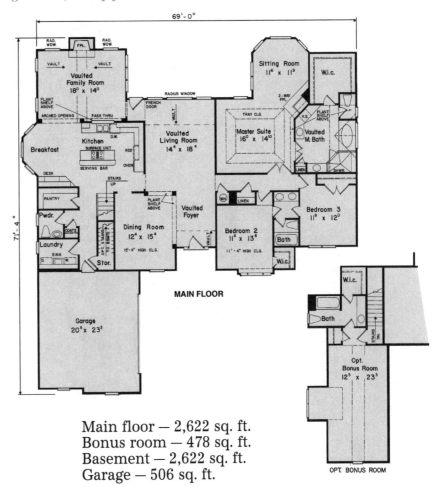

MAIN FLOOR

OPT. BONUS ROOM

Main floor — 2,622 sq. ft.
Bonus room — 478 sq. ft.
Basement — 2,622 sq. ft.
Garage — 506 sq. ft.

An Estate of Epic Proportion

■ *Total living area 3,936 sq. ft.* ■ *Price Code K* ■

UPPER FLOOR

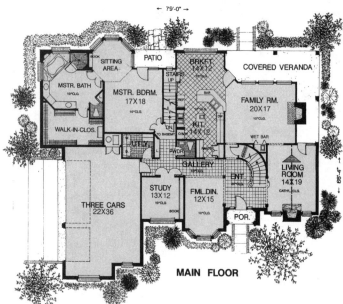

MAIN FLOOR

No. 98539

■ This plan features:

— Four bedrooms

— Three full and one half baths

■ Front door opening into a grand Entry way with a 20' ceiling and a spiral staircase

■ Living Room with cathedral ceiling and fireplace

■ Walk down the Gallery to the Study with a full wall, built-in bookcase

■ The enormous Master Bedroom has a walk-in closet, sumptuous bath and a bayed Sitting Area

■ Family Room has a wetbar and a fireplace

■ An optional basement or slab foundation — please specify when ordering

■ No materials list is available for this plan

Main floor — 2,751 sq. ft.
Upper floor — 1,185 sq. ft.
Bonus — 343 sq. ft.
Garage — 790 sq. ft.

Cozy Cottage with Character

B.NATHAN.

© 1997 Donald A. Gardner Architects, Inc.

■ *Total living area 1,454 sq. ft.* ■ *Price Code C* ■

No. 96485

■ This plan features:

— Three bedrooms

— Two full baths

■ Dormer, gables, and a wrapping front porch giving character to this narrow and cozy cottage.

■ A fireplace as the focal point of the vaulted Great room

■ Kitchen opens to the Dining Room and has a pantry and deck access

■ Master Suite boasting an optional door to the deck, walk-in closet, and a fully equipped bath

■ Two secondary bedrooms share a full bath with dual sink vanity

■ Bonus space stands ready for future expansion

Main floor — 1,454 sq. ft.
Garage & storage — 321 sq. ft.
Bonus room — 424 sq. ft.

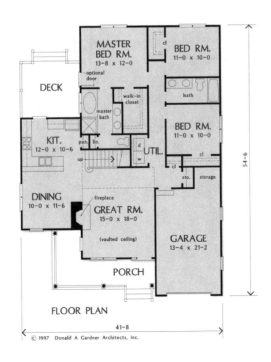

FLOOR PLAN

© 1997 Donald A Gardner Architects, Inc.

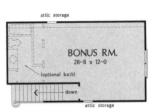

Thoughtfully Designed

■ *Total living area 2,411 sq. ft.* ■ *Price Code E* ■

SECOND FLOOR

FIRST FLOOR

No. 93602

■ This plan features:

— Four bedrooms

— Two full and one half baths

■ Foyer opens to formal Living and Dining rooms

■ Two-story Great Room with an impressive fireplace

■ Hub Kitchen with cooktop work island, built-in pantry and desk

■ Master Bedroom with a tray ceiling, window alcove, walk-in closet and plush bath

■ Three additional bedrooms share a full bath and laundry

■ No materials list is available for this plan

First floor — 1,209 sq. ft.
Second floor — 1,202 sq. ft.
Basement — 1,209 sq. ft.
Garage — 370 sq. ft.

An
EXCLUSIVE DESIGN
By Garrell Associates Inc.

A Comfortable, Informal Design

■ *Total living area 1,300 sq. ft.* ■ *Price Code A* ■

No. 94801

■ **This plan features:**

— Three bedrooms

— Two full baths

■ Warm, Country style front Porch with wood details

■ Spacious Activity Room is enhanced by a pre-fab fireplace

■ Open and efficient Kitchen/ Dining area is highlighted by bay window

■ Corner Master Bedroom offers a pampering Bath with a garden tub and double vanity topped by a vaulted ceiling

■ Two additional Bedrooms with ample closets, share a full Bath

■ An optional crawl space or slab foundation available — please specify when ordering

Main floor — 1,300 sq. ft.
Garage — 576 sq. ft.

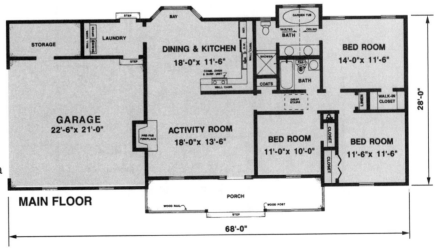

Quaint Starter Home

■ *Total living area 1,050 sq. ft.* ■ *Price Code A* ■

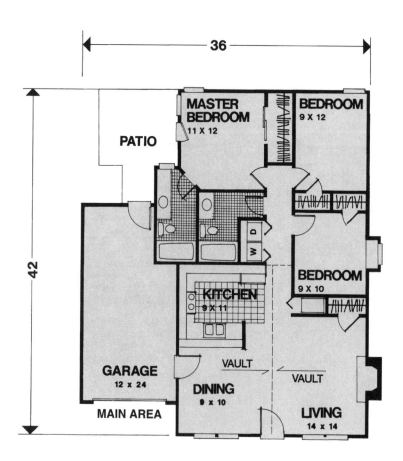

No. 92400

■ **This plan features:**

— Three bedrooms

— Two full baths

■ A vaulted ceiling giving an airy feeling to the Dining and Living Rooms

■ A streamlined Kitchen with a comfortable work area, a double sink and ample cabinet space

■ A cozy fireplace in the Living Room

■ A Master Suite with a large closet, French doors leading to the Patio and a private bath

■ Two additional bedrooms sharing a full bath

■ No materials list is available for this plan

Main area — 1,050 sq. ft.
Garage — 261 sq. ft.

■ *Total living area 4,362 sq. ft.* ■ *Price Code L* ■

No. 98404

■ This plan features:

— Four bedrooms

— Three full and one half baths

■ Grand columns frame the two-story Portico

■ The Living Room is accented by columns, and a fireplace

■ Kitchen with a cooktop island/serving bar and nearby Laundry and Garage entry

■ Secluded Master Suite has a Sitting Area

■ Three second floor bedrooms with walk-in closets and private access to full baths

■ An optional basement or crawl space foundation — please specify when ordering

First floor — 2,764 sq. ft.
Second floor — 1,598 sq. ft.
Garage — 743 sq. ft.
Basement — 2,764 sq. ft.

SECOND FLOOR

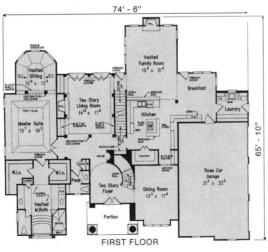

FIRST FLOOR

Mid-Sized Country Style

■ *Total living area 2,126 sq. ft.* ■ *Price Code D* ■

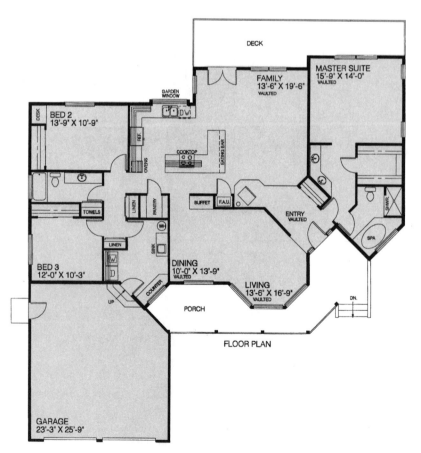

FLOOR PLAN

No. 98748

■ This plan features:

— Three bedrooms

— Two full baths

■ A vaulted ceiling over the Entry, Living Room, Dining Room, Family Room and Master Suite

■ Wide window bay expanding the Living Room

■ Wide garden window expanding the Kitchen while the cook top, L-shaped island/eating bar adds convenience

■ A walk-in closet, oversized shower, a spa tub and a double vanity outside the bath area highlight the Master Suite

■ Two roomy additional bedrooms share the full bath in the hall

Main floor — 2,126 sq. ft.
Width — 64'-0"
Depth — 64'-0"

Towering Windows Enhance Elegance

© Larry E. Belk

■ *Total living area 2,838 sq. ft.* ■ *Price Code G* ■

No. 93034

■ This plan features:

— Four bedrooms

— Three full baths

■ Designed for a corner or pie-shaped lot

■ Spectacular split staircase highlights Foyer

■ Expansive Great Room with hearth fireplace opens to formal Dining Room and Patio

■ Quiet Study can easily convert to another bedroom or home office

■ Secluded Master Suite offers private Porch, two walk-in closets two vanities and a corner whirlpool tub

■ Three second floor bedrooms with walk-in closets, share a balcony and double vanity bath

■ No materials list is available for this plan

First floor — 1,966 sq. ft.
Second floor — 872 sq. ft.
Garage — 569 sq. ft.

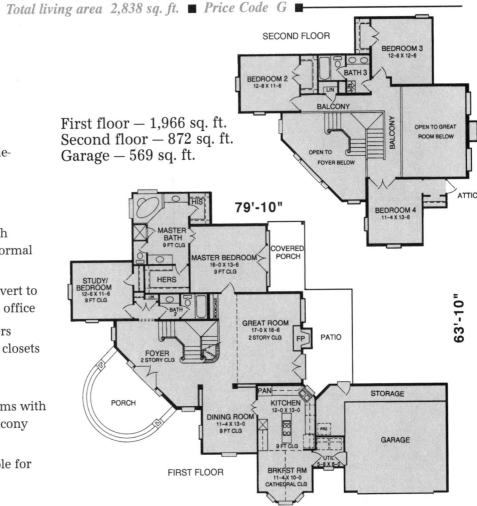

Great Traffic Flow

© 1997 Donald A. Gardner Architects, Inc.

B. NATHAN

■ *Total living area 2,042 sq. ft.* ■ *Price Code F* ■

No. 96486

■ This plan features:

— Three bedrooms

— Two full baths

■ Perfect for narrow lots

■ Side porch leading to the Foyer

■ Great Room boasting a fireplace and built-in cabinets

■ Dining Room sporting an octagonal shape with a tray ceiling and columns

■ U-Shaped kitchen is open to the sunny Breakfast Bay

■ Master Suite features a tray ceiling, back porch access walk-in closet and an indulgent bath

■ Front bedroom doubles as a study, and the bonus room could make a fourth bedrooms upstairs

Main floor — 2,042 sq. ft.
Bonus room — 398 sq. ft.
Garage & storage — 514 sq. ft

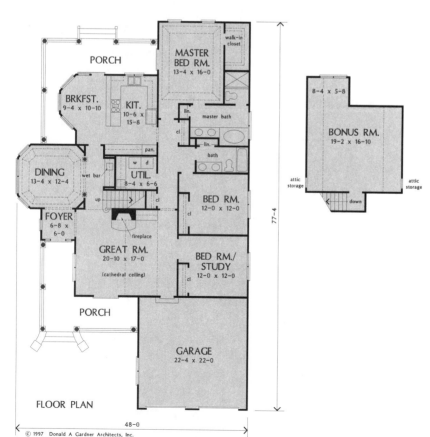

FLOOR PLAN

© 1997 Donald A Gardner Architects, Inc.

Traditional Elements Combine in Colonial

━━ ◼ *Total living area 2,031 sq. ft.* ◼ *Price Code D* ◼ ━━

No. 90606 ✖

◼ This plan features:

— Four bedrooms

— Two full and one half baths

◼ A beautiful circular stair ascending from the central foyer and flanked by the formal Living Room and Dining Room

◼ Exposed beams, wood paneling, and a brick fireplace wall in the Family Room

◼ A separate dinette opening to an efficient Kitchen

First floor — 1,099 sq. ft.
Second floor — 932 sq. ft.
Basement — 1,023 sq. ft.
Garage — 476 sq. ft.

SECOND FLOOR

2x6 studs for added insulation

BED RM
11'-4" x 10'-4"

BED RM
12'-8" x 11'-4"

cl.

W.I.C.

BATH

cl.

cl.

lin.

railing   planter

dn.

MASTER
BED RM
16' x 11'

BED RM
12'-8" x 10'-8"

railing

open

BATH

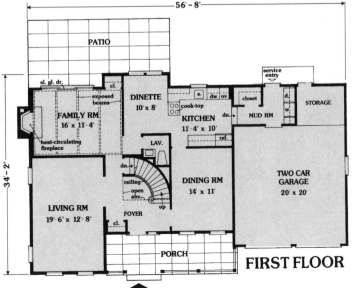

FIRST FLOOR

56'-8"

34'-2"

PATIO

sl. gl. dr.

cl.

exposed
beams

DINETTE
10' x 8'

s.   dw ov

cook-top

KITCHEN
11'-4" x 10'

service
entry

closet

dn.

MUD RM

d.

w.

STORAGE

FAMILY RM
16' x 11'-4"

heat-circulating
fireplace

LAV.

ref.

dn.

railing
open
abv.

up

DINING RM
14' x 11'

TWO CAR
GARAGE
20' x 20'

LIVING RM
19'-6" x 12'-8"

cl.

FOYER

PORCH

283

Warm and Inviting

■ *Total living area 2,548 sq. ft.* ■ *Price Code F* ■

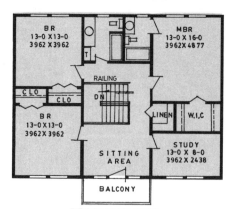

SECOND FLOOR

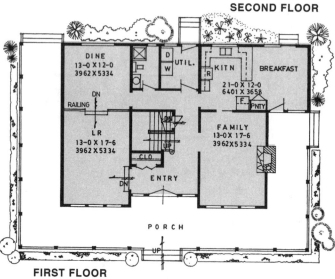

FIRST FLOOR

No. 90827

■ **This plan features:**

— Three bedrooms

— Three full baths

■ A formal sunken Living Room

■ A decorative railing separating the sunken Living Room from the formal Dining Room

■ A Utility/Mudroom at the rear entrance with a laundry center

■ An efficient, country Kitchen with a Breakfast Room flowing from it

■ A fireplaced Family Room

■ A spacious Master Suite

■ Two additional roomy bedrooms share the use of the full hall bath

■ A cozy Sitting Area between the bedrooms

First floor — 1,349 sq. ft.
Second floor — 1,199 sq. ft.
Width — 57'-0"
Depth — 39'-0"

■ *Total living area 2,891 sq. ft.* ■ *Price Code G* ■

No. 94231

■ **This plan features:**

— Three bedrooms

— Two full and one three-quarter baths

■ Glass arch entrance leads into Foyer and Grand Room

■ Decorative windows highlight Study and formal Dining Room

■ Spacious Kitchen with walk-in pantry and peninsula serving counter easily serves Nook, Veranda and Dining Room

■ Luxurious Master Suite with step ceiling, sitting area, his-n-her closets and pampering bath

■ Two additional bedrooms, one with a private Deck, have bay windows and walk-in closets

■ No materials list is available for this plan

First floor — 2,181 sq. ft.
Second floor — 710 sq. ft.
Garage — 658 sq. ft.

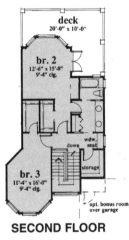

SECOND FLOOR

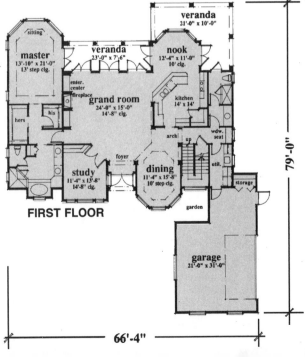

FIRST FLOOR

Stately Columns and Keystones

An EXCLUSIVE DESIGN
By Garrell Associates Inc.

■ *Total living area 3,029 sq. ft.* ■ *Price Code H* ■

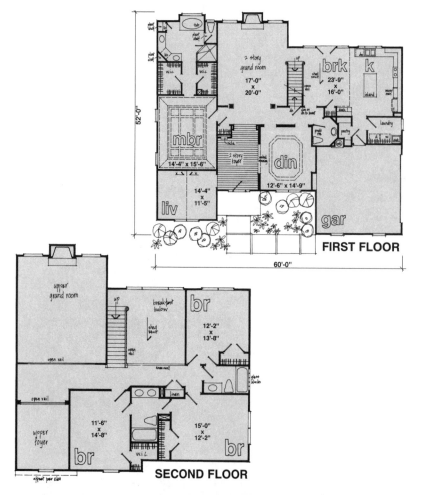

FIRST FLOOR

SECOND FLOOR

No. 93603

■ **This plan features:**

— Four bedrooms

— Three full and one half baths

■ Gracious two-story Foyer opens to vaulted Living Room and arched Dining Room

■ Expansive, two-story Grand Room with impressive fireplace

■ Spacious and efficient Kitchen with a work island, Breakfast area with back yard access, and Laundry/Garage entry

■ Private Master Bedroom offers a decorative ceiling, two walk-in closets and vanities, and a garden window tub

■ Three second floor bedrooms with great closets, share two full baths

■ No materials list is available for this plan

First floor — 2,115 sq. ft.
Second floor — 914 sq. ft.
Garage — 448 sq. ft.

Splendid Appointments

■ *Total living area 3,083 sq. ft.* ■ *Price Code H* ■

No. 98452

■ This plan features:

— Three bedrooms

— Three full and one half baths

■ The two story Foyer is highlighted by a staircase with an open rail

■ The formal Dining Room opens onto a terrace for expanded dining options

■ A two-story Family Room is accented by arched openings from the Dining Room and Foyer

■ The spacious Kitchen/Breakfast Room includes a cook top island and a built-in Pantry

■ The Keeping room with a vaulted ceiling and a cozy fireplace adjoins the Breakfast area

■ An optional basement or crawl space foundation — please specify when ordering

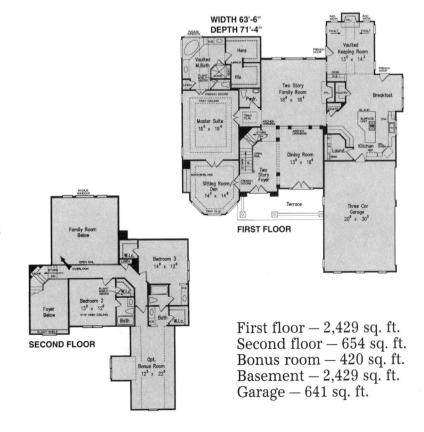

First floor — 2,429 sq. ft.
Second floor — 654 sq. ft.
Bonus room — 420 sq. ft.
Basement — 2,429 sq. ft.
Garage — 641 sq. ft.

Spectacular Stucco and Stone

■ *Total living area 4,106 sq. ft.* ■ *Price Code L* ■

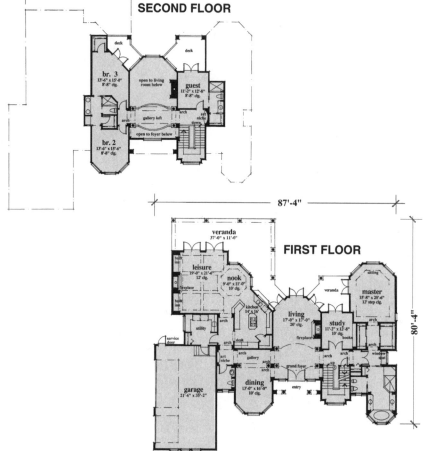

SECOND FLOOR

deck

deck

br. 3
13'-6" x 15'-0"
8'-8" clg.

open to living
room below

guest
11'-2" x 12'-8"
8'-8" clg.

niche

gallery loft

arch

arch

down

br. 2
13'-6" x 15'-6"
8'-8" clg.

open to foyer below

87'-4"

80'-4"

FIRST FLOOR

veranda
37'-0" x 11'-0"

leisure
19'-0" x 21'-6"
12' clg.

nook
9'-0" x 11'-0"
10' clg.

sitting

veranda

master
15'-8" x 20'-6"
12' step clg.

fireplace

kitchen
14' x 16'

living
17'-0" x 17'-0"
20' clg.

study
11'-2" x 12'-8"
10' clg.

books

utility

fireplace

arch

service
door

art
niche

gallery

arch

arch

grand foyer

arch

window
seat

garage
21'-6" x 35'-2"

dining
13'-0" x 16'-0"
10' clg.

entry

No. 94239

■ **This plan features:**

— Four bedrooms

— One full, two three-quarter and one half baths

■ Arches and columns accent Entry, Grand Foyer, Gallery, Living and Dining rooms

■ Open Living Room with fireplace and multiple glass doors

■ Formal Dining Room with bay windows conveniently located

■ Angled Kitchen with walk-in Pantry and peninsula counter

■ Master wing offers a step ceiling, two walk-in closets and a lavish bath

■ No materials list is available for this plan

First floor — 3,027 sq. ft.
Second floor — 1,079 sq. ft.
Basement — 3,027 sq. ft.
Garage — 802 sq. ft.

Country French Design

■ *Total living area 2,714 sq. ft.* ■ *Price Code F* ■

No. 90470

■ This plan features:

— Three bedrooms

— Two full and one half baths

■ Open Foyer receives light from the dormer above

■ Great Room features rear wall hearth fireplace and a built-in media center

■ Breakfast bay is open into the fully equipped U-shaped Kitchen

■ First floor Master Bedroom encompasses entire private wing

■ An optional basement or a crawl space foundation — please specify when ordering

First floor — 1,997 sq. ft.
Second floor — 717 sq. ft.
Bonus room — 541 sq. ft.
Basement – 1,997 sq. ft.
Garage – 575 sq. ft.

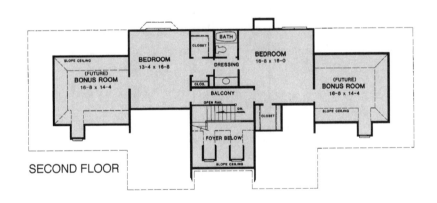

SECOND FLOOR

FIRST FLOOR

A Hint of Victorian Nostalgia

■ *Total living area 2,175 sq. ft.* ■ *Price Code D* ■

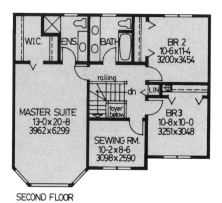

MASTER SUITE
13-0 x 20-8
3962 x 6299

BR 2
10-6 x 11-4
3200 x 3454

BR3
10-8 x 10-0
3251 x 3048

SEWING RM.
10-2 x 8-6
3098 x 2590

W.I.C.   ENS   BATH   railing   dn   LIN

foyer below

SECOND FLOOR

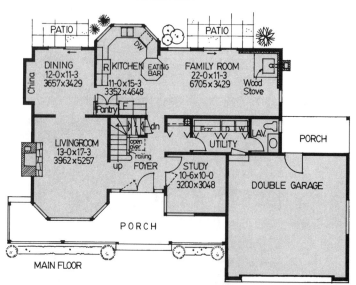

PATIO   PATIO

DINING
12-0 x 11-3
3657 x 3429

China

KITCHEN
11-0 x 15-3
3352 x 4648

EATING BAR   DW

FAMILY ROOM
22-0 x 11-3
6705 x 3429

Wood Stove

Pantry   F

LIVINGROOM
13-0 x 17-3
3962 x 5257

open over   dn

railing

up   **FOYER**

Frzr   W   LAV.

UTILITY

PORCH

STUDY
10-6 x 10-0
3200 x 3048

DOUBLE GARAGE

PORCH

MAIN FLOOR

No. 90909

■ **This plan features:**

— Three bedrooms

— Two full and one half baths

■ A classic center stairwell

■ A Kitchen with full bay window and built-in eating table

■ A spacious Master Suite including a large walk-in closet and full bath

First floor — 1,206 sq. ft.
Second floor — 969 sq. ft.
Garage — 471 sq. ft.
Basement — 1,206 sq. ft.
Width — 61'-0"
Depth — 44'-0"

An
EXCLUSIVE DESIGN
By Westhome Planners, Ltd.

Spacious Country Charm

■ *Total living area 1,887 sq. ft.* ■ *Price Code C* ■

No. 94107

■ This plan features

— Three Bedrooms

— Two full and one half baths

■ Comfortable front Porch leads into bright, two-story Foyer

■ Pillars frame entrance to formal Dining Room

■ Great Room accented by hearth fireplace and triple window

■ Efficient Kitchen with loads of counter and storage space

■ Corner Master Bedroom offers a luxurious Master Bath

■ No materials list is available for this plan

First floor — 961 sq. ft.
Second floor — 926 sq. ft.
Garage — 548 sq. ft.
Basement — 928 sq. ft.

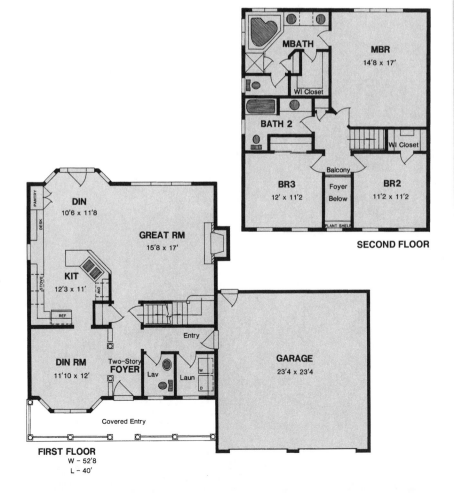

Charming Country Home

■ *Total living area 1,434 sq. ft.* ■ *Price Code A* ■

No. 24711

■ This plan features:

— Three bedrooms

— Two full baths

■ Cozy fireplace below a vaulted ceiling and dormer window in Living Room

■ Kitchen with a peninsula counter/snack bar, built-in pantry and access to laundry, Screened Area-way and Garage beyond

■ Two first floor bedrooms share a full bath and laundry

■ Private second floor Master Suite offers a dormer window, walk-in closet and private bath

■ No materials list is available for this plan

First floor — 1,018 sq. ft.
Second floor — 416 sq. ft.
Basement — 1,008 sq. ft.
Garage — 624 sq. ft.

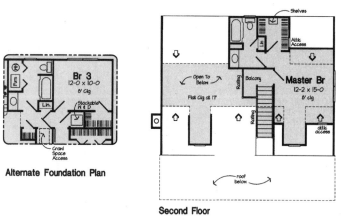

Br 3
12-0 x 10-0
8' Clg

Crawl Space Access

Alternate Foundation Plan

Shelves

Attic Access

Open To Below

Balcony

Flat Clg at 17'

Master Br
12-2 x 15-0
8' clg

Railing

attic access

roof below

Second Floor

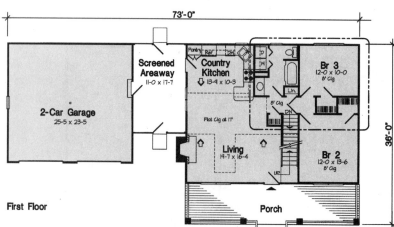

73'-0"

Pantry   Ref

Screened Areaway
11-0 x 17-7

Country Kitchen
13-4 x 10-3

Br 3
12-0 x 10-0
8' Clg

2-Car Garage
25-5 x 23-5

Flat Clg at 17'

Living
14-7 x 16-4

Br 2
12-0 x 13-6
8' Clg

UP

36'-0"

First Floor

Porch

Total living area 2,915 sq. ft. ■ **Price Code G**

No. 97236

■ This plan features:

— Five bedrooms

— Four full baths

■ An 'Old World' feeling with a totally modern floor plan

■ A two-story Foyer adding drama

■ Kitchen with a cook top island/ serving bar and a Breakfast area

■ The two-story Family Room is spacious and includes a cozy fireplace

■ A fifth bedroom or Study is secluded in the front left corner of the home

■ The second floor contains four bedrooms and three bath

■ No materials list is available for this plan

First floor – 1,425 sq. ft.
Second floor – 1,490 sq. ft.
Basement – 1,425 sq. ft.
Garage – 546 sq. ft.

SECOND FLOOR PLAN

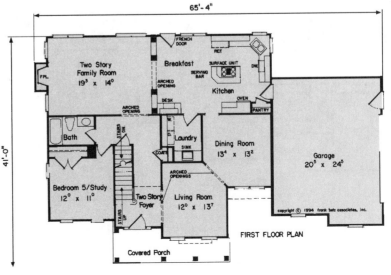

FIRST FLOOR PLAN

Secluded Master Suite

■ Total living area 1,680 sq. ft. ■ Price Code B ■

No. 92527

■ **This plan features:**

— Three bedrooms

— Two full baths

■ A convenient one-level design with an open floor plan between the Kitchen, Breakfast Area and Great Room

■ A vaulted ceiling and a cozy fireplace in the spacious Great Room

■ A well-equipped Kitchen uses a peninsula counter as an eating bar

■ The Master Suite has a luxurious Master Bath

■ Two additional Bedrooms have use of a full hall Bath

■ An optional crawl space or slab foundation — please specify when ordering

Main area — 1,680 sq. ft.
Garage — 538 sq. ft.

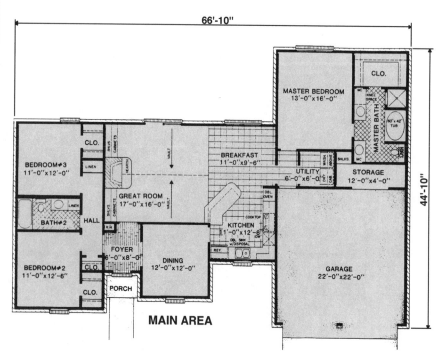

MAIN AREA

Friendly Front Porch

■ *Total living area 3,011 sq. ft.* ■ *Price Code H* ■

No. 96500 ✖

■ This plan features:

— Three bedrooms

— Two full and one half baths

■ Wrap-around front Porch and double French doors are an inviting sight

■ Central Foyer with a lovely landing staircase opens to the Dining and Great rooms

■ The fireplace is framed by a built-in credenza in the Great Room

■ Kitchen has a buffet, pantry and a peninsula counter/snackbar

■ Master Bedroom offers direct access to the Sun Room, a walk-in closet and a luxurious bath

First floor — 2,361 sq. ft.
Second floor — 650 sq. ft.
Carport — 864 sq. ft.

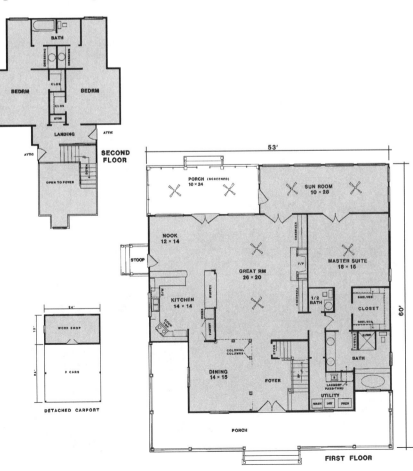

Distinctive Design

■ *Total living area 1,998 sq. ft.* ■ *Price Code C* ■

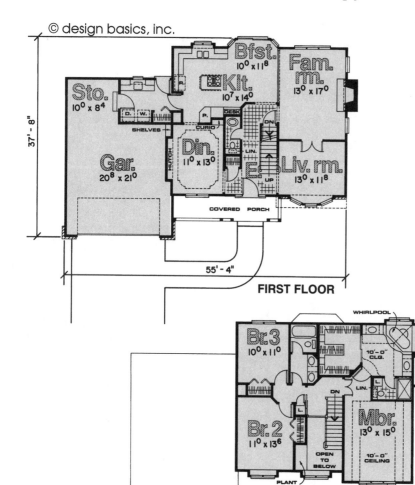

© design basics, inc.

Sto.
10⁰ x 8⁴

Gar.
20⁸ x 21⁰

Bfst.
10⁰ x 11⁸

Kit.
10⁷ x 14⁰

Fam. rm.
13⁰ x 17⁰

Din.
11⁰ x 13⁰

Liv. rm.
13⁰ x 11⁸

37' - 8"

55' - 4"

COVERED PORCH

FIRST FLOOR

Br. 3
10⁰ x 11⁰

WHIRLPOOL

10'-0"
CLG.

Br. 2
11⁰ x 13⁶

Mbr.
13⁰ x 15⁰

10'-0"
CEILING

OPEN TO BELOW

PLANT SHELF

SECOND FLOOR

No. 94904

■ **This plan features:**

— Three bedrooms

— Two full and one half baths

■ Living Room is distinguished by warmth of bayed window and French doors leading to Family Room

■ Built-in curio cabinet adds interest to formal Dining Room

■ Well-appointed Kitchen with island cooktop and Breakfast area designed to save you steps

■ Family Room with focal point fireplace for informal gatherings

■ Spacious Master Suite with vaulted ceiling over decorative window and plush dressing area

■ Secondary bedrooms share a double vanity bath

First floor — 1,093 sq. ft.
Second floor — 905 sq. ft.
Basement — 1,093 sq. ft.
Garage — 527 sq. ft.

Coastal Delight

■ *Total living area 2,376 sq. ft.* ■ *Price Code E* ■

No. 94202 ✕

■ This plan features:

— Three bedrooms

— Two full baths

■ Living area above the Garage offering a "piling" design for coastal, waterfront or low-lying terrain

■ Open Foyer with landing staircase

■ Three sets of double doors below a vaulted ceiling in the Great Room

■ A Dining Room featuring vaulted ceilings and decorative windows

■ A glassed-in Nook flows to the Kitchen with an island work area

■ A second floor Master Suite with a vaulted ceiling, double door to a private Deck, his-n-her closets and a plush bath

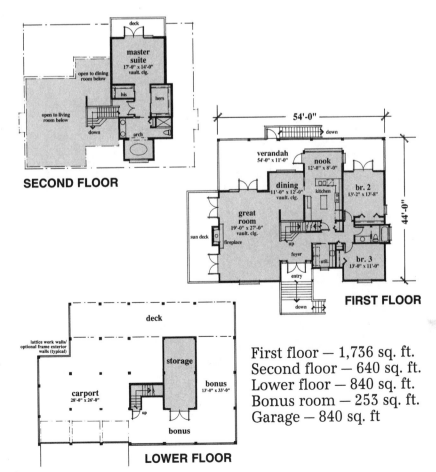

First floor — 1,736 sq. ft.
Second floor — 640 sq. ft.
Lower floor — 840 sq. ft.
Bonus room — 253 sq. ft.
Garage — 840 sq. ft

■ *Total living area 1,310 sq. ft.* ■ *Price Code A* ■

No. 93048

■ **This plan features:**

— Three bedrooms

— Two full baths

■ An efficiently designed Kitchen with a corner sink, ample counter space and a peninsula counter

■ A sunny Breakfast Room with a convenient hide-away laundry center

■ An expansive Family Room that includes a corner fireplace and direct access to the Patio

■ A private Master Suite with a walk-in closet and a double vanity bath

■ Two additional bedrooms, both with walk-in closets, that share a full hall bath

■ No materials list is available for this plan

Main floor — 1,310 sq. ft.
Garage — 449 sq. ft.

WIDTH 49–10

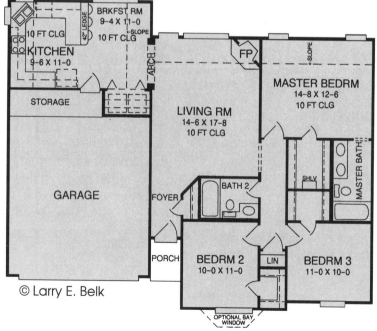

© Larry E. Belk

MAIN FLOOR

■ *Total living area 1,325 sq. ft.* ■ *Price Code A* ■

No. 98912 ✖

■ This plan features:

— Three bedrooms

— Two full baths

■ Quaint front Porch sheltering Entry into the Living Area showcased by a massive fireplace and built-ins below a vaulted ceiling

■ Formal Dining Room accented by a bay of glass with Sun Deck access

■ Efficient, galley Kitchen with Breakfast Area, laundry facilities and outdoor access

■ Secluded Master Bedroom offers a roomy walk-in closet and plush bath with a dual vanity and a garden window tub

■ Two additional bedrooms with ample closets share a full skylit bath

Main floor — 1,325 sq. ft.

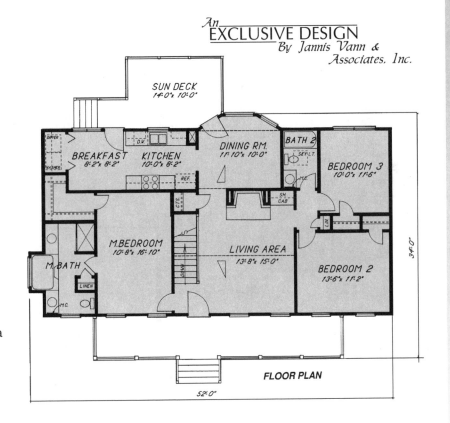

An
EXCLUSIVE DESIGN
*By Jannis Vann &
Associates, Inc.*

FLOOR PLAN

Charming Brick Ranch

Total living area 1,782 sq. ft. ■ *Price Code C*

No. 92630

■ **This plan features:**

— Three bedrooms

— Two full baths

■ Sheltered entrance leads into open Foyer and Dining Room defined by columns

■ Vaulted ceiling spans Foyer, Dining Room and Great Room with corner fireplace and atrium door to rear yard

■ Central Kitchen with separate Laundry and Pantry easily serves Dining Room, Breakfast Area and Screened Porch

■ Luxurious Master Bedroom offers a tray ceiling and French doors to the Bath with a double vanity, a walk-in closet and a whirlpool tub

■ Two additional Bedrooms, one which easily converts to a Study, share a full Bath

■ No materials list is available for this plan

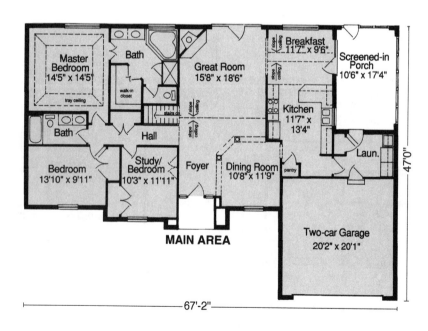

Main area — 1,782 sq. ft.
Garage — 407 sq. ft.
Basement — 1,735 sq. ft.

© 1995 Donald A. Gardner Architects, Inc.

■ *Total living area 1,561 sq. ft.* ■ *Price Code D* ■

No. 96417

■ This plan features:

— Three bedrooms

— Two full baths

■ Arched windows, dormers and charming front and back Porches with columns add country flavor

■ Central Great Room is topped by a cathedral ceiling

■ Breakfast Bay for casual dining is open to the Kitchen

■ Columns accent the entryway into the formal Dining Room

■ Cathedral ceiling crowns the Master Bedroom

■ Master Bath with skylights, whirlpool tub, shower, and a double vanity

Main floor — 1,561 sq. ft.
Garage & Storage — 346 sq. ft.

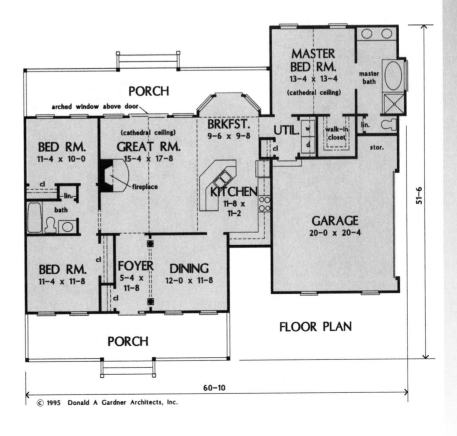

© 1995 Donald A Gardner Architects, Inc.

Quality Inside and Out

■ *Total living area 2,835 sq. ft.* ■ *Price Code G* ■

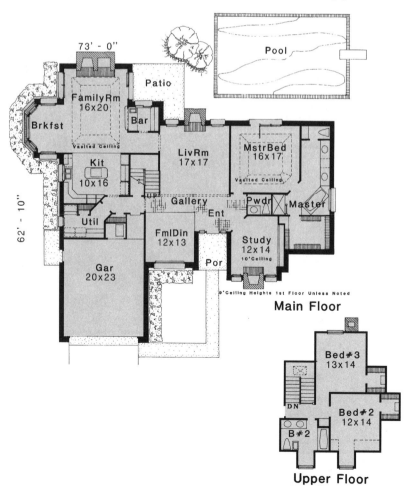

Main Floor

Upper Floor

No. 92269

■ **This plan features:**

— Three bedrooms

— Two full and one half baths

■ The entry/Gallery opens to the Living Room

■ Convenient Study offers built-ins and another fireplace

■ Country Kitchen with work island opens to Breakfast bay, Family Room and Dining Room

■ Expansive Family Room offers access to the Patio

■ Private Master Bedroom suite with a lavish bath and walk-in closet

■ Two second floor bedrooms share a double vanity bath

■ No materials list is available for this plan

Main floor — 2,273 sq. ft.
Upper floor — 562 sq. ft.
Garage — 460 sq. ft.

■ *Total living area 3,335 sq. ft.* ■ *Price Code I* ■

No. 92219

■ This plan features:

— Four bedrooms

— Two full, one three-quarter and one half baths

■ Entry hall with a graceful landing staircase, flanked by formal areas

■ Fireplaces highlight the Living Room/Parlor and Dining Room

■ Kitchen with an island cooktop, built-in pantry and Breakfast area

■ Cathedral ceiling crowns Family Room and is accented by a fireplace

■ Lavish Master Bedroom wing with plenty of storage space

■ Three bedrooms, one with a private bath

■ No materials list is available for this plan

Main floor — 2,432 sq. ft.
Upper floor — 903 sq. ft.
Basement — 2,432 sq. ft.
Garage — 742 sq. ft.

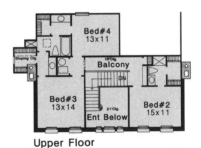

Upper Floor

Main Floor

Quaint and Cozy

B·NATHAN

■ *Total living area 1,864 sq. ft.* ■ *Price Code E* ■

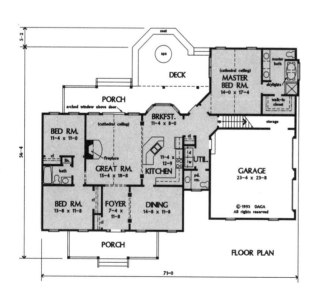

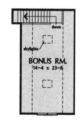

FLOOR PLAN

No. 99878

■ This plan features:

— Three bedrooms

— Two full and one half baths

■ Spacious floor plan with large Great Room crowned by cathedral ceiling

■ Central Kitchen with angled counter opens to the Breakfast Area and Great Room

■ Privately located Master Bedroom has a cathedral ceiling

■ Operable skylights over the tub accent the luxurious Master Bath

■ Bonus Room over the Garage makes expanding easy

■ An optional crawl space or basement foundation — please specify when ordering

Main floor — 1,864 sq. ft.
Garage — 614 sq. ft.
Bonus — 420 sq. ft.

■ *Total living area 2,978 sq. ft.* ■ *Price Code G* ■

No. 94242

■ This plan features:

— Three bedrooms

— Two full, one three-quarter and one half baths

■ Wonderfully balanced exterior highlighted by triple arched glass in Entry Porch, leading into the Gallery Foyer

■ Triple arches lead into Formal Living and Dining Room, Verandah and beyond

■ Kitchen, Nook and Leisure Room easily flow together

■ Owners' wing has a Master Suite with glass alcove to rear yard, a lavish bath and a Study offering many uses

■ No materials list is available for this plan

Main floor — 2,978 sq. ft.
Garage — 702 sq. ft.

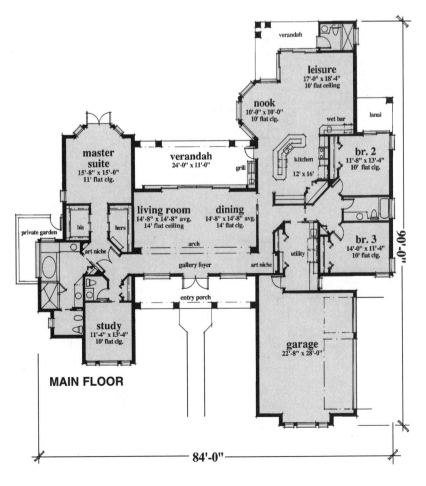

MAIN FLOOR

Rewards of Success

■ *Total living area 2,965 sq. ft.* ■ *Price Code G* ■

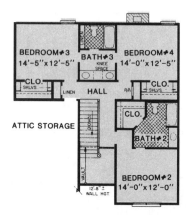

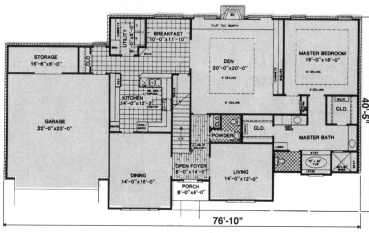

No. 92535 ✖

■ **This plan features:**

— Four bedrooms

— Three full and one half baths

■ An open Foyer flanked by the Dining Room and the Living Room

■ Den with a large fireplace, and built-in cabinets and shelves

■ A well-appointed Kitchen serving the Dining Room

■ A Master Bedroom with a lavish bath and a walk-in closet

■ Three additional bedrooms and two full baths occupying the second floor

■ An optional crawl space or slab foundation — please specify when ordering

First floor — 2,019 sq. ft.
Second floor — 946 sq. ft.
Garage — 577 sq. ft.

© 1997 Donald A. Gardner Architects, Inc.

B. NATHAN

■ *Total living area 2,682 sq. ft.* ■ *Price Code H* ■

No. 96490

■ **This plan features:**

— Four bedrooms

— Three full baths

■ Multiple columns and gables add appeal to traditional style

■ Foyer and Great Room both have two-story ceilings and clerestory windows

■ Great Room highlighted by fireplace, built-in shelves and French doors to back Porch

■ Bright Breakfast bay accesses efficient Kitchen and back stairway to bedrooms and Bonus Room

■ Bedroom/Study and full bath near Master Bedroom suite offers multiple uses

First floor — 2,067 sq. ft.
Second floor — 615 sq. ft.
Bonus room — 433 sq. ft.
Garage & storage — 729 sq. ft.

PORCH

MASTER BED RM.
15-0 x 14-0

GREAT RM.
15-4 x 19-6
(two story ceiling)
fireplace

BRKFST.
13-0 x 11-9

KIT.
13-0 x 12-2

UTILITY
8-0 x 10-0

storage

master bath

walk-in closet

BED RM./ STUDY
12-6 x 11-0

FOYER
8-1 x 10-8

DINING
14-0 x 13-4

GARAGE
22-0 x 23-0

storage

PORCH

FIRST FLOOR PLAN

60-6

73-0

© 1997 Donald A Gardner Architects, Inc.

BED RM.
13-0 x 12-0

walk-in closet

great room below

bath

(optional bedroom)
12-4 x 10-0

down

down

foyer below

BED RM.
14-0 x 13-4

walk-in closet

BONUS RM.
16-8 x 15-0

attic storage

SECOND FLOOR PLAN

Cathedral Ceiling

■ *Total living area 1,346 sq. ft.* ■ *Price Code A* ■

No. 24402

■ **This plan features:**

— Three bedrooms

— Two full baths

■ A spacious Living Room with a cathedral ceiling and elegant fireplace

■ A Dining Room that adjoins both the Living Room and the Kitchen

■ An efficient Kitchen, with double sinks, ample cabinet space and peninsula counter that doubles as an eating bar

■ A convenient hallway laundry center

■ A Master Suite with a cathedral ceiling and a private Master Bath

Main floor — 1,346 sq. ft.
Garage — 449 sq. ft.

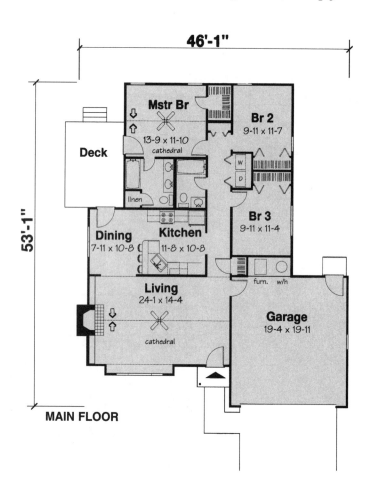

46'-1"

53'-1"

Mstr Br
13-9 x 11-10
cathedral

Deck

Br 2
9-11 x 11-7

linen

Br 3
9-11 x 11-4

Dining
7-11 x 10-8

Kitchen
11-8 x 10-8

furn.   w/h

Living
24-1 x 14-4
cathedral

Garage
19-4 x 19-11

MAIN FLOOR

An
EXCLUSIVE DESIGN
By Upright Design

An **EXCLUSIVE DESIGN**
By Upright Design

■ *Total living area 2,647 sq. ft.* ■ *Price Code F* ■

No. 24403

■ This plan features:

— Three or four bedrooms

— Two full and one three-quarter baths

■ A large Foyer with an attractive staircase

■ Study/Guest Room with convenient access to a full, hall bath

■ Elegant Dining Room topped by a decorative ceiling treatment

■ Expansive Family Room equipped with a massive fireplace with built-in bookshelves

■ Breakfast Room with a convenient built-in planning desk

■ Peninsula counter/eating bar, a built-in pantry, double sink, and ample counter space in the Kitchen

■ A cathedral ceiling crowning the Master Suite

Second Floor

Mstr Bath

Master Br
14-0 x 17-9

Br 2
15-5 x 11-4

Sitting Area
12-2 x 10-9

Br 3
11-8 x 13-6

First floor — 1,378 sq. ft.
Second floor — 1,269 sq. ft.
Basement — 1,378 sq. ft.
Garage — 717 sq. ft.

Shop
14-5 x 15-5

Crawl Space/Slab Option

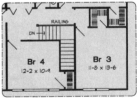

Br 4
12-2 x 10-9

Br 3
11-8 x 13-6

Optional Second Floor

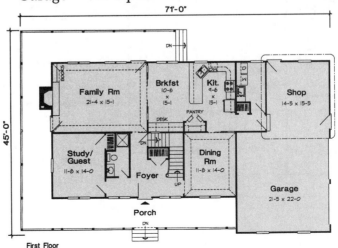

71'-0"

45'-0"

Family Rm
21-4 x 15-1

Brkfst
10-6 x 15-1

Kit.
9-6 x 15-1

Shop
14-5 x 15-5

PANTRY

DESK

Study/ Guest
11-8 x 14-0

Foyer

Dining Rm
11-8 x 14-0

Garage
21-5 x 22-0

Porch

First Floor

Compact Three Bedroom

S. NATHAN
© 1990 Donald A. Gardner Architects, Inc.

■ Total living area 1,452 sq. ft. ■ Price Code C ■

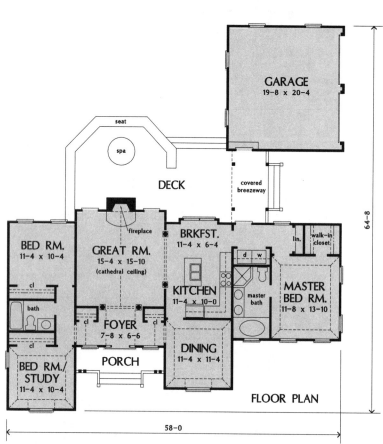

GARAGE
19-8 x 20-4

seat

spa

DECK

covered breezeway

64-8

fireplace

BRKFST.
11-4 x 6-4

lin.

walk-in closet

BED RM.
11-4 x 10-4

GREAT RM.
15-4 x 15-10
(cathedral ceiling)

cl

bath

cl

KITCHEN
11-4 x 10-0

d   w

master bath

MASTER BED RM.
11-8 x 13-10

cl

FOYER
7-8 x 6-6

cl

cl

BED RM./ STUDY
11-4 x 10-4

PORCH

DINING
11-4 x 11-4

FLOOR PLAN

58-0

© 1990 Donald A. Gardner Architects, Inc.

No. 96418

■ **This plan features:**

— Three bedrooms

— Two full baths

■ Contemporary interior punctuated by elegant columns

■ Dormers above the covered Porch light the Foyer leading to the dramatic Great Room crowned in a cathedral ceiling and enhanced by a fireplace

■ Great Room opens to the island Kitchen with Breakfast area and access to a spacious rear Deck

■ Tray ceilings adding interest to the Bedroom/Study, Dining Room and the Master Bedroom

■ Luxurious Master Bedroom highlighted by a walk-in closet and a bath with dual vanity, shower and whirlpool tub

Main floor — 1,452 sq. ft.
Garage & storage — 427 sq. ft.

■ *Total living area 2,485 sq. ft.* ■ *Price Code E* ■

No. 90461 ✕

■ **This plan features:**

— Three bedrooms

— Two full baths

■ Elegant columns on the front
Porch

■ The Study and the Dining room
both overlook the front Porch

■ The Great room has a fireplace,
built-in book shelves and access to
the rear Deck

■ The Kitchen has an angled serving
bar with a double sink

■ The secluded Master suite has
dual walk-in closets, and a bath
with a spa tub

■ An optional basement or crawl
space foundation available —
please specify when ordering

Main floor — 2,485 sq. ft.
Basement — 2,485 sq. ft.
Garage — 484 sq. ft.

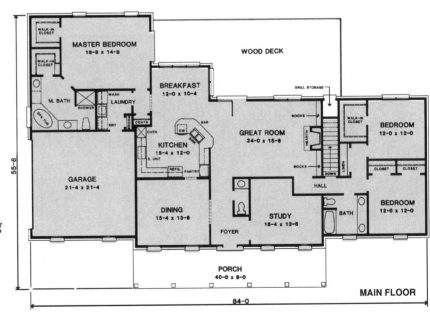

Enjoy a Summer Breeze on the Covered Porch

■ *Total living area 2,209 sq. ft.* ■ *Price Code D* ■

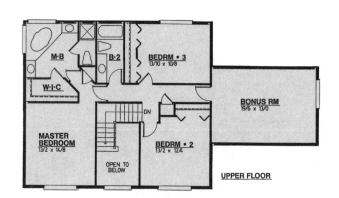

BONUS RM
19/6 x 13/0

M·B   **B·2**   **BEDRM • 3**
13/10 x 10/8

W·I·C

MASTER BEDROOM
13/2 x 14/8

DN

BEDRM • 2
13/2 x 12/4

OPEN TO BELOW

UPPER FLOOR

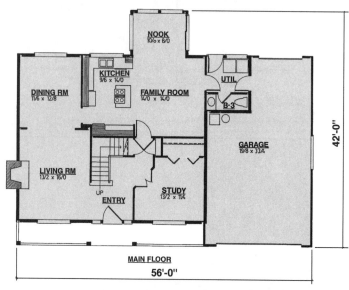

NOOK
10/o x 8/0

KITCHEN
9/6 x 14/0

FAMILY ROOM
14/0 x 14/0

UTIL

B·3

DINING RM
11/6 x 12/8

GARAGE
19/8 x 33/4

LIVING RM
13/2 x 16/0

STUDY
13/2 x 11/4

UP

ENTRY

MAIN FLOOR
56'-0"

42'-0"

No. 91073

■ **This plan features:**

— Three bedrooms

— Two full and one half baths

■ A large Living Room is enhanced by a fireplace

■ An efficient L-shaped Kitchen with cooktop island and open layout to the Family Room

■ Two generously sized bedrooms that share a full bath

■ A Master Suite with a walk-in closet and spa tub

■ A large Bonus Room

■ An optional basement or crawl space foundation — please specify when ordering

■ No materials list is available for this plan

First floor — 1,240 sq. ft.
Second floor — 969 sq. ft.
Bonus Room — 254 sq. ft.
Garage — 550 sq. ft.

■ *Total living area 2,425 sq. ft.* ■ *Price Code E* ■

No. 98419

■ This plan features:

— Three bedrooms

— Two full and one half baths

■ Vaulted Great Room is highlighted by a fireplace

■ Decorative columns define the Dining Room

■ A built-in Pantry and a radius window in the Kitchen

■ The Breakfast Bay is crowned by a vaulted ceiling

■ A tray ceiling over the Master Bedroom and Sitting Area

■ Two additional bedrooms, each with a walk-in closet, share the full, double vanity bath in the hall

■ An optional basement, crawl space or slab foundation — please specify when ordering

■ No materials list is available for this plan

First floor — 1,796 sq. ft.
Second floor — 629 sq. ft.
Bonus room — 208 sq. ft.
Basement — 1,796 sq. ft.
Garage — 588 sq. ft.

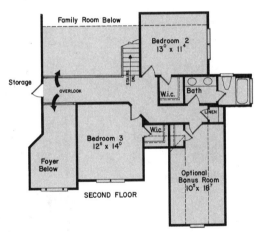

SECOND FLOOR

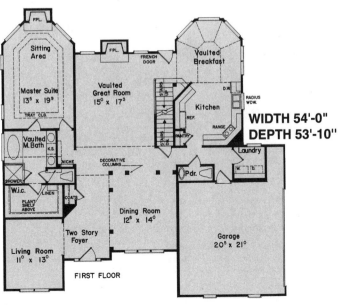

WIDTH 54'-0"
DEPTH 53'-10"

FIRST FLOOR

Farmhouse Flavor

■ *Total living area 1,907 sq. ft.* ■ *Price Code C* ■

An **EXCLUSIVE DESIGN**
By Karl Kreeger

Slab/Crawl Space Option

FIRST FLOOR

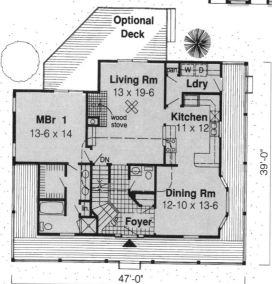

Optional Deck

Living Rm
13 x 19-6

Ldry

MBr 1
13-6 x 14

wood stove

Kitchen
11 x 12

DN

Dining Rm
12-10 x 13-6

Foyer

39'-0"

47'-0"

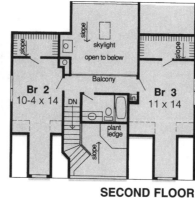

slope slope
skylight
open to below

slope

Balcony

Br 2
10-4 x 14

DN

Br 3
11 x 14

plant ledge

slope

SECOND FLOOR

No. 10785

■ **This plan features:**

— Three bedrooms

— Two full and one half baths

■ A inviting wrap-around Porch with old-fashioned charm

■ Two-story Foyer

■ A wood stove in the Living Room that warms the entire house

■ A modern Kitchen flowing easily into the bayed Dining Room

■ A first floor Master Bedroom with private master bath

■ Two additional bedrooms with walk-in closets and cozy gable sitting nooks

First floor — 1,269 sq. ft.
Second floor — 638 sq. ft.
Basement — 1,269 sq. ft.

■ *Total living area 2,490 sq. ft.* ■ *Price Code F* ■

No. 92549 ⚒

■ This plan features:

— Four bedrooms

— Three full baths

■ Porch entry into open Foyer with a lovely, landing staircase

■ Elegant columns define Dining and Den area for gracious entertaining

■ Efficient, U-shaped Kitchen with a serving counter, Eating bay, and nearby Utility and Garage

■ Decorative ceiling tops Master Bedroom offering a huge walk-in closet and plush bath

■ An optional crawl space or slab foundation — please specify when ordering

First floor — 1,911 sq. ft.
Second floor — 579 sq. ft.
Garage — 560 sq. ft..

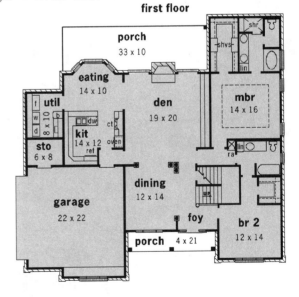

first floor

WIDTH 57'-10"
DEPTH 56'-10"

second floor

Secluded Master Suite

■ *Total living area 1,741 sq. ft.* ■ *Price Code B* ■

Crawl/Slab Plan
NOTE: Mechanicals to be placed in Utility Room with this option.

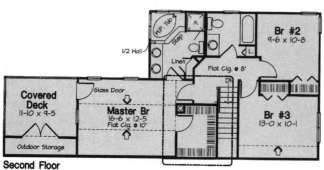

Second Floor

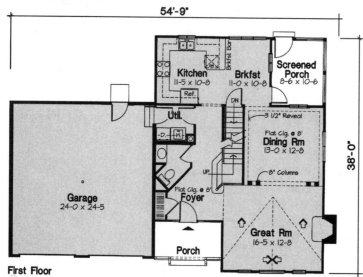

First Floor

No. 24720

■ **This plan features:**

— Three bedrooms

— Two full and one half baths

■ Arched Porch leads into an open Foyer with a cascading staircase

■ Great Room with a vaulted ceiling, sunburst window and hearth fireplace

■ Columns frame entrance to formal Dining Room with decorative ceiling

■ Kitchen with breakfast bar, Breakfast area with Screened Porch access and nearby

■ Master Bedroom has angled ceiling, private Deck

■ No materials list is available for this plan

First floor — 900 sq. ft.
Second floor — 841 sq. ft.
Basement — 891 sq. ft.
Garage — 609 sq. ft.

■ *Total living area 3,352 sq. ft.* ■ *Price Code I* ■

No. 98513

■ This plan features:

— Three bedrooms

— Three full and one half baths

■ Brick and stone blend masterfully for an impressive French country exterior

■ Separate Master Suite with expansive bath and closet

■ Study containing a built-in desk and bookcase

■ Angled island Kitchen highlighted by walk-in Pantry and open to the Breakfast Bay

■ Fantastic Family Room including a brick fireplace and a built-in entertainment center

■ Three additional bedrooms with private access to a full bath

■ No materials list is available for this plan

Main floor — 3,352 sq. ft.
Garage — 672 sq. ft.

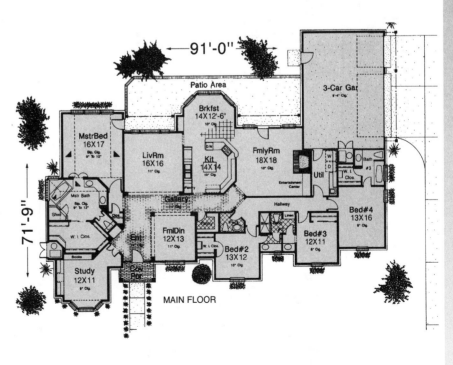

Country-Style Home for Quality Living

■ *Total living area 2,466 sq. ft.* ■ *Price Code E* ■

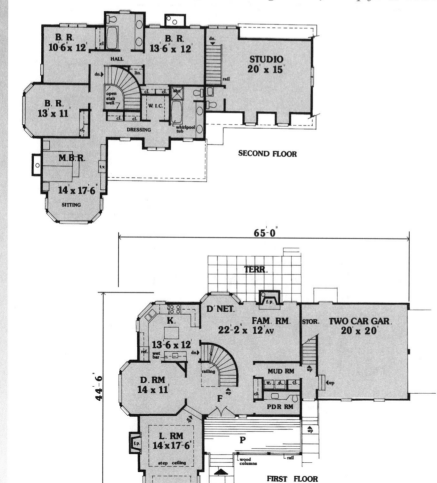

SECOND FLOOR

FIRST FLOOR

No. 99640

■ This plan features:

— Four bedrooms

— Two full and two half baths

■ A spacious central Foyer leads to all rooms

■ A sunken Living Room, enhanced by a focal point fireplace and a large windowed bay

■ An elegant formal Dining Room with interior corners angled to form an octagon

■ A fully equipped Kitchen with a center island

■ A luxurious Master Bedroom includes a dressing area, a walk-in closet and a deluxe bath

■ A Studio area above the Garage that includes a half bath

First floor — 1,217 sq. ft.
Second floor — 1,249 sq. ft.
Bonus — 496 sq. ft.
Basement — 1,217 sq. ft.
Garage — 431 sq. ft.

Total living area 2,263 sq. ft. ■ **Price Code E**

No. 91128

■ This plan features:

— Three bedrooms

— Two full baths

■ An impressive entrance

■ Arched entrances into the Living Room and the Dining Room

■ A corner fireplace in the Living Room with a vaulted ceiling

■ The open Kitchen has a built-in pantry and a desk

■ The Sun Room a quiet location

■ The split bedroom layout provides privacy for parents as well as the children

■ The Master Suite features a large walk-in closet and a vaulted ceiling

■ There is a Bonus room above the garage for future expansion

■ No materials list is available for this plan

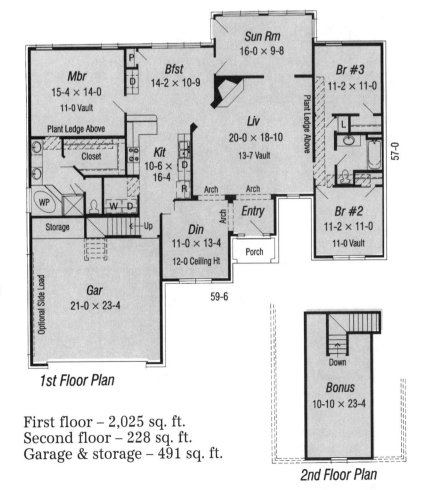

1st Floor Plan

First floor – 2,025 sq. ft.
Second floor – 228 sq. ft.
Garage & storage – 491 sq. ft.

2nd Floor Plan

Classic Country Farmhouse

© 1992 Donald A Gardner Architects, Inc.

■ *Total living area 1,663 sq. ft.* ■ *Price Code D* ■

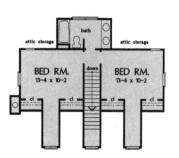

First floor — 1,145 sq. ft.
Second floor — 518 sq. ft.
Bonus room — 380 sq. ft.
Garage & storage — 509 sq. ft.

No. 99800

■ This plan features:

— Three bedrooms

— Two full and one half baths

■ Covered Porch gives classic country farmhouse look, and includes multiple dormers, a great layout for entertaining, and a Bonus Room

■ Clerestory dormer window bathes the two-story Foyer in natural light

■ Large Great Room with fireplace opens to the Dining/Breakfast/ Kitchen space, which leads to a spacious Deck with optional spa and seating for easy indoor/ outdoor entertaining

■ First floor Master Suite offers privacy and luxury with a separate shower, whirlpool tub and a dual vanity

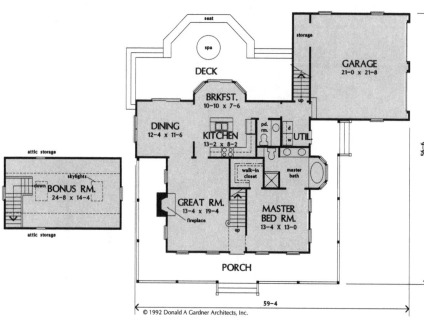

FIRST FLOOR PLAN

© 1992 Donald A Gardner Architects, Inc.

Two-Story Foyer Adds to Elegance

■ Total living area 2,454 sq. ft. ■ Price Code E ■

No. 93240

■ This plan features:

— Four bedrooms

— Two full and one half baths

■ Two-story entrance with lovely curved staircase

■ Family Room enhanced by fireplace and access to Sundeck

■ Country-sized Kitchen with bright Breakfast area, adjoins Dining Room and Utility/Garage entry

■ French doors lead into plush Master Bedroom with decorative ceiling and large master bath

■ Three additional bedrooms with ample closets share a full bath and Bonus Room

■ An optional basement, crawl space or slab foundation — please specify when ordering

First floor — 1,277 sq. ft.
Second floor — 1,177 sq. ft.
Bonus room — 392 sq. ft.
Basement — 1,261 sq. ft.
Garage — 572 sq. ft.

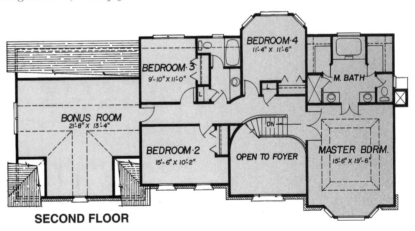

SECOND FLOOR

BEDROOM·3
9'-10" X 11'-0"

BEDROOM·4
11'-4" X 11'-6"

M. BATH

BONUS ROOM
21'-8" X 13'-4"

BEDROOM·2
15'-6" X 10'-2"

OPEN TO FOYER

MASTER BDRM.
15'-6" X 19'-6"

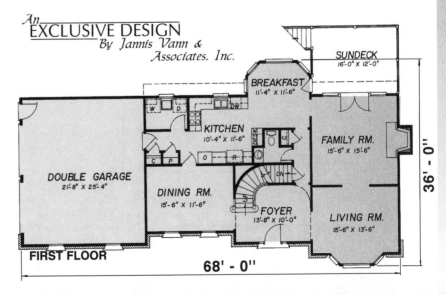

An
EXCLUSIVE DESIGN
By Jannis Vann &
Associates, Inc.

SUNDECK
16'-0" X 12'-0"

BREAKFAST
11'-4" X 11'-6"

KITCHEN
10'-4" X 11'-6"

FAMILY RM.
15'-6" X 15'-6"

DOUBLE GARAGE
21'-8" X 25'-4"

DINING RM.
15'-6" X 11'-6"

FOYER
13'-8" X 10'-0"

LIVING RM.
15'-6" X 13'-6"

FIRST FLOOR

36' - 0"

68' - 0"

321

Cottage Influence

■ *Total living area 2,533 sq. ft.* ■ *Price Code F* ■

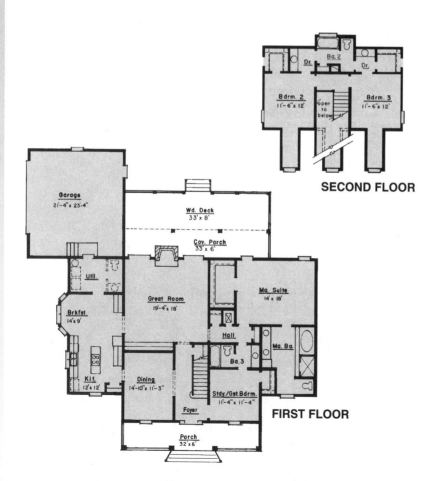

SECOND FLOOR

FIRST FLOOR

No. 94614

■ **This plan features:**

— Three or four bedrooms

— Three full and one half baths

■ Expansive Great Room with focal point fireplace

■ Cooktop island in Kitchen easily serves Breakfast bay

■ Large Master Suite with access to Covered Porch, walk-in closet and double vanity bath

■ Study/Guest Bedroom with private access to a full bath

■ Two second floor bedrooms with dormers

■ An optional slab or crawl space foundation — please specify when ordering

■ No materials list is available for this plan

First floor — 1,916 sq. ft.
Second floor — 617 sq. ft.
Garage — 516 sq. ft.

■ *Total living area 2,690 sq. ft.* ■ *Price Code F* ■

No. 94810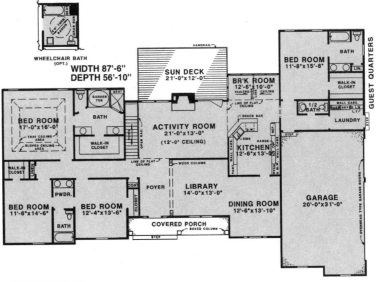

■ This plan features:

— Four bedrooms

— Three full and one half baths

■ Attractive styling using a combination of stone and siding and a covered Porch add to the curb appeal

■ Formal foyer giving access to the bedroom wing, Library or Activity room

■ Activity room showcasing a focal point fireplace and including direct access to the rear Deck and the Breakfast Room

■ Breakfast Room is topped by a vaulted ceiling and flows into the kitchen

■ A secluded Guest Suite is located off the kitchen area

■ Master Suite topped by a tray ceiling and pampered by five-piece bath

Main floor — 2,690 sq. ft.
Basement — 2,690 sq. ft.
Garage — 660 sq. ft.

MAIN FLOOR

Easy One Floor Living

■ Total living area *1,671 sq. ft.* ■ *Price Code B* ■

WIDTH 50'-0"
DEPTH 51'-0"

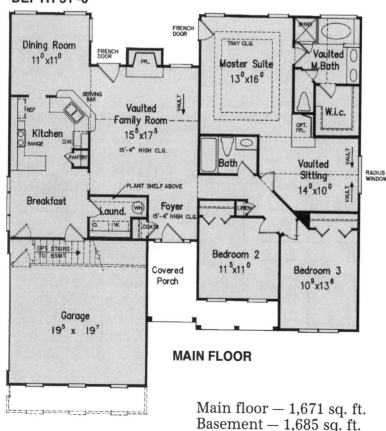

MAIN FLOOR

Main floor — 1,671 sq. ft.
Basement — 1,685 sq. ft.
Garage — 400 sq. ft.

No. 98423

■ **This plan features:**

— Three bedrooms

— Two full baths

■ A spacious Family Room topped by a vaulted ceiling and highlighted by a large fireplace and a French door to the rear yard

■ A serving bar open to the Family Room and the Dining Room, a pantry and a peninsula counter adding more efficiency to the Kitchen

■ A crowning tray ceiling over the Master Bedroom and a vaulted ceiling over the master bath

■ A vaulted ceiling over the cozy Sitting Room in the Master Suite

■ Two additional bedrooms, roomy in size, sharing the full bath in the hall

■ An optional basement, crawl space or slab foundation — please specify when ordering

■ Total living area 2,470 sq. ft. ■ Price Code E ■

No. 92257

■ This plan features:

— Three bedrooms

— Two full and one half baths

■ Arched Portico enhances entry into Gallery and spacious Living Room, with focal point fireplace surrounded by glass

■ Cathedral ceilings top Family Room and formal Dining Room

■ An Kitchen with a breakfast area

■ Corner Master Bedroom suite with access to covered Patio and private bath with a double vanity and garden window tub

■ Two additional bedrooms with walk-in closets share a full bath

■ No materials list is available for this plan

Main Floor — 2,470 sq. ft.
Garage — 483 sq. ft.

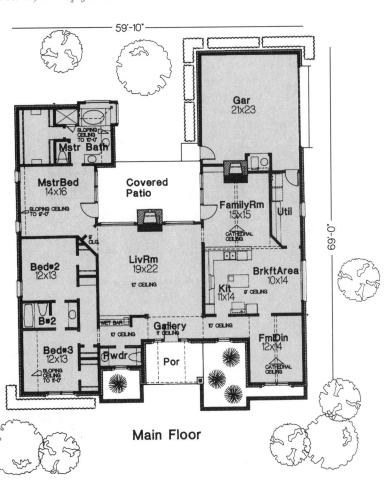

Main Floor

Designed for Today's Family

■ *Total living area 2,192 sq. ft.* ■ *Price Code F* ■

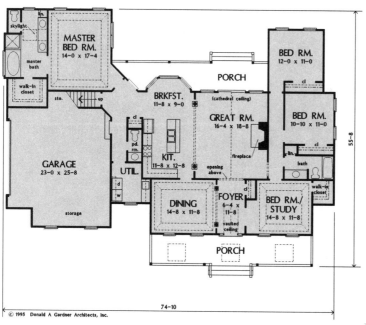

© 1995 Donald A Gardner Architects, Inc.

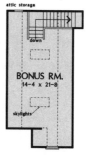

No. 99838

■ This plan features:

— Three bedrooms

— Two full and one half baths

■ Volume and 9' ceilings add elegance to a comfortable, open floor plan

■ Secluded bedrooms designed for pleasant retreats at the end of the day

■ Airy Foyer topped by a vaulted dormer allows natural light to stream in

■ Formal Dining Room delineated from the Foyer by columns topped with a tray ceiling

■ Extra flexibility in the front bedroom which could double as a Study

■ Tray ceiling in the bedroom and skylights and a garden tub in the bath highlight the Master Suite

Main floor — 2,192 sq. ft.
Garage & Storage — 582 sq. ft.
Bonus — 390 sq. ft.

One-Story Country Home

■ *Total living area 1,367 sq. ft.* ■ *Price Code A* ■

No. 99639 ✖

■ This plan features:

— Three bedrooms

— Two full baths

■ A Living Room with an imposing high ceiling that slopes down to a normal height of eight feet, focusing on the decorative heat-circulating fireplace at the rear wall

■ An efficient Kitchen that adjoins the Dining Room

■ A Dinette Area for informal eating in the Kitchen that can comfortably seat six people

■ A Master Suite arranged with a large dressing area that has a walk-in closet plus two linear closets and space for a vanity

Main area — 1,367 sq. ft.
Basement — 1,267 sq. ft.
Garage — 431 sq. ft.

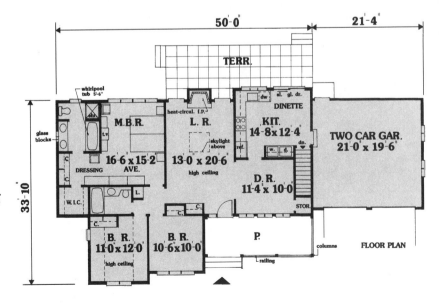

Stunning First Impression

■ *Total living area 2,464 sq. ft.* ■ *Price Code E* ■

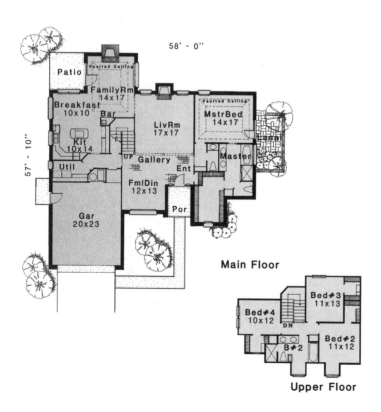

Main Floor

Upper Floor

Main floor — 1,805 sq. ft.
Upper floor — 659 sq. ft.
Basement — 1,800 sq. ft.
Garage — 440 sq. ft.

No. 98540

■ **This plan features:**

— Four bedrooms

— Two full and one half baths

■ Dormer windows on the second floor, arched windows and entrance, brick quoin corners come together for a stunning first impression

■ Large Living Room with a fireplace and an open formal Dining Area

■ Family Room at the rear of home containing a bar

■ Huge island Kitchen with a Breakfast area and plenty of work and storage space

■ Luxurious Master Suite occupying an entire wing of the home and providing a quiet retreat

■ Three additional bedrooms on the second floor sharing a large bath

■ No materials list is available for this plan

For an Established Neighborhood

■ Total living area 1,292 sq. ft. ■ Price Code A ■

No. 93222

■ **This plan features:**

— Three bedrooms

— Two full baths

■ An expansive Living Room enhanced by natural light streaming in from the large front window

■ A bayed formal Dining Room with direct access to the Sun Deck and the Living Room for entertainment ease

■ An efficient, galley Kitchen, convenient to both formal and informal eating areas

■ An informal Breakfast Room with direct access to the Sun Deck

■ A large Master Suite equipped with a walk-in closet and a full private bath

Main area — 1,276 sq. ft.
Finished staircase — 16 sq. ft.
Basement — 392 sq. ft.
Garage — 728 sq. ft.

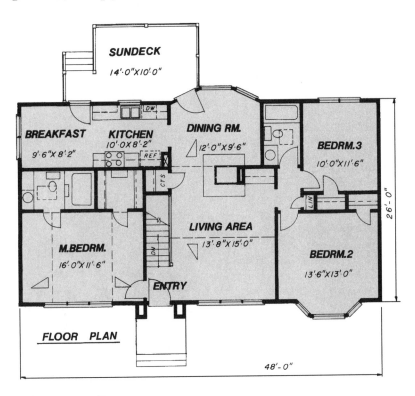

SUNDECK
14'-0"X10'-0"

BREAKFAST
9'-6"X8'-2"

KITCHEN
10'-0X8'-2"

DINING RM.
12'-0"X9'-6"

BEDRM.3
10'-0"X11'-6"

M.BEDRM.
16'-0"X11'-6"

LIVING AREA
13'-8"X15'-0"

BEDRM.2
13'-6"X13'-0"

ENTRY

FLOOR PLAN

48'-0"

26'-0"

An EXCLUSIVE DESIGN
*By Jannis Vann &
Associates, Inc.*

Separate Guest Quarters

■ *Total living area 3,792 sq. ft.* ■ *Price Code K* ■

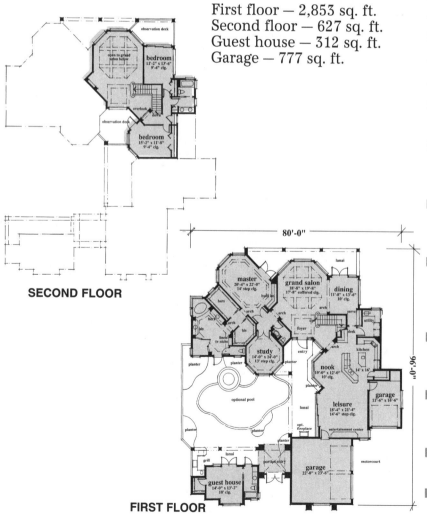

SECOND FLOOR

FIRST FLOOR

First floor — 2,853 sq. ft.
Second floor — 627 sq. ft.
Guest house — 312 sq. ft.
Garage — 777 sq. ft.

No. 94246

■ This plan features:

— Four bedrooms

— Three full and one half baths

■ Portico Entry way opens up to a unique courtyard plan

■ Octagon-shaped Grand Salon overlooks Lanai and opens to formal Dining Area

■ An efficient Kitchen with a walk-in Pantry, built-in desk, island sink and expansive snack bar

■ Open Leisure room with a high ceiling, offers an entertainment center, sliding glass doors to lanai and courtyard

■ Master wing has a large bedroom with a stepped ceiling, a bayed sitting area and lavish bath area

■ Two upstairs bedrooms with private decks, share a double vanity bath

■ Private Guest House offers luxurious accommodations

■ No materials list is available for this plan

■ *Total living area 3,381 sq. ft.* ■ *Price Code I* ■

No. 98514

■ This plan features:

— Five bedrooms

— Two full, one three-quarter and one half baths

■ The Entry/Gallery features a grand spiral staircase

■ The Study has built-in bookcases

■ Formal Living and Dining Rooms each have palladian windows

■ The large Family Room has a fireplace

■ The first floor Master Bedroom contains a luxurious bath with a cathedral ceiling

■ An optional slab or crawl space foundation — please specify when ordering

■ No materials list is available for this plan

Main floor — 2,208 sq. ft.
Upper floor — 1,173 sq. ft.
Bonus — 224 sq. ft.
Garage — 520 sq. ft.

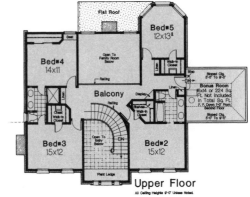

Upper Floor

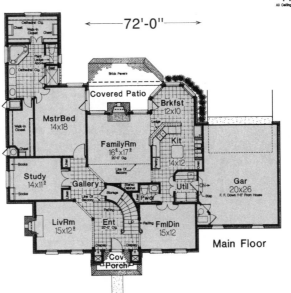

Main Floor

Distinctive Windows Add to Curb Appeal

■ *Total living area 2,735 sq. ft.* ■ *Price Code F* ■

No. 92550

■ **This plan features:**

— Four bedrooms

— Three full baths

■ A private Master Bedroom with a raised ceiling and attached bath with a spa tub

■ A wing of three bedrooms on the right side of the home sharing two full baths

■ An efficient Kitchen is straddled by an Eating Nook and a Dining Room

■ A cozy Den with a raised ceiling and a fireplace that is the focal point of the home

■ A two-car Garage with a storage area

■ An optional crawl space or slab foundation — please specify when ordering

Main floor — 2,735 sq. ft.
Garage — 561 sq. ft.

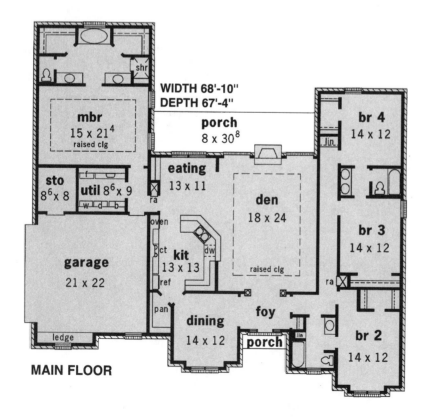

WIDTH 68'-10"
DEPTH 67'-4"

mbr
15 x 21⁴
raised clg

porch
8 x 30⁸

br 4
14 x 12

sto
8⁶ x 8

util 8⁶ x 9

eating
13 x 11

den
18 x 24

br 3
14 x 12

garage
21 x 22

kit
13 x 13

raised clg

dining
14 x 12

foy

porch

br 2
14 x 12

ledge

MAIN FLOOR

Wrapping Front Porch and Gabled Dormers

©1997 Donald A. Gardner Architects, Inc.

■ *Total living area 2,596 sq. ft.* ■ *Price Code H* ■

No. 96411

■ This plan features:

— Four bedrooms

— Three full baths

■ Generous Great Room with a fireplace, cathedral ceiling and a balcony above

■ Flexible bedroom/Study having a walk-in closet and an adjacent full bath

■ Master Suite with a sunny bay window and a private bath topped by a cathedral ceiling and highlighted by his-n-her vanities, and a separate tub and shower

■ Two additional bedrooms, each with dormer windows, sharing a full bath with a cathedral ceiling, palladian window and double vanity

■ Bonus Room over the garage for future expansion

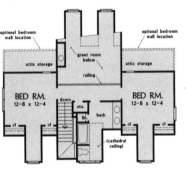

SECOND FLOOR PLAN

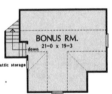

First floor — 1,939 sq. ft.
Second floor — 657 sq. ft.
Garage & Storage — 526 sq. ft.
Bonus room — 386 sq. ft.

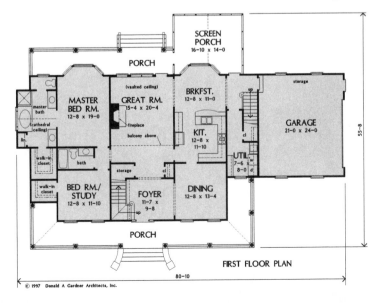

FIRST FLOOR PLAN

© 1997 Donald A Gardner Architects, Inc.

Unique Tower Creates Unique Spaces

■ *Total living area 2,362 sq. ft.* ■ *Price Code E* ■

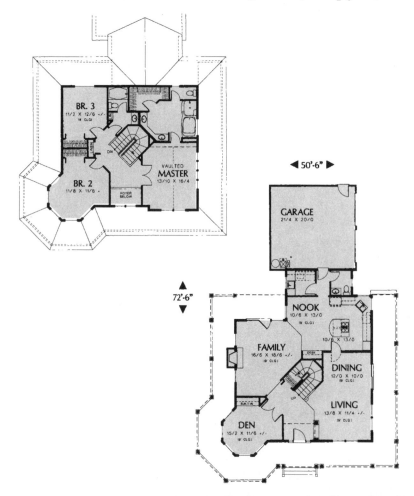

◄ 50'-6" ►

72'-6"

No. 91565

■ **This plan features:**

— Three bedrooms

— Two full and one half baths

■ Extensive porch wraps around and is accessed by active areas of home

■ Combined Living and Dining area offers comfortable entertaining

■ Efficient Kitchen with a cooktop work island, built-in desk, nearby laundry and Garage entry

■ Family Room with a cozy fireplace and atrium door to Porch

■ Unique Den with loads of light and built-in shelves

■ Vaulted ceiling, walk-in closet and a luxurious bath in Master Suite

■ Two bedrooms, one with a unique shape, share a full bath

First floor — 1,337 sq. ft.
Second floor — 1,025 sq. ft.

Total living area 4,125 sq. ft. ■ Price Code L

No. 98439

■ This plan features:

— Four bedrooms

— Three full baths

■ Two-story Foyer leads through arched openings to the formal Living Room and Dining Room

■ An Island Kitchen offers a Pantry and serving bar

■ The Breakfast Room opens to the Kitchen and has a French door to the rear yard

■ A fireplace and built-in shelving highlight the Family Room

■ A home Office or secondary bedroom has a double door entrance for privacy as well as a private full bath

■ The Master Suite has a Sitting Room and lavish bath

■ An optional basement or crawl space foundation — please specify when ordering

First floor — 2,058 sq. ft.
Second floor — 2,067 sq. ft.
Basement — 2,058 sq. ft.
Garage — 819 sq. ft.

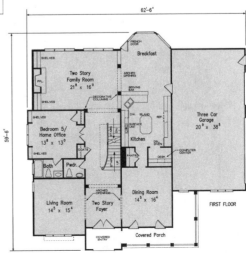

Attractive Hip and Valley Style Roof

■ *Total living area 2,411 sq. ft.* ■ *Price Code E* ■

No. 24262

ALTERNATE KITCHEN

SECOND FLOOR

OPTIONAL RETREAT

FIRST FLOOR

43'-0"

52'-0"

■ This plan features:

— Four bedrooms

— Two full and one half baths

■ A see-through fireplace between the Living Room and the Family Room

■ A gourmet Kitchen with an island, built-in Pantry and double sink

■ A Master Bedroom with a vaulted ceiling

■ A master bath with large double vanity, linen closet, corner tub, separate shower, compartmented toilet and huge walk-in closet

■ Three additional bedrooms, one with walk-in closet, share full hall bath

First floor — 1,241 sq. ft.
Second floor — 1,170 sq. ft.
Garage — 500 sq. ft.

An
EXCLUSIVE DESIGN
By Energetic Enterprises

Moderate Ranch Has Features of a Larger Plan

■ *Total living area 1,811 sq. ft.* ■ *Price Code C* ■

No. 90441 ✕

■ **This plan features:**

— Three bedrooms

— Two full baths

■ A large Great Room with a vaulted ceiling and a stone fireplace with bookshelves on either side

■ A spacious Kitchen with ample cabinet space conveniently located next to the large Dining Room

■ A Master Suite having a large bath with a garden tub, double vanity and a walk-in closet

■ Two other large bedrooms, each with a walk-in closet and access to the full bath

■ An optional basement, slab or crawl space combination — please specify when ordering

Main floor — 1,811 sq. ft.
Basement — 1,811 sq. ft.
Garage — 484 sq. ft.

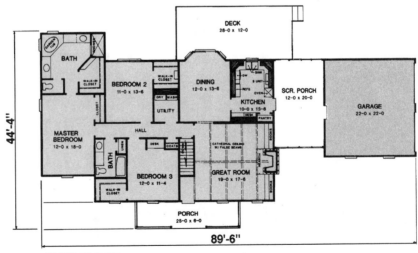

MAIN FLOOR

Traditional Ranch

■ *Total living area 2,275 sq. ft.* ■ *Price Code E* ■

DECK

BR.#2
14x11

BREAKFAST

MASTER
14x18

KITCHEN
10x10

FAMILY ROOM
16X18

Tray Clg.

BR.#3
13x12

Stairs Down

60'

DINING
12x13

FOYER

LIVING
13x13

Cathedral

Tray Clg.

UTILITY

Cathedral

WORKSHOP

MAIN FLOOR

62'

GARAGE
22x19

Drive

No. 92404

■ **This plan features:**

— Three bedrooms

— Two full baths

■ A tray ceiling in the Master Suite

■ A formal Living Room with a cathedral ceiling

■ A decorative tray ceiling in the elegant formal Dining Room

■ A spacious Family Room with a vaulted ceiling and a fireplace

■ A modern, well-appointed Kitchen with snack bar and bayed Breakfast area

■ Two additional bedrooms share a full hall bath

Main floor — 2,275 sq. ft.
Basement — 2,207 sq. ft.
Garage — 512 sq. ft.

■ *Total living area 1,280 sq. ft.* ■ *Price Code A* ■

No. 98747

■ This plan features:

— Three bedrooms

— Two full baths

■ Attractive wood siding and a large L-shaped covered Porch

■ Front entry leading to generous living room with a vaulted ceiling

■ Large two-car Garage with access through Utility Room

■ Roomy secondary bedrooms share the full bath in the hall

■ Kitchen highlighted by a built-in Pantry and a garden window

■ Vaulted ceiling adds volume to the Dining Room

■ Master Suite in an isolated location enhanced by abundant closet space, separate vanity, and linen storage

Main floor — 1,280 sq. ft.

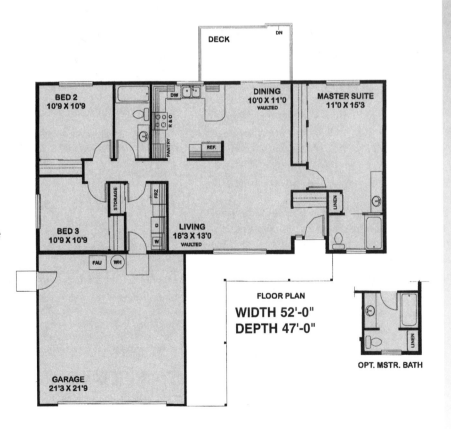

FLOOR PLAN
WIDTH 52'-0"
DEPTH 47'-0"

OPT. MSTR. BATH

Everything You Need...
...to Make Your Dream Come True.

You pay only a fraction of the original cost for home designs by respected professionals.

You've Picked Your Dream Home!

You can imagine your new home situated on your lot in the morning sunlight. You can visualize living there, enjoying your family, entertaining friends and celebrating holidays. All that remains are the details. That's where we can help. Whether you plan to build it yourself, act as your own general contractor or hire a professional builder, your Garlinghouse Co. home plans will provide the perfect design and specifications to help make your dream home a reality.

We can offer you an array of additional products and services to help you with your planning needs. We can supply materials lists, construction cost estimates based on your local material and labor costs and modifications to your selected plan if you would like.

For over 90 years, homeowners and builders have relied on us for accurate, complete, professional blueprints. Our plans help you get results fast... and save money, too! These pages will give you all the information you need to order. So get started now... We know you'll love your new Garlinghouse home!

Sincerely,

President   Chief Executive Officer

EXTERIOR ELEVATIONS

Elevations are scaled drawings of the front, rear, left, and right sides of a home. All of the necessary information pertaining to the exterior finish materials, roof pitches, and exterior height dimensions of your home are defined.

CABINET PLANS

These plans, or in some cases elevations, will detail the layout of the kitchen and bathroom cabinets at a larger scale. This gives you an accurate layout for your cabinets or an ideal starting point for a modified custom cabinet design. Available for most plans. You may also show the floor plan without a cabinet layout. This will allow you to start from scratch and design your own dream kitchen.

TYPICAL WALL SECTION

This section is provided to help your builder understand the structural components and materials used to construct the exterior walls of your home. This section will address insulation, roof components, and interior and exterior wall finishes. Your plans will be designed with either 2x4 or 2x6 exterior walls, but most professional contractors can easily adapt the plans to the wall thickness you require.

FIREPLACE DETAILS

If the home you have chosen includes a fireplace, the fireplace detail will show typical methods to construct the firebox, hearth and flue chase for masonry units, or a wood frame chase for a zero-clearance unit. Available for most plans.

FOUNDATION PLAN

These plans will accurately dimension the footprint of your home including load bearing points and beam placement if applicable. The foundation style will vary from plan to plan. Your local climatic conditions will dictate whether a basement, slab or crawlspace is best suited for your area. In most cases, if your plan comes with one foundation style, a professional contractor can easily adapt the foundation plan to an alternate style.

ROOF PLAN

The information necessary to construct the roof will be included with your home plans. Some plans will reference roof trusses, while many others contain schematic framing plans. These framing plans will indicate the lumber sizes necessary for the rafters and ridgeboards based on the designated roof loads.

TYPICAL CROSS SECTION

A cut-away cross-section through the entire home shows your building contractor the exact correlation of construction components at all levels of the house. It will help to clarify the load bearing points from the roof all the way down to the basement. Available for most plans.

DETAILED FLOOR PLANS

The floor plans of your home accurately dimension the positioning of all walls, doors, windows, stairs and permanent fixtures. They will show you the relationship and dimensions of rooms, closets and traffic patterns. The schematic of the electrical layout may be included in the plan. This layout is clearly represented and does not hinder the clarity of other pertinent information shown. All these details will help your builder properly construct your new home.

STAIR DETAILS

If stairs are an element of the design you have chosen, the plans will show the necessary information to build these, either through a stair cross section, or on the floor plans. Either way, the information provides your builders the essential reference points that they need to build the stairs.

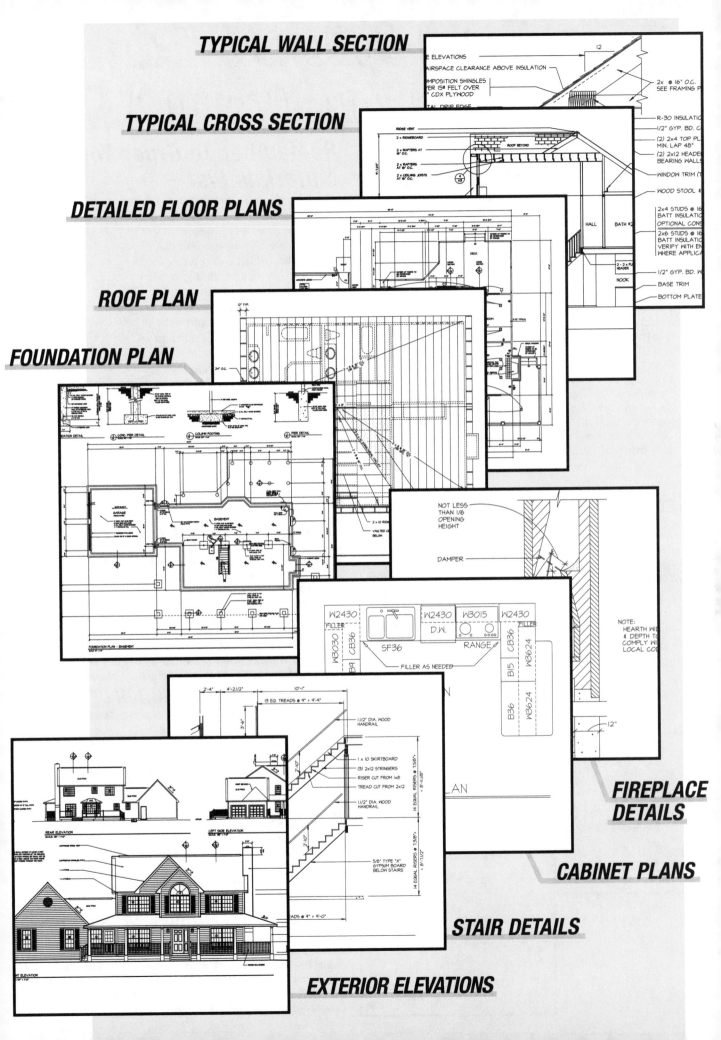

TYPICAL WALL SECTION

TYPICAL CROSS SECTION

DETAILED FLOOR PLANS

ROOF PLAN

FOUNDATION PLAN

FIREPLACE
DETAILS

CABINET PLANS

STAIR DETAILS

EXTERIOR ELEVATIONS

Garlinghouse Options & Extras ...Make Your Dream A Home

Reversed Plans Can Make Your Dream Home Just Right!

"That's our dream home...if only the garage were on the other side!"

You could have exactly the home you want by flipping it end-for-end. Check it out by holding your dream home page of this book up to a mirror. Then simply order your plans "reversed." We'll send you one full set of mirror-image plans (with the writing backwards) as a master guide for you and your builder.

The remaining sets of your order will come as shown in this book so the dimensions and specifications are easily read on the job site...but most plans in our collection come stamped "REVERSED" so there is no construction confusion.

As Shown   Reversed

We can only send reversed plans with multiple-set orders. There is a $50 charge for this service.

Some plans in our collection are available in Right Reading Reverse. Right Reading Reverse plans will show your home in reverse, with the writing on the plan being readable. This easy-to-read format will save you valuable time and money. Please contact our Customer Service Department at (860) 659-5667 to check for Right Reading Reverse availability. (There is a $135 charge for this service.)

Specifications & Contract Form

We send this form to you free of charge with your home plan order. The form is designed to be filled in by you or your contractor with the exact materials to use in the construction of your new home. Once signed by you and your contractor it will provide you with peace of mind throughout the construction process.

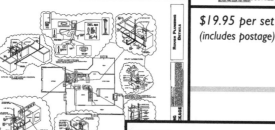

$19.95 per set
(includes postage)

Remember To Order Your Materials List

It'll help you save money. Available at a modest additional charge, the Materials List gives the quantity, dimensions, and specifications for the major materials needed to build your home. You will get faster, more accurate bids from your contractors and building suppliers — and avoid paying for unused materials and waste. Materials Lists are available for all home plans except as otherwise indicated, but can only be ordered with a set of home plans. Due to differences in regional requirements and homeowner or builder preferences... electrical, plumbing and heating/air conditioning equipment specifications are not designed specifically for each plan. However, non-plan specific detailed typical prints of residential electrical, plumbing and construction guidelines can be provided. Please see below for additional information.

Detail Plans Provide Valuable Information About Construction Techniques

Because local codes and requirements vary greatly, we recommend that you obtain drawings and bids from licensed contractors to do your mechanical plans. However, if you want to know more about techniques — and deal more confidently with subcontractors — we offer these remarkably useful detail sheets. These detail sheets will aid in your understanding of these technical subjects. **The detail sheets are not specific to any one home plan and should be used only as a general reference guide.**

RESIDENTIAL CONSTRUCTION DETAILS

Ten sheets that cover the essentials of stick-built residential home construction. Details foundation options — poured concrete basement, concrete block, or monolithic concrete slab. Shows all aspects of floor, wall and roof framing. Provides details for roof dormers, overhangs, chimneys and skylights. Conforms to requirements of Uniform Building code or BOCA code. Includes a quick index and a glossary of terms.

RESIDENTIAL PLUMBING DETAILS

Eight sheets packed with information detailing pipe installation methods, fittings, and sizes. Details plumbing hook-ups for toilets, sinks, washers, sump pumps, and septic system construction. Conforms to requirements of National Plumbing code. Color coded with a glossary of terms and quick index.

RESIDENTIAL ELECTRICAL DETAILS

Eight sheets that cover all aspects of residential wiring, from simple switch wiring to service entrance connections. Details distribution panel layout with outlet and switch schematics, circuit breaker and wiring installation methods, and ground fault interrupter specifications. Conforms to requirements of National Electrical Code. Color coded with a glossary of terms.

Modifying Your Favorite Design, Made *EASY!*

OPTION #1

Modifying Your Garlinghouse Home Plan

Simple modifications to your dream home, including minor non-structural changes and material substitutions, can be made between you and your builder by marking the changes directly on your blueprints. However, if you are considering making significant changes to your chosen design, we recommend that you use the services of The Garlinghouse Design Staff. We will help take your ideas and turn them into a reality, just the way you want. Here's our procedure!

When you place your Vellum order, you may also request a free Garlinghouse Modification Kit. In this kit, you will receive a red marking pencil, furniture cut-out sheet, ruler, a self addressed mailing label and a form for specifying any additional notes or drawings that will help us understand your design ideas. Mark your desired changes directly on the Vellum drawings. NOTE: Please use only a **red pencil** to mark your desired changes on the Vellum. Then, return the redlined Vellum set in the original box to us. **IMPORTANT**: Please **roll** the Vellums for shipping, **do not fold** the Vellums for shipping.

We also offer modification estimates. We will provide you with an estimate to draft your changes based on your specific modifications before you purchase the vellums, for a $50 fee. After you receive your estimate, if you decide to have us do the changes, the $50 estimate fee will be deducted from the cost of your modifications. If, however, you choose to use a different service, the $50 estimate fee is non-refundable. (Note: Personal checks cannot be accepted for the estimate.)

Within 5 days of receipt of your plans, you will be contacted by the Design Staff with an estimate for the design services to draw those changes. A 50% deposit is required before we begin making the actual modifications to your plans.

Once the design changes have been completed to your vellum plan, a representative will call to inform you that your modified Vellum plan is complete and will be shipped as soon as the final payment has been made. For additional information call us at 1-860-659-5667. Please refer to the Modification Pricing Guide for estimated modification costs.

OPTION #2

Reproducible Vellums for Local Modification Ease

If you decide not to use Garlinghouse for your modifications, we recommend that you follow our same procedure of purchasing our Vellums. You then have the option of using the services of the original designer of the plan, a local professional designer, or architect to make the modifications to your plan.

With a Vellum copy of our plans, a design professional can alter the drawings just the way you want, then you can print as many copies of the modified plans as you need to build your house. And, since you have already started with our complete detailed plans, the cost of those expensive professional services will be significantly less than starting from scratch. Refer to the price schedule for Vellum costs.

IMPORTANT POLICY: Upon receipt of your Vellums, if for some reason you decide you do not want a modified plan, then simply return the Kit and the unopened Vellums. Reproducible Vellum copies of our home plans are copyright protected and only sold under the terms of a license agreement that you will receive with your order. Should you not agree to the terms, then the Vellums may be exchanged. For any additional information, please call us at 1-860-659-5667.

CATEGORIES	ESTIMATED COST
KITCHEN LAYOUT — PLAN AND ELEVATION	$175.00
BATHROOM LAYOUT — PLAN AND ELEVATION	$175.00
FIREPLACE PLAN AND DETAILS	$200.00
INTERIOR ELEVATION	$125.00
EXTERIOR ELEVATION — MATERIAL CHANGE	$140.00
EXTERIOR ELEVATION — ADD BRICK OR STONE	$400.00
EXTERIOR ELEVATION — STYLE CHANGE	$450.00
NON BEARING WALLS (INTERIOR)	$200.00
BEARING AND/OR EXTERIOR WALLS	$325.00
WALL FRAMING CHANGE — 2X4 TO 2X6 OR 2X6 TO 2X4	$240.00
ADD/REDUCE LIVING SPACE — SQUARE FOOTAGE	QUOTE REQUIRED
NEW MATERIALS LIST	QUOTE REQUIRED
CHANGE TRUSSES TO RAFTERS OR CHANGE ROOF PITCH	$300.00
FRAMING PLAN CHANGES	$325.00
GARAGE CHANGES	$325.00
ADD A FOUNDATION OPTION	$300.00
FOUNDATION CHANGES	$250.00
RIGHT READING PLAN REVERSE	$575.00
ARCHITECTS SEAL (Available for most states.)	$300.00
ENERGY CERTIFICATE	$150.00
LIGHT AND VENTILATION SCHEDULE	$150.00

Questions?

Call our customer service department at **1-860-659-5667**

"How to obtain a construction cost calculation based on labor rates and building material costs in <u>your</u> Zip Code area!"

ZIP-QUOTE!
HOME COST CALCULATOR

ZIP QUOTE
HOME COST CALCULATOR

WHY?

Do you wish you could quickly find out the building cost for your new home without waiting for a contractor to compile hundreds of bids? Would you like to have a benchmark to compare your contractor(s) bids against? *Well, Now You Can!!,* with **Zip-Quote** Home Cost Calculator. Zip-Quote is only available for zip code areas within the United States.

HOW?

Our new **Zip-Quote** Home Cost Calculator will enable you to obtain the calculated building cost to construct your new home, based on labor rates and building material costs within your zip code area, without the normal delays or hassles usually associated with the bidding process. Zip-Quote can be purchased in two separate formats, an itemized or a bottom line format.

"How does **Zip-Quote** actually work?" When you call to order, you must choose from the options available, for your specific home, in order for us to process your order. Once we receive your **Zip-Quote** order, we process your specific home plan building materials list through our Home Cost Calculator which contains up-to-date rates for all residential labor trades and building material costs in your zip code area. "The result?" A calculated cost to build your dream home in your zip code area. This calculation will help you (as a consumer or a builder) evaluate your building budget. This is a valuable tool for anyone considering building a new home.

All database information for our calculations is furnished by Marshall & Swift, L.P. For over 60 years, Marshall & Swift L.P. has been a leading provider of cost data to professionals in all aspects of the construction and remodeling industries.

OPTION 1

The **Itemized Zip-Quote** is a detailed building material list. Each building material list line item will separately state the labor cost, material cost and equipment cost (if applicable) for the use of that building material in the construction process. Each category within the building material list will be subtotaled and the entire Itemized cost calculation totaled at the end. This building materials list will be summarized by the individual building categories and will have additional columns where you can enter data from your contractor's estimates for a cost comparison between the different suppliers and contractors who will actually quote you their products and services.

OPTION 2

The **Bottom Line Zip-Quote** is a one line summarized total cost for the home plan of your choice. This cost calculation is also based on the labor cost, material cost and equipment cost (if applicable) within your local zip code area.

COST

The price of your **Itemized Zip-Quote** is based upon the pricing schedule of the plan you have selected, in addition to the price of the materials list. Please refer to the pricing schedule on our order form. The price of your initial **Bottom Line Zip-Quote** is $29.95. Each additional **Bottom Line Zip-Quote** ordered in conjunction with the initial order is only $14.95. **Bottom Line Zip-Quote** may be purchased separately and does NOT have to be purchased in conjunction with a home plan order.

FYI

An **Itemized Zip-Quote** Home Cost Calculation can ONLY be purchased in conjunction with a Home Plan order. The **Itemized Zip-Quote** can not be purchased separately. The **Bottom Line Zip-Quote** can be purchased separately and doesn't have to be purchased in conjunction with a home plan order. Please consult with a sales representative for current availability. If you find within 60 days of your order date that you will be unable to build this home, then you may exchange the plans and the materials list towards the price of a new set of plans (see order info pages for plan exchange policy). The **Itemized Zip-Quote** and the **Bottom Line Zip-Quote** are NOT returnable. The price of the initial **Bottom Line Zip-Quote** order can be credited towards the purchase of an **Itemized Zip-Quote** order only. Additional **Bottom Line Zip-Quote** orders, within the same order can not be credited. Please call our Customer Service Department for more information.

Itemized Zip-Quote is available for plans where you see this symbol. 📠
Bottom Line Zip-Quote is available for all plans under 4,000 square feet.

SOME MORE INFORMATION

Itemized and Bottom Line Zip-Quotes give you approximated costs for constructing the particular house in your area. These costs are not exact and are only intended to be used as a preliminary estimate to help determine the affordability of a new home and/or as a guide to evaluate the general competitiveness of actual price quotes obtained through local suppliers and contractors. However, Zip-Quote cost figures should never be relied upon as the only source of information in either case. Land, sewer systems, site work, landscaping and other expenses are not included in our building cost figures. Garlinghouse and Marshall & Swift L.P. can not guarantee any level of data accuracy or correctness in a Zip-Quote and disclaim all liability for loss with respect to the same, in excess of the original purchase price of the Zip-Quote product. All Zip-Quote calculations are based upon the actual blueprints and do not reflect any differences or options that may be shown on the published house renderings, floor plans, or photographs.

What Garlinghouse Offers

Home Plan Blueprint Package

By purchasing a multiple set package of blueprints or a vellum from Garlinghouse, you not only receive the physical blueprint documents necessary for construction, but you are also granted a license to build one, and only one, home. You can also make simple modifications, including minor non-structural changes and material substitutions, to our design, as long as these changes are made directly on the blueprints purchased from Garlinghouse and no additional copies are made.

Home Plan Vellums

By purchasing vellums for one of our home plans, you receive the same construction drawings found in the blueprints, but printed on vellum paper. Vellums can be erased and are perfect for making design changes. They are also semi-transparent making them easy to duplicate. But most importantly, the purchase of home plan vellums comes with a broader license that allows you to make changes to the design (ie, create a hand drawn or CAD derivative work), to make an unlimited number of copies of the plan, and to build one home from the plan.

License To Build Additional Homes

With the purchase of a blueprint package or vellums you automatically receive a license to build one home and only one home, respectively. If you want to build more homes than you are licensed to build through your purchase of a plan, then additional licenses may be purchased at reasonable costs from Garlinghouse. Inquire for more information.

IMPORTANT INFORMATION TO READ BEFORE YOU PLACE YOUR ORDER

How Many Sets Of Plans Will You Need?

The Standard 8-Set Construction Package

Our experience shows that you'll speed every step of construction and avoid costly building errors by ordering enough sets to go around. Each tradesperson wants a set — the general contractor and all subcontractors; foundation, electrical, plumbing, heating/air conditioning and framers. Don't forget your lending institution, building department and, of course, a set for yourself. * Recommended For Construction *

The Minimum 4-Set Construction Package

If you're comfortable with arduous follow-up, this package can save you a few dollars by giving you the option of passing down plan sets as work progresses. You might have enough copies to go around if work goes exactly as scheduled and no plans are lost or damaged by subcontractors. But for only $60 more, the 8-set package eliminates these worries. * Recommended For Bidding *

The Single Study Set

We offer this set so you can study the blueprints to plan your dream home in detail. They are stamped "study set only-not for construction", and you cannot build a home from them. In pursuant to copyright laws, it is <u>illegal</u> to reproduce any blueprint.

An Important Note About Building Code Requirements:

All plans are drawn to conform to one or more of the industry's major national building standards. However, due to the variety of local building regulations, your plan may need to be modified to comply with local requirements — snow loads, energy loads, seismic zones, etc. Do check them fully and consult your local building officials.

A few states require that all building plans used be drawn by an architect registered in that state. While having your plans reviewed and stamped by such an architect may be prudent, laws requiring non-conforming plans like ours to be completely redrawn forces you to unnecessarily pay very large fees. If your state has such a law, we strongly recommend you contact your state representative to protest.

The rendering, floor plans, and technical information contained within this publication are not guaranteed to be totally accurate. Consequently, no information from this publication should be used either as a guide to constructing a home or for estimating the cost of building a home. Complete blueprints must be purchased for such purposes.

Order Form

Order Code No. **CHP20**

____ set(s) of blueprints for plan #_____ $_____

____ Vellum & Modification kit for plan #_____ $_____

____ Additional set(s) @ $50 each for plan #_____ $_____

____ Mirror Image Reverse @ $50 each $_____

____ Right Reading Reverse @ $135 each $_____

____ Materials list for plan #_____ $_____

____ Detail Plans @ $19.95 each
   ❏ Construction ❏ Plumbing ❏ Electrical $_____

____ Bottom line ZIP Quote @ $29.95 for plan #_____ $_____

____ Additional Bottom Line Zip Quote
   @ $14.95 for plan(s) #_____
   $_____

____ Itemized ZIP Quote for plan(s) #_____ $_____

Shipping (see charts on opposite page) $_____

Subtotal $_____

Sales Tax (CT residents add 6% sales tax) (Not required for all states) $_____

TOTAL AMOUNT ENCLOSED $_____

Send your check, money order or credit card information to:
(No C.O.D.'s Please)

Please submit all United States & Other Nations orders to:

Garlinghouse Company
174 Oakwood Drive
Glastonbury, CT. 06033

ADDRESS INFORMATION:

NAME: _____

STREET: _____

CITY: _____ **STATE:** _____ **ZIP:** _____

DAYTIME PHONE: _____ **EMAIL ADDRESS** _____

Credit Card Information

Charge To: ❏ Visa   ❏ Mastercard

Card # | | | | | | | | | | | | | | | | | |

Signature _____ Exp. _____ / _____

ORDER TOLL FREE — 1-800-235-5700
Monday-Friday 8:00 a.m. to 8:00 p.m. Eastern Time
or FAX your Credit Card order to 1-860-659-5692
All foreign residents call 1-860-659-5667

Please have ready: 1. Your credit card number 2. The plan number 3. The order code number ⇨ CHP20

Garlinghouse 2001 Blueprint Price Code Schedule

	1 Set	4 Sets	8 Sets	Vellums	ML	Itemized ZIP Quote
A	$350	$395	$455	$550	$60	$50
B	$390	$435	$495	$600	$60	$50
C	$430	$475	$535	$650	$60	$50
D	$470	$515	$575	$700	$60	$50
E	$510	$555	$615	$750	$70	$60
F	$555	$600	$660	$800	$70	$60
G	$600	$645	$705	$850	$70	$60
H	$645	$690	$750	$900	$70	$60
I	$690	$735	$795	$950	$80	$70
J	$740	$785	$845	$1000	$80	$70
K	$790	$835	$895	$1050	$80	$70
L	$840	$885	$945	$1100	$80	$70

Shipping — (Plans 1-59,999)

	1-3 Sets	4-6 Sets	7+ & Vellums
Standard Delivery (UPS 2-Day)	$25.00	$30.00	$35.00
Overnight Delivery	$35.00	$40.00	$45.00

International Shipping & Handling

	1-3 Sets	4-6 Sets	7+ & Vellums
Regular Delivery Canada (7-10 Days)	$25.00	$30.00	$35.00
Express Delivery Canada (5-6 Days)	$40.00	$45.00	$50.00
Overseas Delivery Airmail (2-3 Weeks)	$50.00	$60.00	$65.00

Shipping — (Plans 60,000-99,999)

	1-3 Sets	4-6 Sets	7+ & Vellums
Ground Delivery (7-10 Days)	$15.00	$20.00	$25.00
Express Delivery (3-5 Days)	$20.00	$25.00	$30.00

Our Reorder and Exchange Policies:

If you find after your initial purchase that you require additional sets of plans you may purchase them from us at special reorder prices (please call for pricing details) provided that you reorder within 6 months of your original order date. There is a $28 reorder processing fee that is charged on all reorders. For more information on reordering plans please contact our Customer Service Department.

Your plans are custom printed especially for you once you place your order. For that reason we cannot accept any returns.

If for some reason you find that the plan you have purchased from us does not meet your needs, then you may exchange that plan for any other plan in our collection. We allow you sixty days from your original invoice date to make an exchange. At the time of the exchange you will be charged a processing fee of 20% of the total amount of your original order plus the difference in price between the plans (if applicable) plus the cost to ship the new plans to you. Call our Customer Service Department for more information. Please Note: Reproducible vellums can only be exchanged if they are unopened.

Important Shipping Information

Please refer to the shipping charts on the order form for service availability for your specific plan number. Our delivery service must have a street address or Rural Route Box number — never a post office box. (PLEASE NOTE: Supplying a P.O. Box number *only* will delay the shipping of your order.) Use a work address if no one is home during the day.

Orders being shipped to APO or FPO must go via First Class Mail.

For our International Customers, only Certified bank checks and money orders are accepted and must be payable in U.S. currency. For speed, we ship international orders Air Parcel Post. Please refer to the chart for the correct shipping cost.

Thank you

INDEXINDEXINDEX

Legend:
- ⊠ Materials List Available
- ⚡ZIP Zip Quote Available
- R Right Reading Reverse
- 🏠 Duplex Plan

Plan#	Page#	Price Code	Square Footage	Icons
10534	30	F	3440	⊠
10548	33	B	1688	⊠
10610	50	D	2346	⊠
10663	32	E	3176	⊠
10674	57	B	1600	⊠ ⚡ZIP
10689	264	E	2744	⊠ ⚡ZIP
10690	4	D	2281	⊠ ⚡ZIP
10748	228	B	1540	⊠
10780	155	F	4217	⊠
10785	314	C	1907	⊠ ⚡ZIP
10805	60	E	2778	⊠
20070	31	B	1787	⊠ R
20093	31	C	2001	⊠
20100	85	B	1737	⊠ ⚡ZIP R
20136	95	C	2095	⊠
20144	10	D	2563	⊠ ⚡ZIP
20158	199	C	1819	⊠
20161	24	A	1307	⊠ ⚡ZIP R
20198	38	B	1792	⊠ ⚡ZIP
20219	124	C	2041	
20221	135	D	2300	⊠
20403	40	B	1734	⊠ ⚡ZIP
24243	143	G	1644	⊠ ⚡ZIP 🏠
24245	63	C	2083	⊠ ⚡ZIP R
24250	29	B	1700	⊠ ⚡ZIP R
24259	122	C	2010	⊠
24262	336	D	2411	⊠ ⚡ZIP
24302	236	A	988	⊠ ⚡ZIP
24326	259	B	1505	⊠ ⚡ZIP
24400	156	C	1978	⊠ ⚡ZIP
24402	308	A	1346	⊠ ⚡ZIP
24403	309	E	2647	⊠ ⚡ZIP
24404	34	D	2356	⊠ ⚡ZIP
24563	167	E	2861	⊠ ⚡ZIP
24700	21	A	1312	⊠ ⚡ZIP
24701	43	B	1625	⊠ ⚡ZIP
24706	58	A	1470	⊠ ⚡ZIP
24708	26	B	1576	
24711	292	A	1434	
24717	191	B	1642	
24718	79	A	1452	
24720	316	B	1741	
24726	272	D	2201	
26001	192	C	2005	⊠
34005	215	A	1441	⊠ ⚡ZIP R
34027	16	C	1960	⊠ ⚡ZIP R
34029	148	B	1686	⊠ ⚡ZIP 🏠
34043	23	B	1583	⊠ ⚡ZIP R
34150	75	A	1492	⊠ ⚡ZIP R
34154	71	A	1486	⊠ ⚡ZIP R
34328	29	A	1092	⊠ ⚡ZIP R
34600	255	A	1328	⊠ ⚡ZIP R
34601	25	A	1415	⊠ ⚡ZIP R
34602	81	B	1560	⊠ ⚡ZIP
34603	74	B	1560	⊠ ⚡ZIP
34705	223	D	2224	⊠ ⚡ZIP R
34878	8	C	1838	⊠
34901	70	B	1763	⊠ ⚡ZIP R
34926	12	D	2525	⊠ ⚡ZIP R
90353	96	A	1246	⊠
90406	158	B	1737	⊠
90409	65	B	1670	⊠
90412	149	A	1454	⊠
90413	168	D	2440	⊠
90420	216	D	2473	⊠
90423	76	B	1773	⊠
90433	36	A	928	⊠
90436	83	C	2181	⊠
90439	237	D	2562	⊠
90440	146	B	1764	⊠
90441	337	C	1811	⊠
90443	107	E	2759	⊠
90444	180	D	2301	⊠
90450	220	D	2398	⊠
90454	154	D	2218	⊠
90458	157	D	2263	⊠
90461	311	D	2485	⊠
90470	289	E	2714	⊠
90606	283	C	2031	⊠
90616	249	C	1992	⊠
90622	263	C	2095	⊠
90827	284	D	2548	⊠
90838	77	E	2685	⊠
90909	290	C	2175	⊠
91053	97	C	2099	⊠
91073	312	D	2209	
91109	61	E	2747	
91111	99	E	3034	
91128	319	D	2263	
91565	334	D	2362	⊠
91700	160	D	2406	⊠
91731	46	B	1857	⊠
91746	39	B	1717	⊠
91749	88	E	3051	⊠
91753	126	A	1490	
91797	187	A	1485	⊠
92209	183	F	3292	
92219	303	F	3335	⚡ZIP
92220	72	C	1830	
92237	171	F	3783	⚡ZIP
92238	224	B	1664	
92239	145	A	1198	
92248	49	F	3921	⚡ZIP
92257	325	D	2470	
92265	86	F	3818	
92269	302	E	2835	
92274	121	F	3870	
92275	179	E	2675	
92277	78	E	3110	⚡ZIP
92279	54	E	3079	
92281	150	A	1360	
92283	154	B	1653	
92400	278	A	1050	
92404	338	D	2275	⊠
92405	145	B	1564	
92501	84	F	2727	⊠
92504	234	F	3813	⊠
92505	51	F	3504	⊠
92508	62	F	2951	⊠
92509	269	E	2551	⊠
92525	149	B	1484	⊠
92527	294	C	1680	⊠
92531	151	C	1754	⊠
92535	306	F	2965	⊠
92536	64	D	1869	⊠
92538	175	F	2733	⊠
92539	157	D	2033	⊠
92544	142	D	1987	⊠
92546	227	E	2387	⊠
92549	315	E	2490	⊠
92550	332	F	2735	⊠
92552	153	D	1873	⊠
92576	42	E	2858	⊠
92609	94	B	1768	⚡ZIP
92610	18	C	2101	⚡ZIP
92619	19	E	2692	
92622	15	D	2217	
92625	27	B	1710	
92630	300	B	1782	
92642	82	C	2082	⚡ZIP
92651	108	D	2403	⚡ZIP
92653	80	D	2443	⚡ZIP
92655	244	B	1746	
92657	98	F	4328	
92660	44	C	1964	
92663	114	E	2725	
92674	112	C	1876	
92685	116	A	1442	
92902	89	E	2787	
93000	150	C	1862	
93015	142	A	1087	
93017	158	A	1142	
93021	47	A	1282	
93034	281	E	2838	
93035	67	D	2545	
93041	129	E	3034	
93042	144	E	2995	
93048	298	A	1310	
93059	140	D	2559	
93182	6	F	3650	
93205	66	D	2588	⊠
93206	103	E	2645	⊠ ⚡ZIP
93209	141	D	2464	⊠ ⚡ZIP
93212	203	C	2091	⚡ZIP
93219	252	B	1668	⊠ ⚡ZIP
93222	329	A	1292	⊠ ⚡ZIP R
93240	321	D	2454	⊠
93247	219	F	3840	
93261	231	B	1778	⊠ ⚡ZIP
93265	146	A	1325	
93269	20	B	1735	⊠
93279	123	A	1388	⊠ ⚡ZIP
93287	153	C	2024	⊠ ⚡ZIP
93306	163	B	1672	
93311	212	C	1810	
93330	258	F	3620	
93333	251	E	3198	
93349	195	C	1961	
93413	185	C	1808	
93415	204	B	1714	
93416	235	A	1475	
93422	247	A	828	
93424	256	A	1028	
93432	169	C	1833	⊠
93602	276	D	2411	
93603	286	E	3029	
94104	128	C	1813	
94105	159	B	1792	
94107	291	C	1887	
94202	297	F	3216	⊠
94230	93	F	4759	
94231	285	E	2891	

Legend: Materials List Available | Zip Quote Available | Right Reading Reverse | Duplex Plan

Plan#	Page#	Price Code	Square Footage	Icons
94233	35	D	2527	
94239	288	F	4106	
94242	305	E	2978	
94246	330	F	3792	
94248	190	C	1853	
94614	322	D	2533	
94615	164	E	2665	
94622	211	E	3149	
94640	253	D	2558	
94641	73	D	2400	
94715	55	E	3012	Materials List
94721	102	E	2832	Materials List
94749	196	B	1589	Materials List
94800	170	B	1199	Materials List
94801	277	B	1300	Materials List
94810	323	E	2690	Materials List
94811	178	D	2165	Materials List
94902	104	C	1931	Materials List
94904	296	C	1998	Materials List, Zip Quote
94906	111	C	1957	Materials List
94907	130	B	1768	Materials List, Zip Quote
94908	138	B	1642	Materials List
94911	184	C	1858	Materials List, Zip Quote, Right Reading Reverse
94932	208	D	2594	Materials List, Right Reading Reverse
94943	207	D	2377	Materials List
94984	240	C	2042	Materials List, Right Reading Reverse
94996	250	C	2115	Materials List
96402	189	D	2027	Materials List
96403	56	E	2832	Materials List
96404	186	D	2301	Materials List
96405	182	D	1903	Materials List
96407	200	E	2772	Materials List
96408	173	D	2164	Materials List
96411	333	E	2596	Materials List
96413	161	D	2349	Materials List, Zip Quote
96417	301	C	1561	Materials List, Zip Quote
96418	310	B	1452	Materials List
96421	162	D	2045	Materials List
96423	214	D	2218	Materials List
96435	100	E	2526	Materials List
96442	194	D	2182	Materials List
96446	248	D	2144	Materials List
96449	218	D	2211	Materials List
96452	205	B	1475	Materials List
96454	257	D	1537	Materials List
96456	209	C	1639	Materials List
96457	197	C	1843	Materials List
96462	221	C	1846	Materials List
96468	206	C	1864	Materials List
96476	226	C	1823	Materials List
96478	177	D	2203	Materials List
96479	189	C	1883	Materials List
96485	275	B	1454	Materials List
96486	282	D	2042	Materials List
96487	174	C	1669	Materials List
96488	271	C	1695	Materials List
96489	132	C	1609	Materials List
96490	307	E	2682	Materials List
96491	165	D	2250	Materials List
96493	193	C	1770	Materials List
96500	295	E	3011	Materials List
96503	210	D	2256	Materials List
96505	37	D	2069	Materials List
96506	217	B	1654	Materials List
96509	198	A	1438	Materials List
96513	268	B	1648	Materials List
96522	229	B	1515	Materials List
97236	293	E	2915	
97237	131	A	1283	
97240	133	F	3407	
97241	241	A	1489	
97247	246	A	1466	
97250	260	A	1492	
97254	266	B	1692	
98211	253	E	3063	
98231	232	E	2980	
98400	68	F	3262	Materials List
98402	118	F	3027	Materials List
98403	48	F	3395	Materials List
98404	279	F	4362	Materials List
98405	152	F	3039	Materials List
98406	213	B	1600	Materials List
98407	197	C	2052	Materials List
98408	92	C	1856	Materials List
98410	201	D	2389	Materials List
98411	120	A	1373	Materials List
98414	218	B	1575	Materials List
98415	188	A	1429	Materials List
98416	202	B	1619	Materials List
98419	313	E	2425	
98423	324	B	1671	Materials List
98425	209	C	1845	Materials List
98426	273	E	2622	Materials List
98427	222	C	2051	Materials List
98429	205	C	1906	Materials List
98430	217	C	1884	Materials List
98431	193	B	1675	Materials List
98434	225	A	1346	Materials List
98435	230	C	1945	Materials List
98437	134	F	3949	Materials List
98438	110	F	3525	Materials List
98439	335	F	4125	Materials List
98441	226	B	1502	
98443	229	A	1359	
98445	222	C	1913	
98447	194	C	2155	Materials List
98452	287	E	3083	Materials List
98454	202	C	1874	Materials List
98455	221	D	2349	Materials List
98456	210	B	1715	Materials List
98457	105	E	2686	Materials List
98460	225	B	1544	
98462	214	B	1750	
98463	206	B	1505	
98503	201	C	1876	
98508	239	F	3480	Zip Quote
98511	265	D	2445	
98512	213	C	2167	
98513	317	F	3352	
98514	331	F	3381	Zip Quote
98518	53	D	2455	Zip Quote
98519	69	D	2524	
98522	230	B	1528	
98524	261	E	2902	
98528	136	E	2748	
98533	176	D	2567	
98534	267	E	2959	
98535	242	F	3512	
98536	243	F	3423	Zip Quote
98538	245	F	4082	
98539	274	F	3936	Zip Quote
98540	328	D	2464	
98733	115	D	2496	Materials List
98742	262	B	1664	
98747	339	A	1280	Materials List
98748	280	C	2126	Materials List
98904	2	D	2614	Materials List
98912	299	A	1325	Materials List
99022	254	A	1494	Materials List
99045	125	B	1767	
99057	117	B	1720	Materials List
99431	59	D	2277	Materials List
99432	19	D	2562	Materials List
99450	14	E	2695	Materials List, Zip Quote
99457	17	D	2270	Materials List
99500	101	C	2082	
99620	127	D	2212	Materials List
99639	327	A	1367	Materials List
99640	318	D	2466	Materials List
99641	147	B	1567	Materials List
99661	106	A	1387	Materials List
99796	139	D	2598	Materials List
99800	320	C	1663	Materials List
99801	52	D	2188	Materials List, Zip Quote
99803	91	C	1977	Materials List, Zip Quote
99804	113	C	1815	Materials List, Zip Quote
99805	161	C	1787	Materials List, Zip Quote
99806	178	B	1246	Materials List
99807	233	C	1879	Materials List, Zip Quote
99808	41	C	1832	Materials List, Zip Quote
99809	185	B	1417	Materials List, Zip Quote
99810	22	C	1685	Materials List, Zip Quote
99811	186	B	1699	Materials List
99812	270	B	1386	Materials List, Zip Quote
99813	173	C	1959	Materials List
99815	169	D	1912	Materials List, Zip Quote
99824	162	D	2121	Materials List
99825	90	E	2869	Materials List
99829	177	C	1972	Materials List
99830	181	B	1372	Materials List, Zip Quote
99831	170	C	1699	Materials List
99835	174	C	1515	Materials List
99836	190	C	1792	Materials List
99837	137	C	1743	Materials List
99838	326	D	2192	Materials List
99840	28	C	1632	Materials List
99843	45	E	2563	Materials List
99845	198	C	1954	Materials List, Zip Quote
99852	109	C	1898	Materials List
99853	119	E	2692	Materials List, Zip Quote
99857	166	C	1865	Materials List
99859	165	C	1831	Materials List, Zip Quote
99860	172	B	1498	Materials List
99871	181	C	1655	Materials List
99873	182	C	1778	Materials List
99878	304	C	1864	Materials List, Zip Quote
99891	87	E	2561	Materials List
99895	238	D	2435	Materials List

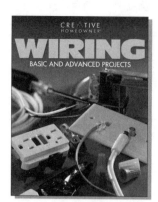
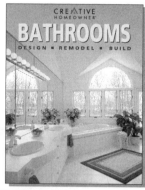
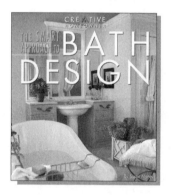

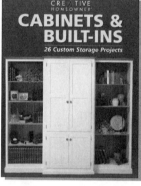

the Home Planner, Builder & Owner

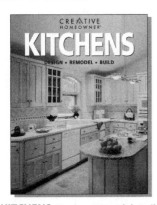

KITCHENS: Design, Remodel, Build

This is the reference book for modern kitchen design, with more than 100 full-color photos to help homeowners plan the layout. Step-by-step instructions illustrate basic plumbing and wiring techniques; how to finish walls and ceilings; and more.

BOOK #: 277065   192pp.   8½"x10⅞"

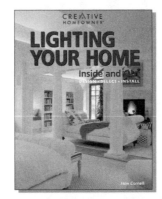

LIGHTING YOUR HOME: Inside and Out

Lighting should be selected with care. This book thoroughly explains lighting design for every room as well as outdoors. It is also a step-by-step manual that shows how to install the fixtures. More than 125 photos and 400 drawings.

BOOK #: 277583   176pp.   8½"x10⅞"

MASONRY: Concrete, Brick, Stone

Concrete, brick, and stone choices are detailed with step-by-step instructions and over 35 color photographs and 460 illustrations. Projects include a brick or stone garden wall, steps and patios, a concrete-block retaining wall, a concrete sidewalk.

BOOK #: 277106   176pp.   8½"x10⅞"

The Smart Approach to KITCHEN DESIGN

Transform a dated kitchen into the spectacular heart of your home. Learn how to create a better layout and more efficient storage. Find out about the latest equipment and materials. Savvy tips explain how to create style like a pro. More than 150 color photos.

BOOK #: 279935   176 pp.   9"x10"

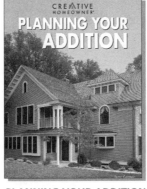

PLANNING YOUR ADDITION

Planning an addition to your home involves a daunting number of choices, from choosing a contractor to selecting bathroom tile. Using 280 color drawings and photographs, architect/author Jerry Germer helps you make the right decision.

BOOK #: 277004   192pp.   8½"x10⅞"

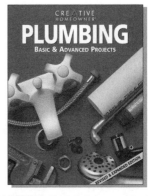

PLUMBING: Basic & Advanced Projects

Take the guesswork out of plumbing repair and installation for old and new systems. Projects include replacing faucets, unclogging drains, installing a tub, replacing a water heater, and much more. 500 illustrations and diagrams.

BOOK #: 277620   176pp.   8½"x10⅞"

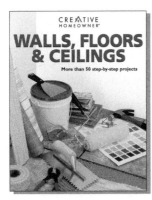

WALLS, FLOORS & CEILINGS

Here's the definitive guide to interiors. It shows you how to replace old surfaces with new professional-looking ones. Projects include installing molding, skylights, insulation, flooring, carpeting, and more. Over 500 color photos and drawings.

BOOK #: 277697   176pp.   8½"x10⅞"

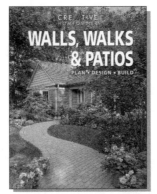

WALLS, WALKS & PATIOS

Learn how to build a patio from concrete, stone, or brick and complement it with one of a dozen walks. Learn about simple mortarless walls, landscape timber walls, and hefty brick and stone walls. 50 photographs and 320 illustrations, all in color.

BOOK #: 277994   192pp.   8½"x10⅞"

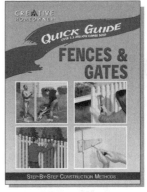

QUICK GUIDE: FENCES & GATES

Learn how to build and install all kinds of fences and gates for your yard, from hand-built wood privacy and picket fences to newer prefabricated vinyl and chain-link types. Over 200 two-color drawings illustrate step-by-step procedures.

BOOK #: 287732   80pp.   8½"x10⅞"

Place Your Order ...

WORKING WITH TILE

Design and complete interior and exterior tile projects on walls, floors, countertops, shower enclosures, more. 425 color illustrations and over 80 photographs.

BOOK #: 277540   176pp.   8½"x10⅞"

COLOR IN THE AMERICAN HOME

Find out how to make the most of color in your home. Over 150 photographs of traditional and contemporary interiors.

BOOK #: 287264   176pp.   9"x10"

The Smart Approach to HOME DECORATING

Learn how to work with space, color, pattern, and texture with the flair of a professional designer. More than 300 color photos.

BOOK #: 279667   256pp.   9"x10"

CREATIVE HOMEOWNER®

BOOK ORDER FORM
Please Print

SHIP TO:

Name:

Address:

City: State: Zip: Phone Number:

(Should there be a problem with your order)

Quantity	Title	Price	CH #	Cost
	375 Southern Home Plans	$9.95	277037	
	400 Affordable Home Plans	9.95	277012	
	408 Vacation & Second Home Plans	8.95	277036	
	508 One-Story Home Plans	9.95	277030	
	508 Two-Story Home Plans	9.95	277031	
	600 Most Popular Home Plans	9.95	277029	
	Adding Value to Your Home	16.95	277006	
	Advanced Home Gardening	24.95	274465	
	Annuals, Perennials, and Bulbs	19.95	274032	
	Bathrooms: Design, Remodel, Build	19.95	277053	
	Better Lawns, Step by Step	14.95	274359	
	Bird Feeders	10.95	277102	
	Build a Kids' Play Yard	14.95	277662	
	Cabinets & Built-Ins	14.95	277079	
	Color in the American Home	19.95	287264	
	Complete Guide to Wallpapering	14.95	278910	
	Complete Guide to Water Gardens	19.95	274452	
	Complete Home Landscaping	24.95	274615	
	Creating Good Gardens	16.95	274244	
	Custom Closets	12.95	277132	
	Decks: Planning, Designing, Building	16.95	277162	
	Decorating with Paint & Paper	19.95	279723	
	Decorating with Tile	19.95	279824	
	Decorative Paint Finishes	10.95	287371	
	Drywall: Pro Tips for Hanging & Finishing	14.95	278315	
	Easy-Care Guide to Houseplants	19.95	275243	
	Fences, Gates & Trellises	14.95	277981	
	Furniture Repair & Refinishing	19.95	277335	
	Gazebos & Other Outdoor Structures	14.95	277138	
	Home Book	40.00	267855	
	Home Landscaping: California Reg.	19.95	274267	
	Home Landscaping: Mid-Atlantic Reg.	19.95	274537	
	Home Landscaping: Midwest Reg./S Can.	19.95	274385	
	Home Landscaping: Northeast Reg./SE Can.	19.95	274618	
	Home Landscaping: Southeast Reg.	19.95	274762	
	House Framing	19.95	277655	
	Kitchens: Design, Remodel, Build (New Ed.)	16.95	277065	
	Lighting Your Home Inside & Out	16.95	277583	
	Lyn Peterson's Real Life Decorating	27.95	279382	
	Masonry: Concrete, Brick, Stone	16.95	277106	
	Mastering Fine Decorative Paint Techniques	27.95	279550	
	Planning Your Addition	16.95	277004	
	Plumbing: Basic and Advanced Projects	14.95	277620	
	Remodeling Basements, Attics & Garages	16.95	277680	
	Smart Approach to Bath Design	19.95	287225	
	Smart Approach to Home Decorating	24.95	279667	
	Smart Approach to Kitchen Design	19.95	279935	

Quantity	Title	Price	CH #	Cost
	Smart Approach to Window Decor	$19.95	279431	
	Trees, Shrubs & Hedges for Home Landscaping	19.95	274238	
	Walls, Floors & Ceilings	16.95	277697	
	Walls, Walks & Patios	16.95	277994	
	Wiring: Basic and Advanced Projects	19.95	277049	
	Working with Tile	16.95	277540	
	Yard and Garden Furniture (Plans & Projects)	19.95	277462	

Quick Guide Series

Quantity	Title	Price	CH #	Cost
	Quick Guide - Attics	$7.95	287711	
	Quick Guide - Basements	7.95	287242	
	Quick Guide - Ceramic Tile	7.95	287730	
	Quick Guide - Decks	7.95	277344	
	Quick Guide - Fences & Gates	7.95	287732	
	Quick Guide - Floors	7.95	287734	
	Quick Guide - Garages & Carports	7.95	287785	
	Quick Guide - Gazebos	7.95	287757	
	Quick Guide - Insulation & Ventilation	7.95	287367	
	Quick Guide - Interior & Exterior Painting	7.95	287784	
	Quick Guide - Masonry Walls	7.95	287741	
	Quick Guide - Patios & Walks	7.95	287778	
	Quick Guide - Plumbing	7.95	287863	
	Quick Guide - Ponds & Fountains	7.95	287804	
	Quick Guide - Pool & Spa Maintenance	7.95	287901	
	Quick Guide - Roofing	7.95	287807	
	Quick Guide - Shelving & Storage	7.95	287763	
	Quick Guide - Siding	7.95	287892	
	Quick Guide - Stairs & Railings	7.95	287755	
	Quick Guide - Storage Sheds	7.95	287815	
	Quick Guide - Trim (Crown Molding, Base & more)	7.95	287745	
	Quick Guide - Walls & Ceilings	7.95	287792	
	Quick Guide - Windows & Doors	7.95	287812	
	Quick Guide - Wiring, Fourth Edition	7.95	287884	

Number of Books Ordered _____   Total for Books _____

NJ Residents add 6% tax _____

Prices subject to change without notice.   Subtotal _____

Postage/Handling Charges _____
$3.75 for first book / $1.25 for each additional book

Total _____

Make checks (in U.S. currency only) payable to
CREATIVE HOMEOWNER®
P.O. BOX 38, 24 Park Way
Upper Saddle River, New Jersey 07458-9960

Please visit us at our Web site: **www.creativehomeowner.com**